Register Your Book

at ibmpressbooks.com/ibmregister

Upon registration, we will send you electronic sample chapters from two of our popular IBM Press books. In addition, you will be automatically entered into a monthly drawing for a free IBM Press book.

Registration also entitles you to:

- Notices and reminders about author appearances, conferences, and online chats with special guests

- Access to supplemental material that may be available

- Advance notice of forthcoming editions

- Related book recommendations

- Information about special contests and promotions throughout the year

- Chapter excerpts and supplements of forthcoming books

Contact us

If you are interested in writing a book or reviewing manuscripts prior to publication, please write to us at:

Editorial Director, IBM Press
c/o Pearson Education
800 East 96th Street
Indianapolis, IN 46240

e-mail: IBMPress@pearsoned.com

Visit us on the Web: ibmpressbooks.com

Implementing ITIL® Configuration Management

Implementing ITIL® Configuration Management

Larry Klosterboer

IBM Press
Pearson plc
Upper Saddle River, NJ • Boston • Indianapolis • San Francisco
New York • Toronto • Montreal • London • Munich • Paris • Madrid
Cape Town • Sydney • Tokyo • Singapore • Mexico City

Ibmpressbooks.com

IBM Press Program Managers: Tara Woodman, Ellice Uffer
Cover design: IBM Corporation

Associate Publisher: Greg Wiegand
Marketing Manager: Kourtnaye Sturgeon
Publicist: Heather Fox
Acquisitions Editor: Greg Wiegand
Development Editor: Kevin Howard
Managing Editor: Gina Kanouse
Designer: Alan Clements
Project Editor: Jovana San Nicolas-Shirley
Copy Editor: Lori Lyons
Indexer: Lisa Stumpf
Compositor: Nonie Ratcliff
Proofreader: Kristy Hart
Manufacturing Buyer: Dan Uhrig

Published by Pearson plc
Publishing as IBM Press

This Book Is Safari Enabled

The Safari® Enabled icon on the cover of your favorite technology book means the book is available through Safari Bookshelf. When you buy this book, you get free access to the online edition for 45 days. Safari Bookshelf is an electronic reference library that lets you easily search thousands of technical books, find code samples, download chapters, and access technical information whenever and wherever you need it.

To gain 45-day Safari Enabled access to this book:

- Go to http://www.awprofessional.com/safarienabled.

- Complete the brief registration form.

- Enter the coupon code BWB7-2SEB-CVRW-3DB4-YG36.

If you have difficulty registering on Safari Bookshelf or accessing the online edition, please e-mail customer-service@safaribooksonline.com.

Library of Congress Cataloging-in-Publication Data

Klosterboer, Larry.
  Implementing ITIL configuration management / Larry Klosterboer.
        p. cm.
    ISBN 0-13-242593-9
    1. Configuration management. 2. Information technology—Management. 3. Management information systems. I. Title.
    QA76.76.C69K66 2008
    658.4'03—dc22

                                                          2007042071

    ISBN-13: 978-0-13-242593-3
    ISBN-10: 0-13-242593-9

Text printed in the United States on recycled paper at R.R. Donnelley in Crawfordsville, Indiana.
First printing: December 2007

To Janet, who makes this (and everything else) possible.

Contents

Part I: Planning for Configuration Management   17

Part II: Implementing Configuration Management   97

Preface

Welcome to the frustration, tedium, and hard work that is configuration management. If you've picked up this book, you probably have some notion of what it means to manage Information Technology (IT) configurations—and you are probably hoping I'll tell you that it can be easy to set up and manage a configuration management service.

Unfortunately, I can't say it will be easy, but I can at least report that it is possible to have an effective process that results in an accurate Configuration Management Database (CMDB) and useful information that produces real benefit for your total IT services. This book is born from the crucible of real-world experience. You won't find sugar coating and you won't find magic formulas. Instead you'll find hard-won lessons and danger signs posted by a fellow traveler.

You know I would be lying if I told you that I have implemented a perfect configuration management service. Each implementation I've done has its own particular blemishes and shortcomings. Some have been called successful, and hoping for anything beyond that seems unreasonable.

Organization of the Book

We begin in Chapter 1, "Overview of Configuration Management," with a general overview of the landscape. There is an introduction to the IT Infrastructure Library (ITIL) along with a more in-depth look at configuration management. You look at both the business value you can gain from a well-implemented program and the challenges you're likely to encounter in putting the program in place. Also in Chapter 1 is a maturity scale you can use to understand how well your organization has done thus far. This material serves as a background before you dive into the depths.

Like every good IT project, putting a configuration management service in place happens in three stages. After Chapter 1, this book is organized into three parts representing the planning stage, the implementation stage, and the operational stage.

First you sit in a quiet spot and think deeply about what you want to accomplish. You tell three or four others and together you brainstorm about what is possible. You talk to some managers and get a dose of what is realistic. You bring in some experts who help you flesh out the details of how to go about the work. You make estimates, start to lay out a schedule, and ultimately figure out the details. Out of all this activity, a plan is formed. The many pieces of assembling a plan are documented in the first section of this book.

I've personally been involved in a variety of IT projects that started off with good intentions but poor requirements, and those projects never ended in success. Based on this experience, Chapter 2, "Gathering and Analyzing Requirements," focuses on defining the requirements for configuration management. Although you may already have a handle on requirements definition and management, you should still browse through Chapter 2 for a few tips on gathering and analyzing configuration management requirements.

We get specific in Chapter 3, "Determining Scope, Span, and Granularity," where we tackle the hardest part of configuration management. This chapter introduces a three-dimensional way of thinking about the structure of your CMDB. You find very practical advice on how to set up the scope, granularity, and span of the database. While I can't tell you exactly what should and should not be in your particular database, the rules of thumb in Chapter 3 should help you get to a workable definition that is custom tailored to your situation.

People often are eager to start putting configuration items into a database, and they have no idea of how those configuration items (CIs) will stay accurate as changes happen in the real world. To help you avoid this rookie mistake, Chapter 4, "Customizing the Configuration Management Process," describes how to plan for your very own configuration management process. You learn how to tailor the process to meet your specific requirements and how to build out an effective process without getting carried away with too much detail.

Although the process work is certainly important, you eventually will need to gather data and store it in a database. You'll need to know what kind of database is right for you, where to look for existing data, and how to merge data into a cohesive set of information. Chapter 5, "Planning for Data Population," describes exactly those steps.

By the end of Chapter 5, you will have lots of good planning information but still won't have a plan. You need to assemble all the information from the previous chapters, and that is exactly what Chapter 6, "Putting Together a Useful Project Plan," helps you to do. You find information on work breakdown structure, schedule, scope, communications, and all the rest of the pieces of a full project plan. Chapter 6 also serves to recap the first section of the book.

After the plan has been committed using whatever governance mechanisms your organization uses, you start the real work of executing the plan. You pull together a team with the best intention of doing everything right, but the real world intrudes and you progress with wild rushes of progress interspersed with missteps and rework. During this second stage, the going is hard, but you have a specific goal and end date in mind, thanks to your careful planning work. Part II of the book provides information on the actual implementation work.

It would be impossible to implement configuration management without solid tools to implement the CMDB. There are many good tools in the marketplace, and I'm not going to advocate any single tool over the rest. Instead, Chapter 7, "Choosing the Right Tools," provides you with some common characteristics to think about in selecting a configuration management tool set. As an added bonus, I provide you with a very simple way to document your tool decision without emotion or undue vendor influence.

As important as the tools are, they must automate the process that you've decided to use. If you let the tools dictate the process, you'll inevitably find a disjointed and incomplete process. Chapter 8, "Implementing the Process," focuses again on the process—this time from the standpoint of how to actually implement what you planned in Chapter 4. You learn how to communicate with the organization, how to build training materials, and what level of detail is sufficient for your overall process work.

If your implementation is like all those I've been associated with, the actual population of the CMDB is the longest and most visible step in the implementation. That's the topic of Chapter 9, "Populating the Configuration Management Database." Here you learn about two different population approaches and how to make sure that the data you put in is clean and useful from the start. Of course, I'll continue my theme that putting data into a database is useless without a way to maintain its accuracy. So, you'll find some discussion in Chapter 9 about integrating the incident, change, and release management processes with configuration management data.

One of the best ways to improve your chances of success in almost any IT project is to perform some kind of pilot program. In Chapter 10, "Choosing and Running a Pilot Program," you look at how to shape, advertise, and execute a configuration management pilot. I describe how to evaluate the success of a pilot and make an educated decision on whether or not to push forward to a full production roll out.

Assuming your pilot is successful, you'll want to expand out to the rest of the organization. You need to think about a broad range of issues, including communications, training, and some obstacles you might face that weren't resolved from the pilot. Those topics are discussed in Chapter 11, "Communication and Enterprise Roll Out," where I describe the move from a small, isolated pilot to a broad enterprise configuration management service. This chapter touches on most of the key themes from the second part of the book and serves as a summary to Part II.

You might think that you've earned a rest after a successful configuration management implementation, and you're probably right. But we all know that the real work comes after implementation, when you've settled into day-by-day operations. It isn't glamorous, but somebody has to keep the lights on and the database clean. That's why there is a third part to this book. In this final part, you learn how to mature your configuration management service and exploit its full value.

We start with a peek at the configuration management organization. Rather than simply focus on the operational roles, I've summarized all of the roles from implementation through operations in Chapter 12, "Building a Configuration Management Team." I present the standard responsibilities and the skills needed to make the program successful. If your job is to hire a group of people to make configuration management real for your organization, I give you permission to skip ahead to Chapter 12.

Next we think about some good uses for all of the data you've been so careful to gather, cleanse, and store. Chapter 13, "The Many Uses for Configuration Information," describes not only some reports you may want to create, but also some real-world ways in which you can use configuration information to help your overall IT effectiveness. If you're interested in how configuration management can help with IT charge back or software license compliance, you'll find great information in this chapter.

Chapter 14, "Measuring and Improving CMDB Accuracy," tackles the critical question of database accuracy. There is no more certain path to failure than the one that starts with incorrect data. I describe various methods for defining and tracking accuracy, and give you concrete ways to improve the accuracy of the CMDB.

Finally, this book concludes with a chapter on some of the things you'll be able to tackle after you have good configuration management data. In Chapter 15, "Improving the Business Value of Configuration Management," you find extended discussions of an IT services catalog and using configuration management to help in your corporate compliance programs. Although these aren't strictly configuration management discussions, they are intended to give you added motivation to get configuration management completely under control.

Throughout the book, I include examples of situations where our teams made the right decisions and some where we made the wrong decisions. My hope is that you'll view this book as a set of lessons others have learned so that you won't have to repeat my mistakes.

Let me repeat one more time that configuration management is possible. It isn't easy, and doesn't happen without hard work, but you can have an accurate, reliable source of IT information that will dramatically help in many of the decisions you need to make as a technical or business leader in the IT community.

Acknowledgments

One of the greatest privileges in life is working side by side with bright, talented, and dedicated people. That has been my privilege in creating this book. I especially want to thank Brian, Jay, and Rob for their patience in correcting my many mistakes and their persistence in helping me clarify the message. I've gained much from their insights. Despite their immense help, the opinions remaining in this book are those of the author and should not be construed as the opinions of the reviewers or any other person or organization.

Thanks are also due to my various managers at IBM who have continually given me opportunities to grow and learn. Without their guidance and enablement, I would not have any knowledge to pass on to the reader.

Finally, to every customer I've had the pleasure to work with, learn from, and serve—thank you. Ultimately it is your stories and the lessons I've learned on your time that are shared in this book. You know better than anyone else which things worked and which ones didn't because you have had to live with the results.

About the Author

Larry Klosterboer is a certified IT architect specializing in systems management. He works for IBM's global service delivery team out of Austin, Texas. Larry has more than 18 years of experience in service delivery, spanning technologies from mainframe to networking to desktop computing. His areas of focus have included network design, UNIX® systems administration, asset management, and most recently, implementing IT service management.

CHAPTER 1

Overview of Configuration Management

This book will help you make better information technology (IT) decisions. That's a big promise, but it's not my promise. The IT Infrastructure Library® (ITIL®) is a compendium of best practices from many companies in many industries. It represents the best thinking of thousands of people about how IT should be run, what impact IT can have on the business it supports, and how to gain the most value from your IT investments. One of the stated goals of ITIL is to help decision makers make better decisions by ensuring that adequate IT information is available to support those decisions. *Configuration management* is the discipline of identifying, tracking, and controlling the various components of the IT environment, and it is this information that enables decision making.

As you can imagine, however, making better decisions does not come without some hard work. Implementation of the full set of ITIL best practices, or reengineering your process to fit the ITIL model, involves a long and often confusing journey. That's where this book comes in. It will help clarify the jargon, establish the roadmap, and warn of the pitfalls along the way. Rather than a generic work that repeats much of what is already documented in the ITIL, this book focuses specifically on configuration management and helps you to implement this core discipline, which will enable the rest of your ITIL journey. By focusing on configuration management, we enable you to build the critical set of information that will be the foundation for better decision making.

Figure 1.1 shows the four areas we cover in this chapter. We'll get a basic understanding of ITIL and configuration management. Then we'll look at the benefits and challenges of implementing a configuration management service. Throughout this chapter and all those that follow, we'll focus on practical experience rather than memorized theories.

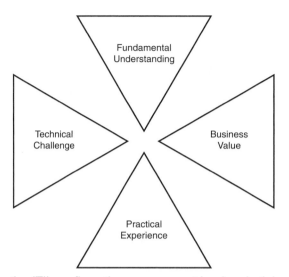

Figure 1.1   Implementing ITIL configuration management involves both benefits and challenges.

ITIL Background

The ITIL implementation is one of the hottest topics in IT today. In order to gain a good understanding of the value of configuration management, we must clearly understand what ITIL is and what it is not. Fundamentally, ITIL is exactly what its name implies—a collection of books. The common theme of the library is that all of the books provide guidelines that can help organizations implement the best practices that have been learned the hard way by the pioneering few. There is a volume about security, one about planning, one about software assets, and one about managing applications. The library continues to grow as more successful techniques are documented and guidelines established for what can make others successful.

The latest information on ITIL comes from the UK Office of Government Commerce (OGC) through its web site at http://www.best-management-practice.com/. Be sure to visit the "Terms and Conditions" link at the bottom of the page for the appropriate uses of that web site.

This book focuses on two volumes of the library: "Service Support" and "Service Delivery," the combination of which is called "IT Service Management." Together these two volumes form the core of ITIL—the piece with which most enterprises begin their implementations. Collectively, the service support and service delivery volumes describe the collected best practices in these IT disciplines. Five processes are described in service support:

- Incident Management
- Problem Management
- Change Management
- Release Management
- Configuration Management

Five additional processes are defined in service delivery:

- Capacity Management
- Availability Management
- Service Continuity Management
- Service Level Management
- Financial Management

The guidelines offered for these ten process areas cover what any IT shop, large or small, must do to effectively provide service to the enterprise it supports. Figure 1.2 shows this categorization of the ITIL service management processes.

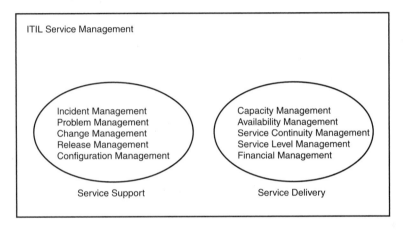

Figure 1.2   ITIL categorizes service management processes into two groups.

As this book is being written, the next release of ITIL is being readied for release. This book assumes the reader is familiar with ITIL Version 2, but where significant differences exist in the next release (Version 3), they will be pointed out. The structure of the library is different in Version 3, with the assumption that all books focus on service management, and the underlying organization is based on the service life cycle.

So rather than service delivery and service support, ITIL Version 3 contains volumes on service strategy, service design, service transition, service operation, and service improvement. By adopting this life cycle-based approach, the library becomes more useful to organizations at various stages of the journey. This book focuses on organizations that are actively implementing configuration management, and thus elaborates on the guidance that will be found in the Version 3 Service Transition book.

This isn't a book about ITIL, but it is important to understand the high-level purpose of each process area to better understand how configuration management relates to each process. The service delivery processes are those that directly impact the running of servers and software.

- **Capacity management**—Aims to understand how much capacity (measured in memory, bandwidth, storage, and variety of other units) is currently available, how much will need to be available in the future, and how best to manage so that capacity shortfalls don't occur and excessive capacity isn't acquired.

- **Availability management**—Deals with maximizing the availability of the IT infrastructure through trend analysis and proactive elimination of single points of failure.

- **Service continuity management**—Proactively plans for component outages and includes everything involved in ensuring the business keeps getting the IT services it needs despite the lack of one or more IT components. It consists of disaster recovery and contingency planning.

- **Service level management**—Defines and monitors the value which IT is providing to the business through setting and reporting on targets called service levels.

- **Financial management**—Deals with understanding the costs of IT and appropriately funding the IT infrastructure in the most efficient way.

The service support processes are centered on the record keeping, tracking, and process improvements that make IT successful.

- **Incident management**—Captures the details associated with a service outage, communicating those details to the appropriate parties so that service can be restored as quickly as possible.

- **Problem management**—An information analysis function that determines the root cause of any highly impacting or frequently recurring outage and then tracks corrective actions to correct that root cause.

- **Change management**—A critical discipline that controls and communicates the changes occurring in the IT environment.

- **Release management**—A disciplined approach to organizing changes to make better use of the resources involved.

- **Configuration management**—Fundamentally the science of tracking the exact state of the overall IT environment at any point in time.

All of these process areas will be referenced frequently in examples throughout this book.

Although it is easiest to consider ITIL as made up of separate process areas, real life isn't always that simple. In many cases a particular activity will encompass more than one process area, and the interplay between processes is at least as important as understanding any single area. For example, suppose a server is supporting a major business application, and the server suffers a catastrophic failure. The incident management process comes to the forefront by attempting to restore service. But at the same time, availability management is invoked in an attempt to maximize the availability of the overall service, and service level management tracks the impact to both operations level and service level agreements. As part of restoring the service, changes may need to be managed, the service continuity plan may need to be invoked, extraordinary costs might need to be tracked, and it might be desirable to check capacity plans to find another server capable of picking up at least part of the load

Along the way, configuration management provides information about the impact of the service interruption, including whether there will be a complete failure of a service or simply a degradation, and also provides options for restoring service. Thus, a single IT event (the crashing of a server) actually involves many of the ITIL defined process areas. It is exactly this interplay between processes that makes configuration management and the information it provides so important, as we see repeatedly in the chapters that follow.

Configuration Management

Why focus on configuration management? Honestly, this book focuses on configuration management because not very many organizations have successfully implemented this central process discipline. It is proving to be one of the more challenging processes to do well. First, it is important because it is the center of the ITIL information universe. It attempts to build a process to gather, manage, and link information vital to every other ITIL process discipline.

Second, it is challenging because it is often a new way of thinking for IT groups. Traditionally IT has been much more concerned with the financial value of the environment than with the operational value of information about the environment. It is true that technical teams have often felt the need for better data, but the resulting mixture of spreadsheets, tribal knowledge, and incomplete databases simply adds to the challenge rather than providing a useful base to build on. Technicians have a vague notion of "IT infrastructure," but seldom do they have a complete and accurate picture of what the infrastructure consists of outside the silo in which they operate.

Finally, while configuration management is a familiar term, the definition outside of ITIL has been very vague at best. Outside of software development and mainframe data centers, configuration management has never been standardized in any meaningful way.

So, what is meant by configuration management specifically in an ITIL context? According to the ITIL Service Support book, "Configuration Management covers the identification, recording and reporting of IT components, including their versions, constituent components and relationships." In other words, anything that makes up the IT environment should be recorded as part of configuration management. Most importantly, the physical relationships and logical dependencies between components, subcomponents, applications, servers, networks, documentation, and the myriad of parts of the IT environment must be tracked.

It wouldn't be unusual in a fairly large organization for the IT environment to be made up of millions of individual items to be tracked. Of course, with several million items to be tracked, it shouldn't surprise anyone that there could be five million or more relationships to be tracked. While this sounds like a tremendous amount of effort, remember that your existing staff is trying to track this information in their heads today! Configuration management is intended to take away the burden of mental tracking, and with it the mistakes that can cost time and extra effort.

Fortunately, this book describes a way to build up to this kind of complexity without having to tackle all those details at the very beginning.

Perhaps the best way to understand the centrality of configuration management in the ITIL process framework is to walk through concrete examples of the ways the ITIL processes interact with the Configuration Management Database (CMDB).

Anyone who has used a computer has felt the pain associated with incident management. A router goes down, and suddenly you have a storm of frustrated users calling the service desk, lights flashing on the monitoring consoles, and executives calling the IT managers demanding to know what's happening. Incident management in ITIL terms is about restoring service, and the key metric is how quickly service can be restored.

The CMDB provides information to help the incident management team isolate the source of the problem more quickly. The better system administrators or application managers track some pieces of the information, or recall the last time this incident occurred, but they still don't have the complete picture that enables them to deal with new kinds of incidents. With configuration management data, the same IT manager simply looks at a few servers and/or applications that are down, and quickly sees that they are all related to the same router. With an accurate CMDB, the source of the incident can be isolated quickly, and then details about the failing component, such as software and firmware levels, can be viewed. Having configuration data in place can literally cut hours off the time it takes to resolve a complex incident.

The CMDB—or more specifically, the information it contains—is equally important to change management. A change review board might be reviewing tens or even hundreds of potential changes in a meeting. On the surface it might look like approving two changes for two separate business applications would be unrelated tasks, and both might get approved. By looking at an accurate CMDB, however, the change board can quickly see that both applications depend on the same database server, and one change record has asked to have the server backed up while the other change record has asked to have the same database server taken out of service. Clearly both changes cannot be implemented at the same time; but without configuration management data, these conflicts can be all too common.

In the security domain, when vulnerability is uncovered, it becomes vital to understand exactly what applications and infrastructure components are exposed. If the IT manager needs to go through an inventory exercise to find the affected components, the company is left vulnerable far too long, and even then some significant relationships might be missed. Accurate configuration data allows everyone to understand exactly how serious the vulnerability is and quickly plan the level of effort required to secure the environment.

Or consider the application software manager who is tasked with platform conversion. All Visual Basic applications must be converted to C# to meet new corporate standards. But this task is impossible without an accurate inventory of which applications exist, and details about which of these are written in Visual Basic. Many key decisions in the release management domain are affected by configuration management information.

And on it goes. Every process defined by the ITIL framework gains concrete benefits from accurate and timely configuration management data, and those other processes will never function effectively without configuration data. These key dependencies are facilitated by relating the configuration items (CIs) to key concepts in other processes, as shown in Figure 1.3. Once populated, your CMDB will be the most frequently accessed set of tables in the entire systems management solution. Because configuration data is so vital and used for so many purposes, it is critical that it be accurate and complete—a recurring theme in this book. Many more examples of the interlocking of configuration management and other ITIL disciplines will be presented in the chapters that follow.

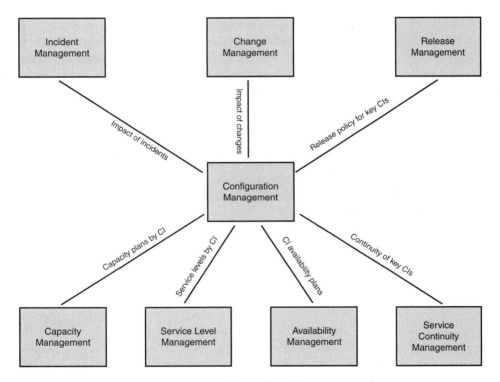

Figure 1.3   Each other process interacts with configuration management.

The Business Value

Beyond the operational processes, however, there is a significant business value to having complete and accurate configuration management data. The old saying "time is money" was never truer than in systems management. Having timely and accurate data at the point of resolving an incident or considering a change will result in huge savings. As everyone knows, having information is critical to making good decisions, and this is certainly the case with configuration information.

Making Good Decisions

Consider, for example, the many decisions that are made around the cost of support. Should we outsource our IT support? Perhaps we can move some of the support off shore to leverage lower labor rates. How much longer should we support those old dot-matrix printers? Is the value of the redundancy really worth the cost of supporting the load balancer? These are just a few of the many questions that come up around support costs in IT shops every day. In an era of global economic competition, making wise decisions can be a matter of survival. But wise decisions are fueled by adequate information. Having an accurate CMDB allows the IT manager to understand which components of the infrastructure fail most often, how much change activity is occurring to antiquated equipment, and when to drop support of certain applications or types of equipment.

Although configuration management should never be confused with IT asset management, there is certainly value to having more information as part of the IT purchase cycle. The CMDB can help determine when it's appropriate to refresh hardware sooner than expected, or when it is acceptable to let the refresh cycle lag behind the original schedule. If a server is hosting business-critical applications and has had a whole series of minor incidents reported against it, it might be time to escalate the refresh time of that server, or perhaps swap it into a less critical part of the environment. But rather than simply deciding based on the annoyance of the most recent incident, you can have concrete information from the CMDB on which to base this kind of decision.

On the other hand, if a router has been running perfectly for four years, and it supports only a handful of user networks, it probably doesn't make sense to replace it with a newer model just because policy says that four years is long enough for routers. Of course, none of these decisions can be made without good data on the environment, including relationships of components to applications and users, and a good track of the incidents and changes by component. Without configuration management information, you won't have solid information on when to shift your IT policies, and you will have to rely on instinct or emotion.

If your organization has adopted grid computing to any extent, you already understand the significant decisions around this utility-based computing model. Because the basic tenet of grid computing is massively parallel computing, you must have an easy way to understand the configurations available for use. Accurate configuration information will allow for rapid decisions about how much work can be directed to the overall grid, and which potential hosts can support the additional workload. Without having adequate information about the configurations involved, it would be virtually impossible to make workload decisions for the entire grid.

Another kind of decision that is enabled by configuration management data is investment decisions. By looking at the data available, and particularly at the relationships between IT components as captured in the CMDB, it's possible to isolate single points of failure and see redundancies. Examining the number and criticality of applications related to a server can show potentially under- or overutilized servers. Seeing the links between routers can show where additional firewalls might improve IT security. This type of information helps to determine which projects are worthy of funding and which projects can safely be delayed until the following year. In this way, the CMDB and discipline helps to support the decision making around your IT investments.

Process Effectiveness

The business value of configuration management is not limited to making decisions. Configuration management is truly a service support process. It supports all other processes by helping them meet their goals more easily. As an example, consider again the incident management process. Typically during a service disruption, information is in short supply and demands for action are frequent and loud. Knowing which applications run on the downed server, which LAN segments are supported by the failing hub, or which business processes depend on the bug-ridden application can be the difference between a temporary inconvenience and a prolonged, revenue-losing outage. When the organization trusts the CMDB and can rely on its accuracy, every incident will be understood and repaired more quickly. This more rapid understanding allows technicians to recover service instead of trying to discover (once again) how things are pieced together.

The key to really understanding how things are pieced together is a complete business service model. In such a model, IT infrastructure components such as servers, routers, and operating systems are linked to the business application software they support. This application software, in turn, is linked to the specific function or process within the wider organization that uses those applications.

As a simple example of a business service model, consider the payroll function present in most organizations. The business functions of payroll are to compensate employees, make sure taxing authorities get paid, and record disbursements to various insurance, pension, and charitable causes made on the employees' behalf. Assume that the payroll function uses a primary payroll application, as well as a health insurance application that links via EDI with an insurance company. The payroll application runs on a set of UNIX-based servers, including a database server, several web servers, and an application server. Each of these servers runs an operating system and one or more middleware products. The health insurance application can be similarly broken down, and here we even include the direct network links that support the EDI transactions. A simple schematic might look like Figure 1.4. By linking all these individual IT components together with the payroll business functions, we have created a service model that demonstrates directly how IT supports payroll. Service models will be a recurring theme throughout this book, but it is easy to see how the existence of such models, and gathering them together into a services catalog, can be a key enabler to make all IT processes more effective.

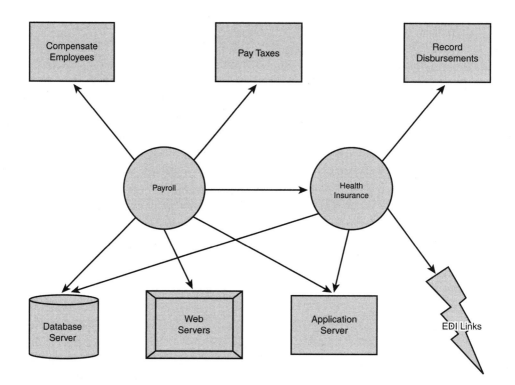

Figure 1.4   A simple example of an environment to be recorded in configuration management.

Release management can also be made more effective by accurate configuration management data. Imagine a major application consisting of a database, an application server tier, and a web-based presentation tier. Each piece of the application may run on one or more servers, and all those servers might host other applications beyond the one being considered part of the release. A release manager needs complete and accurate information about this entire environment, including the dependencies of one part of the application on another, before scheduling the series of changes needed to put a new release of this application into production. On a much smaller scale, consider the release of a new security patch to Microsoft® Windows®. Without adequate and near real-time configuration information, it is extremely difficult to determine where the patch has been installed and where it is still needed. Inadequate data could lead to a continued security exposure as well as embarrassing and expensive security breaches.

As another example of the support that configuration management gives to all other process areas, consider service continuity management. Being proactive, a continuity planner could look through the CMDB for likely points of failure by navigating the relationships between IT components. Seeing those potential failures allows the continuity plans to include redundancy or hot standby spares as appropriate. In addition, when a disaster does happen, if the CMDB can be restored in the recovery environment, it can serve as a valuable double check that all critical components are indeed restored to service after the plan is invoked.

Finally, consider the significant advantage that configuration management data provides in making outsourcing more effective. In the simplest case where a single outsourcing vendor is involved, configuration information provides a solid baseline for understanding the services being provided. In a more complex situation where multiple vendors provide different services, configuration management can enable the communication between vendors. Rather than pointing fingers or placing blame, each vendor can take responsibility for specific configuration items, and the scope of duties can be very clear. For such multivendor environments, configuration information is critical.

The Technical Challenges

So given all of the many benefits and advantages, why doesn't every organization have a complete and accurate CMDB? Because it's hard! There certainly are challenges associated with implementing the organization, the process, and the tools needed to achieve all these benefits. But don't despair—this book will guide you through the challenges and show how you can achieve the benefits of configuration management for your organization.

An underlying assumption throughout this book is that you have the sponsorship of key decision makers for your organization. Technical and business challenges can be overcome, but if there are political barriers outside of direct project control, you need a strong sponsor who can sweep those barriers away before they block the project. We'll return to the theme of sponsorship many times in the chapters that follow.

Data Overload

The single largest obstacle to creating a CMDB is the sheer volume of data that can be collected. Even a relatively small organization must track thousands of individual items, and in larger enterprises the number can quickly grow to more than a million. The challenge is exacerbated by the variety of items that need to be counted, and the technical knowledge needed to understand what to count and in what order.

For example, suppose a server cluster has four physical boxes and runs twelve virtual operating system images along with a cluster control program that manages swapping resources like memory and CPU power among the virtual images. It takes a technically adept person to recommend how to account for that cluster in the CMDB. It might be described as 4 servers, 12 servers, or perhaps 1 server. The number of items to be cataloged multiplied by the difficulty of determining what to track results in a very large obstacle to correctly creating and maintaining a CMDB.

The key to overcoming data overload is to break down the environment into manageable pieces and decide that it's better to have good information about some things than no information about everything. The key to breaking down any IT environment is in understanding the appropriate scope and granularity for your needs. Scope involves deciding which IT objects to manage in the configuration database, whereas granularity involves determining how much and what kind of information will be maintained about each of those objects. Chapter 3, "Determining Scope, Span, and Granularity," provides details of how to determine the appropriate scope and granularity.

Dynamic Environments

A second technical hurdle is the frequency of change in most IT environments and the fact that many changes are decentralized. Individual users can install programs on their PC, and sometimes on shared spaces of servers; business needs drive the maintenance and upgrade releases of all business applications; technical obsolescence dictates that hardware be refreshed constantly; and ongoing projects introduce new levels of automation and new layers of complexity. All of these sources of change may be controlled to a greater or lesser extent by formal processes, but each results in changes to the IT environment that must be recorded into the CMDB. Sometimes it seems that you need an army of record keepers just to keep the data up to date with all these changes going on. Many configuration management projects have a solid plan for getting all the data populated, only to find out that what they populated in the first days of the project has turned to hopelessly out-of-date garbage by the time the project ends.

Change management provides the freedom to make all of the required and requested changes to the IT environment without worrying about losing control of the situation. The key to long-term success of the configuration management process is the linkage between that process and change control. The linkage must be established so that every change record results in at least one update to the CMDB, and every update to the CMDB can be traced back to at least one change record.

When this linkage is in place, you can be confident that every change will be well understood and can be executed with full knowledge of its impact on the environment. Without that strong linkage, and all of the audits and controls that should be inherent in the change management process itself, maintaining accurate configuration control will be extremely difficult. Chapter 4, "Customizing the Configuration Management Process," has much more to say about integrating the configuration management process with other ITIL process areas.

Many organizations are experimenting with autonomic computing or other means of dynamically installing technology. In its simplest form, this involves setting up a controlling system that will deploy standardized software packages quickly to other computers. While this deployment technology can greatly reduce costs, it introduces a new technical challenge for configuration management. Unless the automatic process includes some way to read from the CMDB prior to taking actions and update the CMDB with the results of the actions taken, the accuracy of configuration information can be jeopardized. This kind of automatic provisioning makes an environment even more dynamic and tracking of configuration information even more challenging.

Failures in Tool Integration

Another technical challenge for those wishing to implement configuration management is the immaturity and especially the lack of integration between tools in this arena. There are strong discovery-type tools that can scan a network to find hardware devices and scan storage media to find software programs. There are integrated suites of tools that allow incident and change records to be tied to configuration records. There is even a developing class of tools that claim to be able to detect the relationships between some of these entities. But the challenge is to find or build a complete end-to-end tool set that will discover data, move it to a repository, link in with data about other ITIL processes, and allow strong capabilities to retrieve and visualize that data in necessary ways. The problem is confounded greatly by the need to both filter discovered data and marry it to undiscoverable data, such as the business unit associated with a piece of software or the physical location of a server. Even the best tools available today need to be heavily modified or programmatically integrated with other tools in order to meet the needs of a complete configuration management process.

The tools problem becomes even greater when organizations are focused on necessary security problems. In the most extreme cases, tools that automatically discover configuration information over the network aren't even allowed. Even where discovery tools are supported, they are often located behind firewalls that cannot transport their data to other parts of the enterprise. An integration strategy is needed to define how data from different network security zones can be combined and transferred to the enterprise CMDB. This adds a new dimension of complication to the overall tool integration exercise.

Choosing the correct combination of tools becomes a matter of understanding exactly which roles those tools will play. Chapter 2, "Gathering and Analyzing Requirements," helps you define good requirements—not just for tools, but for your entire configuration management program. And in Chapter 7, "Choosing the Right Tools," you learn much more about the types of tools available and how to assemble a complete system to accomplish your objectives.

The Journey to Maturity

The one thing to take away from this chapter is that configuration management is a significant business advantage, but one that presents significant obstacles. Always bear in mind that configuration management, like all the ITIL disciplines, is not a binary entity. You don't either have it or not have it. Everyone does some kind of configuration management, even if it is only remembering where you left the server after you installed it. Rather, there is a continuum from the organization which has only the faintest notion of what their environment looks like to the highly disciplined enterprise that closely controls all configuration items and uses the information mined from their CMDB to make significant business decisions.

Experience shows that there are four milestones of maturity in the configuration management discipline. Of course, like any good continuum, the stages blend together and it's sometimes difficult to discern one stage from another as you're doing your best to progress through them. But most organizations will recognize one of these milestones as the "good enough" point—that place where the value gained from the configuration management work is sufficient and further effort doesn't produce commensurate business value. Although this book provides advice for reaching all these milestones, each organization must assess for itself the value it gains against the effort needed to get that value. This is another point at which your key decision maker can help. Your sponsor will determine whether to expend the additional energy to gain the next maturity level or to be content with the gains already achieved.

The first stage of configuration management is characterized as an inventory exercise. Data is gathered and categorized into a CMDB. At this stage, the organization defines some kinds of configuration items—usually servers, business applications, commercial software packages, and workstations—and goes about collecting the information about those types of things. The information may be collected afresh with inventory techniques and tools, or it may be gathered from diverse existing systems that each contain part of the data. The key milestone for this first stage is in classifying the data that will be gathered and starting the data-gathering activities. The classification scheme is important and will generate a lot of healthy discussion, even in the smallest organizations. This is as it should be because the classification is ultimately more important than the actual data gathered. Changing the types of data gathered after the configuration management process has begun is extremely difficult.

The second stage is characterized by the documentation of dependencies between the configuration items. This is a major step because these relationships hold the real power of the CMDB. Although IT asset management systems typically relate hardware to software or users to workstations, a mature CMDB will hold a richer set of relationship types that can be used to really understand the full operational picture. Building this richer set of relationships shows that your organization has moved beyond the first stage and is really beginning to understand the uses of configuration management. Relating CIs to one another will require an entirely new way of thinking for any organization that has not been doing configuration management before.

Relationships offer a very rich and flexible way to describe the IT environment, just as relational databases opened up a much more flexible way of storing data. But just like the change from the old indexed databases to the more modern relational schemes, using relationships to describe an environment requires new techniques and thought processes. You will find much in this book to help you make that shift in the way your organization thinks.

The third milestone along the configuration management journey is one in which the organization finds itself maturing and perhaps even reengineering its processes. Accurate configuration data, including relationships, will help align other IT processes with the industry best practices which ITIL represents. Systems monitoring tools can relate events directly to specific configuration items to help technicians more quickly find failing components. Rather than classify the incident with a product type classification scheme, the service desk can depend on the CMDB to populate the categorization of the incident. Similarly, in stage three, the change management, capacity management, and even service level management processes can be reworked to leverage the configuration information that is available. Rather than have service levels on items with somewhat random names, services levels are based on specific configuration items, and outages to those configuration items can immediately trigger the service level managers to know that their targets are in danger. When you look at the other ITIL process areas and realize that they depend heavily on configuration management data, you've reached the third milestone along your journey to maturity. This maturity of process is where the most significant benefits of the configuration management discipline are measurable, and many organizations decide this is the end of their investment in configuration management.

For the organizations that choose to go forward, the fourth milestone empowers business decisions. Specific projects are executed to enable business transformation based on IT knowledge. Such a project might be to create business processes in your CMDB, and link together groups of business applications into a business process. Using an appropriate indicator of the relevance of each application to the overall process, you could create business value chains to show the impact of any IT component on the overall business it serves. As another example, the organization can establish capacity plans that reflect the real importance of a component rather than simply assuming any device running near its capacity must be augmented. The configuration management information and mature processes present at this stage allow for clear planning of IT projects and a proactive analysis of those projects real impact on both the IT environment and the overall capability of the business. Reaching stage four will help you make the better decisions I promised at the beginning of this chapter. These four stages are displayed in Figure 1.5.

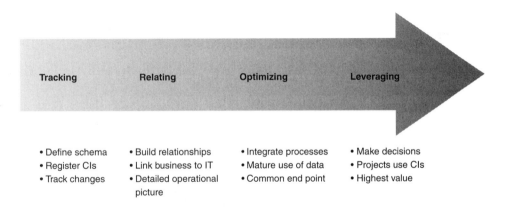

Figure 1.5   Maturity is reached through a series of phases.

So while configuration management is not easy, it is worthwhile and has proven to be cost effective for hundreds of organizations. This book leads you through the key decision points and helps you to understand some of the lessons that others have learned about implementing this key ITIL discipline.

PART I

Planning for Configuration Management

17

Gathering and Analyzing Requirements

The reason most organizations don't end up with a satisfying configuration management process is that they don't begin by identifying the needs that must be satisfied. It is important to define the criteria for success explicitly.

Everyone has a different understanding of what configuration management can do, and expectations generally are high. Each stakeholder group believes they know what configuration management should do for them, but very seldom are these expectations and assumptions clearly documented, or even consistently understood, within the group. This chapter describes how to corral all of your organization's visions and hopes for configuration management and wrangle them into a solid set of requirements that are achievable and realistic.

It is important to understand at the outset that requirements management techniques are not dependent on the subject matter of the requirements. This chapter provides some general information about requirements management and systems engineering along with describing specific experiences in gathering and analyzing configuration management requirements. If requirements management is a strength for your organization and these techniques are second nature to every project, you can just skim this chapter quickly to gather the bits that are important for configuration management. On the other hand, if you are unfamiliar with the cycle of eliciting, documenting, prioritizing, and sizing requirements, read carefully. Better yet, get a requirements management expert to join your project team. The only proven way to control the cost and quality of your overall configuration management effort is to define good requirements up front and put them under strict change control throughout the project.

Gathering

Requirements management generally falls into two areas: what you do before you have requirements, and what you do after you have them. This first section describes how to distill configuration management requirements out of all the expectations and hopes that might be swirling around. This process of gathering all the wishes of all the stakeholders is critical because until everything is put on the table, there is no way to really understand what the end goal of configuration management should be for your organization.

Figure 2.1 shows the gathering part of the requirements cycle. I call this "gathering" because the purpose is to initiate communication with as many stakeholders as possible and to clarify that communication enough to document specific needs for the project. Although many textbooks on requirements management discount the dreams and hopes of your stakeholders, experience shows that many requirements can be lost if you discount dreams and hopes too soon.

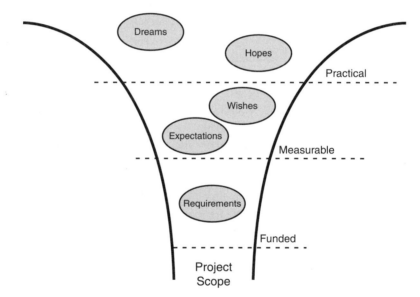

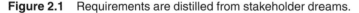

Figure 2.1   Requirements are distilled from stakeholder dreams.

Eventually, though, you must start to focus on those dreams and hopes and get to specific wishes and expectations. The difference here is one of practicality. Although a stakeholder might dream of a configuration management system that automatically detects and documents every new business application installed on every server, even the most optimistic wouldn't expect that kind of system to grow where the organization is still struggling just to catalog all of the available servers. The horizontal lines in Figure 2.1 indicate filters that must be applied to get to the next step. Only the practical dreams and hopes will be expressed as wishes and expectations.

This first filter is where a strong project sponsor comes into play. The sponsor needs to judge what is and is not going to be practical for the project. This difference between practical and impractical is often measured in degrees of desire, the amounts of effort to be expended, and the general size of the project that the sponsor desires. All these factors will help determine which dreams and hopes are worth pursuing.

After all the wishes and expectations have been put on the table, the second filter is measurability. Those expectations that cannot be measured cannot be fulfilled. Only the wishes and expectations that can be put into concrete, measurable terms will become requirements. This isn't to say that the other expectations and wishes aren't important—they should be saved and used in presentations as descriptions of the benefits of your project. These "soft" benefits, where you can fairly claim them, will help greatly with stakeholder concurrence at various decision check points along your project path. Never discount what a stakeholder expects—just don't promise to deliver on it by putting it into your requirements document.

Finally, not all of the requirements are going to be fulfilled in your project scope. Funding is the filter which determines which requirements actually get built. Although all requirements are practical and measurable, not all are important enough to be funded in your project. This final filter, analyzing requirements, is the subject of the second half of this chapter.

The Need for Requirements

The need for good requirements should be obvious. Without a vision of where the project is headed, it's likely to go nowhere. It is critical to have clear, specific, measurable, and documented statements about what the configuration management process and the Configuration Management Database (CMDB) should do.

Without good requirements, the implementation team will not know when they've finished their work. Instead, they will continue implementing until they feel their work is "good enough." Of course, the opinion of what is enough will be different between the implementation team and the test team, and there will be inevitable debates about whether what was implemented really completes the needed tasks.

If you don't have good requirements, validation of the final work product becomes a long, difficult negotiation session with users telling you that it isn't correct, and you saying that it is exactly what you intended. Testing should always be based on whether requirements have been met or not. Without adequate or measurable requirements, testing is simply an opinion poll indicating whether the test team likes what they see. Testing normally results in a set of defects, where a defect is defined as an area in which requirements are not met. Without requirements, the test team has no basis on which to raise defects. This results either in no defects being raised at all, negating the purpose of testing, or in defects being endlessly debated between the implementation team and the test team.

Without good requirements, the project manager will have to make up tasks in the project plan. A good plan should be based on meeting stated requirements, and fulfillment of each requirement should be documented as a deliverable in the plan. If there are no requirements, you'll most likely end up with a project plan to produce project-oriented deliverables such as communications plans and test results, but without concrete tasks to actually implement configuration management.

Good requirements will serve as a project measuring stick throughout all the stages, and as we see later in this chapter, serve as a boundary between what gets into the first release and what can wait until later releases. If someone asks you to start building a configuration management process, organization, or tool without good requirements, it's time to educate him or find another project to work on.

A LESSON LEARNED

We had a major customer, where we were pressed for time and needed to get a configuration management plan put together to meet a contractual deadline. We talked briefly to the central office team who had been thinking about configuration management, but completely ignored the people out in the business units and geographical regions of the customer. We didn't even document what we heard from central office in the form of requirements.

Of course, the results were predictable. We struggled to figure out what might be of value. We debated about whether things would really satisfy the customer. We produced what we thought might be wanted. We produced the document describing exactly what would be in the CMDB in great detail, *and then spent the next 12 months defending and rationalizing it!* In the end, the customer decided we should start over and take a more careful, requirements-based approach.

The lesson learned is that by not taking the time to document requirements up front, we ended up needing much more time to accomplish our task, and even then it didn't meet the customer's needs.

So we know we need requirements, but what kind do we need? We need statements that are clear, unambiguous, and pertinent. Hopefully you've learned clear and unambiguous language from your English teacher. A requirement that states "Present a screen to the user" is unclear and ambiguous. A much better wording is "The system shall render an HTML page containing form A7." Clarity is normally gained through adding more descriptive words. Never use words like *page, field, table, column, box, picture,* or *icon* without additional text to say what these should look like, what they should contain, and how they should be defined. Remove ambiguity by choosing words more carefully. Avoid words such as *some, much, many, often,* and *about* in your requirements, and replace them with exact numbers.

Pertinent is just as important—each requirement must apply to configuration management. You'll be amazed at how easy it is to start specifying requirements for change management, incident management, or any of a number of other disciplines. Although all process disciplines within the IT Infrastructure Library (ITIL) framework clearly integrate with one another, you must doggedly insist that configuration management not try to accomplish more than it is capable. Be on your guard especially for requirements that sound like they fit, but fundamentally deal with another process area.

For example, "The CMDB shall relate each incident record to one or more configuration items." That almost sounds like a configuration management requirement, but look more closely. Can the CMDB relate anything to anything? How would that work? In reality, when an incident record is recorded is the perfect time to find out which configuration item (CI) is broken and record the relationship between the CI and the incident. That specific instance in time happens as part of the incident management process, and the service desk agent recording the incident is using an incident management tool. This can't be a requirement against the configuration management process or tool because they won't even be in play at the time. Be careful to insist that all of your requirements actually can be filled by the process or tool you're putting in place.

Where to Look

So where do you go to get good requirements? The best place to start is where you are. Most likely you are involved in building configuration management because of your role in the enterprise. Look at your job description. If it says anything about configuration management, those are probably some requirements. Look at the problems that you, your team, and your organization are experiencing because you don't have good configuration data. Those problems are a great place to look for a description of what's needed. Attend some incident management meetings—document what you learn about how configuration data could help, being careful to get only configuration management requirements. Do the same with meetings regarding change approvals, capacity planning, or service levels. In each of these disciplines, you're likely to discover some way in which configuration management data could help. In addition to these formal meetings, you also want to talk to people both inside your organization and in other organizations who are implementing ITIL. All these areas will help you when looking for requirements.

Certainly you'll want to schedule time with your stakeholders. Anyone who has a dream, hope, wish, or expectation of configuration management is a stakeholder, and the more of them you can listen to, the better you'll be able to compile a complete picture of what will satisfy your organization. Be sure to consider those stakeholders outside of information technology (IT). Although you may need to educate them a bit about what configuration management is and why you're interested in it, you'll often find the fresh perspective they can bring worth the effort of seeking them out. Also don't get bound to a single geography. If your organization spans the world, you should talk to people all across the world and not just in your home country. In this exploratory stage of requirements gathering, you will most likely get a much better education about how your organization thinks, and not just about configuration management. Any time spent seeking out your stakeholders will be returned threefold in time saved getting your project approved and keeping it moving forward when obstacles arise.

Beyond talking to people, you can also look at documents for clues to the requirements. Is there a configuration management process description somewhere? It probably has a lot of requirements in it. Descriptions of related processes can also be sources for good requirements. Look up configuration management tools and read the descriptions of the features they support. Which of those features are requirements for your tool set? By all means read the ITIL volume on service support. You'll find some general guidelines there for what the configuration management process should be, and those guidelines can be distilled into requirements for your organization. If you have been handed any project description or scope documentation for the configuration management project, those would be excellent sources of requirements. While you're between appointments with all your stakeholders, take the time to read all the documents you can find.

The key thing to remember is that when looking for requirements, it is impossible to cast your net too broadly. Every corner you fail to examine has the potential to unleash a project-crippling surprise later. Every person you fail to ask will come in at the eleventh hour with a completely new thought that needs to be implemented. Remember that the filters defined in Figure 2.1 and explained earlier will help center these discussions and provide actual requirements. Skipping directly to the easy requirements without considering some of the less obvious sources will leave you with an incomplete picture of the project.

Techniques for Eliciting Requirements

Just as there are many places to look for requirements, there are many ways to find requirements after you get to those places. The techniques you use are critical to getting key business people to open up and share their dreams, which is the only way your project will be able to satisfy them. There is little more frustrating than meeting all of the stated requirements, only to find out that you "missed the mark." This can happen too easily if you ask the wrong questions or use the wrong techniques. The following sections describe some techniques that will help you avoid this trap.

Requirements Workshops

One important technique for getting a solid set of requirements is to hold a requirements workshop. The purpose of the workshop technique is to bring together people so that they can share their ideas on what configuration management should become. The format and participation in the workshop will be dictated by what your organization typically supports, but the following paragraphs will give you some of the techniques that have proven effective in large projects.

Most of the success of a workshop approach to requirements gathering is dependant on getting the right participation. Ideally you'd like to have every stakeholder for the project, but that usually isn't practical because of the number of stakeholders and other demands on their time. The most important participants in a requirements workshop are the project sponsor, the requirements analyst, and anyone who is known as the greatest skeptic in your organization. The first two are obvious choices, but it has been proven repeatedly that workshops are more effective if you include the skeptic as well. Maybe you have someone who has been particularly vocal that configuration management will never work. Perhaps you know of someone who believes the task is just too big. Those are exactly the points of view you need in the workshop because they provide the best grounding in reality for the dreams and hopes of the optimists.

Along with those three roles, you should seek as much diversity as possible in your workshop participants. If your company is international, make sure that each country, or at least each geographic region, is represented. By all means seek participants from outside the IT organization. It is often these "business" people who have the clearest ideas of what IT projects should accomplish, and usually these same business people will make the final evaluation of your project's success.

Also invite people from different levels in the organization structure. A workshop with all executives will be out of touch with what can truly be accomplished, whereas recommendations from a group with no managers at all will not be as easy to sell come funding time.

Workshops are always more effective if they can be conducted face to face. The travel costs for a well-run workshop are saved in labor later in the project as clear requirements make implementation, testing, and deployment much easier. The typical requirements workshop should be two or three days. If the participants are new to configuration management, you may need a bit more time and be able to combine the requirements gathering with some good education for your stakeholders. If this is part of your plan, make sure to leave time and have the appropriate expert supply the education. The workshop should also include one or two people designated to take notes and capture requirements.

The agenda for the workshop should be based on a breakdown of the scope of your overall configuration management effort. If you're starting at ground zero, that means part of the workshop should focus on the process, part on data sources, part on tools, and part on identifying the people who will benefit and exactly how they will get those benefits. For example, your agenda might start with a high-level view of the configuration management process from the ITIL service support book, followed by an open discussion on which pieces need more definition for your organization—that would result in a list of process requirements. The next item on the agenda might be a discussion of the kinds of decisions people would like to be able to make with more data. That could lead to some interesting requirements on both data sources and users of the data. The workshop should include discussion of the roles that are expected to be played, and where those roles will fit within your organization. Organizational requirements and labor requirements often are ignored, but this is a mistake. Remember that the purpose of the workshop is to cast a broad net and get as many ideas about what needs to be accomplished as you possibly can.

In very large, global enterprises, a modified form of workshop can be useful. We call this a *road show* approach. In this approach, you make a world tour to the various locations where concentrations of stakeholders can be found, and conduct basically the same workshop at each location. At each stop on the tour you present the current state of thinking, including the cumulative knowledge from previous meetings, and then solicit feedback that can be used to shape the thinking. This global approach allows a much wider group to participate in face-to-face meeting formats while incurring travel expenses for only a small team of core people. One of the most fatal mistakes in gathering requirements is to ask everyone at the "home office" what they need while completely ignoring the 90 percent of the stakeholders who don't work at corporate headquarters. The format of the road show needs to be adapted to review the results obtained from previous stops on the tour, but for large organizations this type of workshop will get the best possible results without having one large free-for-all session.

Storyboarding

Storyboarding is another technique that can be useful for getting people to talk about their wishes and expectations. This involves having one of the team members create a set of scenarios, or storyboards, describing potential ways in which configuration management information could be gathered, used, reported, or some other aspect. For example, you might prepare a storyboard describing a typical change event in your organization. The general outline of the storyboard might look like this:

1. A change is proposed by the server administrator to add memory to the CashFlow server.
2. The change is sent to the architecture team, who evaluates it against standards found in the CMDB.
3. The architecture team approves the technology behind the change and forwards the record to the Change Approval Board (CAB) for business direction.
4. The CAB checks in the CMDB for other servers that already have additional capacity. Finding one, they ask whether CashPro could be moved to a different server.
5. The server administrator checks the configuration of the other server and finds that it doesn't have enough memory.
6. The CAB approves the proposed change.

Storyboards do not have to describe in detail the existing procedures or even the new procedures. They simply need to cover enough ground so that they can generate conversation about the requirements. This kind of a "straw man" approach often helps people explain their own expectations more clearly than a simple discussion. Experience shows that people more readily criticize an existing concept than create a brand new concept.

After the storyboards are in place, you can either send them around in email for discussion or use them as the basis for workshop type sessions. Regardless of the format, it is important to let everyone know that your purpose is *not* to make the storyboard perfect, but to generate discussion and capture requirements for the configuration management project. You can use the tendency to want to improve the storyboards, however, by evolving naturally from the raw storyboards to the more refined format of use cases.

Interviews

In some cases, one or more senior leaders in your organization might intimidate others in a workshop format. Rather than turning a workshop into an interview with one lead speaker and many spectators, it is sometimes better to schedule individual interviews with people whose position and personality make this a better approach. Direct interviews also can be useful when key stakeholders are too busy to attend a workshop or comment on a package of storyboards.

The interview takes no less preparation than the workshop and should cover many of the same topics. When using interviews in conjunction with workshops, always include workshop results as part of the agenda for the interviews. The ideas generated by the many might spark the thoughts of the interviewee and lead to more productive discussions. Unfortunately, because the interview has only one person generating ideas, it is likely to provide less quantity of requirements than a workshop. On the other hand, because the interviewee is likely to be in a higher leadership position, the requirements probably will be more important than those generated at a group workshop.

The disadvantage with interviews is that communication of the results is not as easy as those for workshops. After a workshop, all the participants know the results immediately and most likely will begin talking about them to their peers and their management team. After an interview, you simply have a set of notes and need to work hard to get the ideas generated out to others. It is quite possible that a single idea heard only in an interview doesn't represent the wishes of the organization at all. In fact, many times I've had ideas from one interview directly conflict with ideas from a separate interview. In this case, it is even more important to get the notes out for review to determine which ideas should be turned into legitimate requirements.

Whether you use a workshop, a road show, storyboards, or individual interviews, one of the most important techniques in soliciting requirements is to loop back and make sure you've accurately and completely captured what you heard. Certainly this involves documenting the requirements (more on that in a moment), but more importantly it involves reviewing the documents with the original sources. There is nothing quite as satisfying as being understood. Accurately capturing and playing back the requirements you hear will go a long way toward building your support base among the stakeholders. On the flip side, there is nothing quite as alienating as being misquoted and left feeling misunderstood. Always take time to put the requirements in writing and validate that you captured them accurately.

How to Document Requirements

At first glance, it might seem from the previous discussion that requirements are simply meeting notes. I've left the impression that by listening to lots of conversations and keeping careful notes, you will have created a workable set of requirements. It is now time to correct that misconception. To really be usable and helpful, requirements should be documented more carefully than just as a set of notes. This section describes some of the best practices in documenting requirements and helps you to move from notes to a set of specific requirements on which you can build a project.

Levels and Categories

A simple list of requirements, starting from the first thing you hear and ending with the last thing someone asks for, is probably the most inefficient way to document your requirements. You need a way to organize information that will be helpful in managing the requirements later. Most requirements systems feature at least some notion of levels and some idea of categories.

Levels indicate the degree of specificity of a requirement, and *categories* are used to group requirements along architectural lines. The following sections deal with requirement levels and categories.

Level indicates the degree of generality or specificity of a requirement. Business requirements typically are at the highest level and express general needs about what the business functions of configuration management will be. A business requirement might say "Each update to the CMDB must be traceable to a specific request for change." This is general in several ways: it defines a policy statement, it leaves the notion of "traceable" open to further definition, and it allows for many different implementations through either processes or tools. This concept of business level requirements generates much confusion because it seems to violate the earlier rule that requirements should be unambiguous. In reality, however, there is a difference between a requirement that is general and one which is ambiguous. An ambiguous requirement can be interpreted in different specific ways, whereas a general requirement doesn't provide details but also doesn't suggest multiple interpretations. The distinction isn't all that important in practice because business requirements are always made more specific by requirements at lower levels.

The next level of requirements is typically the "system" level, where most of the overall details of the total configuration management project are defined. These requirements should be more specific than the business requirements and will necessarily be more numerous. System requirements normally are defined at a level of detail that allows the implementation team to fulfill them in some verifiable way. Adding to the earlier example, here is a system requirement that would be at a lower level than the business requirement: "When a user attempts to update a configuration item from the Update screen, the system shall read the value of the RFC field. If the value is not valid in the systemRFC table, the system shall respond with a message indicating that updates are not allowed without a valid RFC." This requirement is clearly at a lower level of detail than the business requirement that spawned it, but it is also a direct result of something the business requirement asks for. It is important that requirements at a lower level be directly traceable to higher level requirements.

In documenting system requirements, you might decide that one or more pieces of the overall architecture need to be defined at a still lower level of detail. This can lead to the third level of requirements, often called component requirements. Not every project will have component requirements, and even when you choose to use component requirements, not every component will require them. Component requirements are most often useful for components that must interface with people or tools outside of your configuration management team. User interfaces and external tool integration points are examples of situations that frequently require component level requirements.

Now that we understand requirement levels, *categories* are much simpler. When speaking of requirements, the best practice is to split categories along architectural lines. If your project will involve building a complete configuration management solution from nothing, your architectural categories might include process requirements, tool requirements, organization requirements, and data requirements. If, on the other hand, your job is to develop the next release of a configuration management tool, the categories might be user interface, database, external interfaces, and reporting. The essential thing is that you define a set of categories that will make sense to everyone working on the project. After the requirements are organized by categories, the implementation project plan, the testing cycle, and even deployment can be organized along the same lines. This kind of architecture-driven project helps to ensure that no tasks are missed and all requirements are fully implemented, tested, and deployed.

Documentation Techniques

There are a couple of special purpose requirements documentation techniques that deserve special attention. The first is called *use cases*. Use cases essentially are sequential descriptions of how something is supposed to work. They describe how a person or tool (called the actor) relates to the thing being built. Use cases are especially good for describing transaction- or workflow-oriented requirements because they help everyone understand the flow and sequencing better than a simple list of system or component requirements. Many volumes are written about using the use case technique in documenting requirements, but the basic steps are fairly simple:

1. Document who the actor is.
2. Describe the normal or typical set of steps that happen in order.
3. Think about any deviations from the normal steps, and document those paths.
4. Go back and flesh out the use case with enough text to make it a useful requirement set.

The other special technique that can be used to document requirements is a *prototype*. Especially in the case of defining web pages or other user interface elements of the configuration tools, you can often start with a "low fidelity" prototype, which is no more than a few slides put together in a presentation. Where your project team has the skills, you can go further to a "high fidelity" prototype by actually using rapid prototyping tools. The process of building a prototype, getting feedback, modifying the prototype, and repeating until all the stakeholders are satisfied is a great way to document exactly what the interface is supposed to look like. In this case, it really is true that the picture is worth a thousand words.

When to Stop Gathering Requirements

All this focus on gathering requirements might make it seem that you are never going to actually implement configuration management. In reality, the requirement process can take several weeks to several months, depending on the maturity of thinking around configuration management in your enterprise. If your stakeholders know about configuration management and understand what the project should accomplish in principle, you will get to the end of requirements relatively quickly. They probably already know what they want, and your mission simply will be to capture it on paper and move on to the analysis phase.

In some cases, however, the requirements gathering process must be combined with an education process. In this situation, the best thing you can do is to get together whatever experts you have to help you prepare completely. Workshops, storyboard sessions, and interviews that you conduct will need to be much more basic to start out. In some cases you may need to have an initial session to establish the subject matter in people's minds, and then a follow-up session where you can actually gather requirements. In the questions you ask and the categories you choose, you are teaching the organization to have a common vocabulary and a consistent idea of what configuration management is and does. If that is your situation, don't be afraid to let the requirements gathering stage go on for several months.

But how do you know when you are finished with requirements? That is actually a rather difficult question. The simplest answer is that when you've asked everyone you can think of and none of them have new ideas, you're finished getting requirements. But we all know that someone who ran out of ideas yesterday might think of something new tomorrow. Requirements can't be a boundless process. If the requirements gathering phase lasts too long, your stakeholders will get the impression that your project will take too long to return significant value, and may even decide that there are higher priorities than endless requirements gathering. On the other hand, if you cut off the requirements gathering too soon, you run the risk of significant stakeholders feeling their voice wasn't heard and thus withholding support from the project. A delicate balance is clearly required.

The best practice is to gather the requirements by level, and let each level mature appropriately. This means that you first gather the business requirements and steadfastly refuse to talk about lower-level details until everyone believes they have exhausted all the general requirements. Make sure to include reporting, administration of tools, data sources, procedures, organizational roles, and everything else mentioned in this book to cover the entire waterfront. When you're convinced that you've achieved the full breadth of coverage and have all the business requirements documented, go through a few reviews. First, review with the project team and see whether any new ideas emerge. Then review with your project sponsors—the people who are funding your project and making key decisions about whether to go on. Finally, review with the widest possible list of interested and affected stakeholders. At each stage of the review, look for new requirements. This isn't the time for rewording or redefining the existing requirements—that comes in the analysis phase. By the time you've concluded those three reviews, you should have a fairly mature set of business requirements and everyone will be more than ready to dig in at a lower level.

Next, define the system requirements category by category. Decide at this stage whether you need component requirements or not, but don't start defining them until you've finished with all the requirements that apply at the system level. Again, go through a series of reviews, although the reviews might need to be split into multiple meetings to accommodate the larger number of requirements anticipated at this level. The lower-level requirements will dictate that more people from the implementation teams are involved to really understand whether the requirements are unambiguous enough to be directly implemented. The review process lets the system requirements mature, and as they do, people will decide they have no further system-level requirements to add. Repeat the process again for each set of component requirements you want to define. Eventually you'll get the feeling of a solid, completed set of requirements. This is admittedly more art than science, but it does become easier with practice.

Gathering and documenting requirements is a lot like making popcorn in the microwave. You start simply with setting up things. Pretty soon things are popping along nicely, and before you know it requirements are springing up everywhere. But after a bit, the pace slows and not many new requirements are popping. With enough experience, you'll learn to let the last ideas mature without waiting too long and burning the popcorn.

Analyzing

Congratulations! By now you're the proud owner of at least a couple articulate, well-written requirements documents. That's great work. The next step is to turn those documented requirements into a configuration management organization running a configuration management process to collect and manage configuration management data. The best way to do that is to spend some time in requirements analysis.

Analysis can conjure a picture of endless studies conducted by countless committees. That isn't at all what is intended here. Requirements analysis is simply the act of deciding the right order to approach things and breaking large endeavors into smaller projects to demonstrate small steps toward the overall goal. This section describes several techniques that will enable you to clearly understand how to build a workable configuration management service, whether in one single project or as part of a multiyear program.

Requirements Prioritization

When people document requirements, they tend to end up with lists of individual functions that have various degrees of importance to the organization. The first thing you want to do is organize the requirements by importance. This is called requirements prioritization, and is the first stage of analysis.

To allocate requirements to different priorities, you need to define what the different values can be. Some like to use "low," "medium," and "high." Others choose "deferred," "optional," and "required," or perhaps "possible," "important," "critical," and "vital." The labels you choose to use are not nearly as important as the policies behind using those labels. If this is a new step to you, and you are unable to find any requirements that have been prioritized in your organization before, do everyone a favor and take time to document the policy around choosing different priorities. It sounds trivial, but having a consistent way to decide between a high priority and a medium priority will save your project and future projects hours of time in haggling and debating. If clear policies already exist for your organization, then simply review the policy to make sure it fits the context of your requirements.

The next issue is to decide who gets to specify the priorities. Sometimes a "one person, one vote" approach works well. If you feel there may be significant conflicts in the priorities of different groups, you might want to establish a more sophisticated weighting system allowing more powerful groups a stronger voice in the prioritization. The team that doesn't need a vote is the implementation team—they will get their say in the next phase of analysis when they specify how difficult the requirements will be to implement.

Requirements should be prioritized by levels, starting with business requirements. After all the business requirements have been prioritized, next prioritize all the system requirements that relate to each business requirement. For example, suppose you have business requirements A, B, and C. Business requirement A has system requirements a and b; requirement B has system requirements c, d, and e; and requirement C has system requirements f, g, h, i, and j. Once you've determined that A and C are high priority and B is medium priority, then determine which of a and b is the highest priority and which of f through j is highest priority. This seems obvious, but it is surprising how often people spend time prioritizing dozens or even hundreds of detailed system requirements without ever realizing that the business requirement is low priority and probably will not get implemented in the coming project.

A common problem is that everything seems a high priority. You may end up with 5 percent low priority requirements, 15 percent medium priority, and 80 percent high priority. This can happen if you have weak or nonexistent policies for choosing priorities. If you find your requirements analysis taking this direction, you simply insist that instead of several priority categories, you use a strict numerical ranking. Take the entire highest priority category and rank them from the most urgent to the least urgent. This enforces the idea that some requirements have a higher priority than others.

A second issue that can arise is that people will be hesitant to use the lowest priority category because they believe this is equivalent to making a decision that the requirement won't be fulfilled. This isn't so, because prioritization is only the first part of the analysis phase. Many times smaller requirements at a lower priority will get implemented before larger requirements at a higher priority. Just because a requirement gets assigned to a lower priority does not mean it won't get built into your configuration management project.

Sizing the Requirements

Knowing the priority of the requirements gives you half the information you need to properly scope your configuration management project. The other half of the equation is an estimate on how long it will take to fulfill each requirement. This estimate is referred to as the *size* of a requirement. When you know the size and priority of each requirement, you can assemble these pieces together into a coherent plan to meet the most important requirements in the shortest time possible while expending the least amount of resources possible.

In order to assign the correct size to each requirement, you need to turn over the requirements over to the team responsible for implementing them. For tools requirements, this might be a development or customization team. For process requirements, this is most likely a process engineer. For organization requirements, you might need an HR specialist who can estimate how long it will take to find people to fill the roles indicated in the requirements. At this early stage, these estimates are not commitments to specific days in a project schedule, but indicators of the level of effort that will be needed for each requirement.

Ask the teams doing these estimates to provide only a rough order of magnitude at this point. Remember that some of the requirements being estimated will not be implemented in the first release, or possibly not at all, so you don't want someone spending hours getting to a very accurate estimate of how long it will take to implement. A rough guess is all you want during requirements analysis phase, and a more detailed estimate will come during project planning.

Be sure to get the estimates back in consistent units. Most often this means asking everyone to estimate the number of days required to fulfill the requirements they are sizing. To provide estimates as a number of hours is probably too fine grained, but going to weeks or months will end up having too many requirements with exactly the same size. If days of effort will be difficult or expensive to estimate, you can also choose to start by categorizing the requirements into tiny, small, medium, large, and extra large. Should too many requirements fall into the same sizing category (such as all of them are medium), you can do more specific sizing on just those requirements.

If your organization is not accustomed to providing estimates, it would be best to document some policies in this area as well. For example, if a developer is providing an estimate for writing a bit of code, should they also include hours for testing that code? Or will you get a separate testing estimate from someone else? Should hours be included in the estimates for reviews of the work products, such as code reviews and document reviews? Making the wrong assumptions about what should be included in the size of a requirement will result in an inflated or deflated size when compared to other estimates. Simple policy statements help to avoid these kinds of inconsistencies and mistakes in sizing requirements. Those mistakes will lie hidden until the actual project execution uncovers them and pays for them with the realization that the schedule will slip or more work could have been done in the time allotted.

Deriving Additional Requirements

Many times in the course of analyzing requirements, the experts will discover that something is unclear or missed entirely. This happens most frequently in the estimation phase, where deep subject matter experts are looking at the requirements more critically. This isn't a problem, but it definitely should be addressed when found. When something appears unclear, or additional details need to be decided, the best way to handle this is by adding more requirements, called *derived* requirements. Rather than springing from workshops or interviews, they come from the implementation team and serve to fill in any gaps in the original requirements documents.

Rather than simply slipping them in, these requirements should be integrated into the requirements documents through a controlled change process. The stakeholders who helped to define and prioritize the requirements should get a chance to review the proposed new requirements before they are adopted officially into the documents. This prevents an implementation team from "gold plating" the requirements and thus delivering capabilities that actually are not needed. The change can be proposed by the expert finding the omission, and a small core group of stakeholders can quickly review and determine whether to add more detail.

Most often these requirements that are derived later will have the same priority and category as the requirement originally being examined. As an example, suppose you find a system requirement stating "The CMDB shall store a name for every configuration item." Our customization team is estimating the amount of time it will take to make our tool satisfy this requirement when they realize that they will need to know how many characters a name can be, whether the name should allow mixed case, and if any special characters like underscores and hyphens can be part of a name. The team leader proposes an additional requirement that says "The name of a configuration item shall be no more than 40 characters long, and shall be made of upper- and lowercase letters and numerals, but no other characters." The priority and category of the new requirement would be the same as the original requirement, and the two should be linked to indicate that one cannot be done without the other. An alternative is to change the wording of the original requirement, in essence making it more specific and measurable.

The process of deriving additional requirements can happen throughout the analysis cycle. The more eyes you have on the requirements, the greater likelihood that these kinds of insertions will occur—this is a good thing. Remember that the purpose of analyzing the requirements is to decide what will eventually get built by the configuration management project. Greater clarity in analysis now will always lead to less cost in implementation later.

Gaps occasionally are found even after the analysis phase has been completed and the requirements are agreed to. When additional requirements are necessary after the start of the project, they should be introduced through a carefully controlled change process which makes sure that everyone is informed of the change. Major shifts, such as adding additional business requirements, need to be reviewed with your project sponsor because they will most likely impact the project schedule and budget, whereas minor changes to the content of system or component requirements usually can be handled by the project team directly during implementation. Either way, the stakeholders should be made aware of the changes, no matter how subtle.

Gaining Project Approval

The central goal of requirements analysis is to produce an exact project scope that can get funded so you can move forward. Looking back at this chapter, you'll realize you have quite a bit of information that can help you put together a recommended scope. You have notes from workshops and interviews, many of which will put context around what your stakeholders feel are the important groups of requirements. You have the reviewed requirements documents, consisting of a full set of everything that could possibly be done by your project. Most importantly, you have assigned a priority and a size to each requirement, and through the set of reviews you have confidence that you haven't missed anything.

Using the information you've gathered, you now undertake the creative exercise of finding the right project scope. You've been given general outlines by your sponsor, but now you are going to get precise about exactly which business, system, and component requirements you will implement. More importantly, you're going to decide which requirements you will not be implementing in the first configuration management project. Whether you're developing a tool or implementing an entire service, you should always begin with the idea that there will be a second release. That is, always assume that you cannot implement all requirements in a single, monolithic project and that follow-up projects will be needed to completely fill all of the organization's needs.

Many people like to set the scope based on a given set of resources over a specified period of time. In other words, how much can my implementation team of six people accomplish given a four-month project life? Using that scheme, you can simply look down the list of requirements by priority, putting in the highest priority ones that fit in the number of effort days allotted. When you have all the highest priority requirements in that will fit, look across the next highest priority set and see if any are small enough to still fit inside the box. Following this method will get you to a project that fits your predetermined criteria.

Other organizations prefer to work along functional lines. Here you look at your requirements lists by category, and which architectural function has been determined as the highest priority overall. After you've identified the highest priority functional set, you then include all the requirements needed to fully implement that function. Often you'll find that you need to include requirements from other categories to truly implement the high priority function.

Whichever method you choose to assemble a "good" project, you will probably have some juggling to do. The more familiar you are with the requirement set, the better you'll be able to do this juggling.

As an example, you might have documented a requirement for graphic visualization of relationships between configuration items. In the system requirements, you explored exactly what was needed and found that you need the ability to search for a single CI, and then show that CI at the center of a radial diagram with the various relationships in a circle around the single CI. This is a common requirement, and one that can be accomplished by several of the leading tools. In your organization, this requirement has been prioritized with a medium priority, and the estimate to fulfill the requirement has come back at 22 days of effort. At the same time, you have a requirement to produce essentially the same information in a list format, which has come back as a high priority but will take 30 days of effort.

You could choose to include neither requirement in your proposed scope, which would clearly make for a lower cost project with a shorter implementation time, but this would reduce the overall function provided to a level that might not be acceptable. You could choose to do both requirements, but at a higher cost in terms of resources and/or schedule. Or you could choose just one or the other presentation formats, citing the rationale that they really provide the same information. Using a decision-making process like this, the team should assemble an overall project scope, determining exactly which requirements will hold together to produce the right balance of function versus cost.

While the proposed scope is being assembled, don't forget to document the rationale used to put it together. That rationale will help in selling the proposal to all of your stakeholders. Many of the questions that your stakeholders will have will already be covered because the team has considered and responded to them in assembling the project proposal. If you assembled the project using time and resource constraints, be sure to tell everyone what those constraints are. If you selected a set of functionality as the highest priority, document why those functions were chosen and how each requirement contributes to those functions. Logical and well-documented rationale will make the proposal much stronger than a simple list of requirements.

LOOK INTO THEIR EYES

On one project, the approval of the scope came at a very bad time for me. Rather than travel to meet with the sponsor face to face, I settled for a conference call that I could squeeze into my schedule. The call seemed to go well, with the sponsor replying "OK" and "Yes" at all the appropriate points, so I thought the scope must have hit the mark. We went on to organize the project plan and start executing the project. Only later did we learn that I had missed some reports that our sponsor thought were the most crucial part of configuration management. Two months into the project, the sponsor introduced five new business requirements, essentially changing the entire shape of the project. This cost several hundred hours in reworking the plan, the budget, and even the design.

The moral of the story is that whenever possible, you should insist on a face-to-face meeting with your sponsor, and directly ask whether he or she is completely happy with the project.

After you've put together your specific list of requirements to be implemented and the rationale for why you've chosen those and excluded others, you're ready to see your sponsor. This is a critical meeting for the entire implementation of configuration management. The sponsor certainly saw some value to the project to even let you go this far, but here is where your sponsor and key decision maker will measure your proposal against his or her own expectations. If your proposal disappoints those expectations, you'll have long, difficult climb to get each subsequent part of the project supported and approved. On the other hand, if your sponsor believes you're being too ambitious and doesn't really believe you can accomplish everything you've promised, you're going to suffer more scrutiny at each checkpoint. It is vital at this point that you get frank feedback on the proposed scope. If the scope isn't satisfactory, ask for an opportunity to correct it and come back. There is nothing that can sabotage your implementation quite as thoroughly as a sponsor who seems to agree with the scope, but isn't quite satisfied with it.

When the project scope has been defined by a set of solid requirements that have already been reviewed by the stakeholders and approved by the sponsor, you've built the strongest possible base for implementing configuration management.

CHAPTER 3

Determining Scope, Span, and Granularity

After gathering and documenting effective requirements, you have a solid foundation on which to build a configuration management system. Some of those requirements most likely deal with the data you will put into the Configuration Management Database (CMDB). This chapter explores that topic in much more depth, recommending that you look at the shape of the CMDB as a three-dimensional matrix.

The first dimension of the matrix is called *scope*. Scope indicates what the potential contents of the CMDB will be—that is, the categories of objects that will be included and what kinds of relationships you can capture between those categories. Scope provides the general outline of your database schema and is easiest to think of using object-oriented terms. Scope indicates the object classes that will be included.

Span is used to indicate which specific groups will be tracked within each object you've defined in the scope. We'll learn that span is a necessary dimension because there are many cases where you want to track some members of a group, but not all of them. A classic example is documentation, where you certainly want to track some very important documents as configuration items, but it would be outrageously expensive to track every single document that the information technology (IT) organization produces.

The third dimension of the matrix is called *granularity*. While scope indicates what will be contained, granularity determines what will be known about each configuration item or relationship. Most people relate to a computer screen, so think of the granularity as a definition of which specific fields will be on a screen whose purpose is to show a single configuration item (CI) or relationship. If you are familiar with object-oriented programming terms, the granularity indicates the attributes of each object.

We cover scope and granularity in separate sections in this chapter, and then pull together some thoughts on the entire CMDB schema at the end of the chapter.

Scope

Although a CMDB can be extremely complex, it is built of only two elementary constructs, called *configuration items* and *relationships*. Configuration items represent static portions of the IT environment, such as computers, software programs, or process documents. Relationships, as the name implies, track how these configuration items are related to one another, and are much more dynamic because these relationships can change frequently. Given these simple building blocks, defining the scope of a configuration management system is as simple as deciding which types of configuration items you want to track and which relationships will be important.

Note that we define scope as which *types* of configuration items will be tracked, not which configuration items. Once we decide that a particular type of thing is going to be tracked, it becomes part of our scope, even if we choose to track only a single instance of that type of thing. The choice of how many of each type, and exactly which ones, is part of the span of the CMDB, and is discussed later in this chapter.

Although scope is a very simple concept, it can be extremely difficult to define for your organization. Because scope gives the CMDB its shape, you should choose a set of categories that are easy to understand and demonstrate complete coverage of the IT space. You will certainly want to include types of objects from the different areas you manage—servers, mainframes, data networks, telephony, packaged software, developed software, and whatever else is part of the purview of your organization. Additionally, you may want to consider a set of categories for documentation because IT Infrastructure Library (ITIL) best practice describes configuration management as including control of the user guides, process documents, and other artifacts that are part of the operational space.

Fortunately, help is available in determining which categories to use. The Desktop Management Task Force (DMTF) has created a standard called the Common Information Model (CIM), which conveniently enough is a set of categories for describing an IT environment. If you would like to see the full standard, visit the DMTF web site at www.dmtf.org/standards/cim/. The standard can be somewhat daunting because it covers a very wide range of situations and is necessarily complex, but it is well worth considering. Increasingly, tool vendors are adopting the CIM as the basis of their "out-of-the-box" database, which can greatly reduce your implementation time if you adopt the model. Most organizations will not select a scope that covers the entire standard but will choose a subset of the available categories from the model.

One very good aspect of the DMTF standard that should be part of your configuration management scope is the inclusion of what the DMTF calls associations, and what we've been calling relationships. It is hard to overemphasize the role that these relationships between configuration items play in the overall CMDB. A beginner's mistake would be to focus on the configuration item scope but overlook the importance of defining which relationship categories will be used. Be sure to carefully consider which kinds of associations you will include.

Let's consider some specific examples of scope decisions. Some obvious configuration items to include are UNIX servers, licensed software packages, and your organization's key process documents. In the relationship area, you will most certainly want to include relationships between software and hardware and between servers and the networks they reside on. But there is also plenty of gray area. Take, for example, the hard disk that comes in each personal computer. You could call this a separate configuration item and potentially get important information about which machines will need to have more disk space to accommodate the latest operating system. On the other hand, do you really want the complication and expense of tracking every disk replacement done throughout the organization? A cost analysis might show it is less expensive to just bump up the size of ALL disk drives purchased than it would be to track all the change records needed to replace workstation disks. It is easy to see that setting the scope of the configuration management process can involve hundreds of business decisions.

One distinct possibility to keep in mind is that you might have a multi-tiered CMDB system—that is, you might have a CMDB dedicated to each smaller domain of information such as servers, business applications, network equipment, and others. These "sub-CMDBs" could then have a much lower level of scope than is needed or wanted at the enterprise CMDB. This kind of model requires that you think about cross-CMDB relationships as well as those relationships that fit neatly within a single sub-CMDB, requiring a much more elaborate scope definition.

Examples of Included and Excluded Scope

As a further illustration of choosing the appropriate scope, let's look at some broad categories that are most often included or excluded. This is not meant to be a comprehensive list of possibilities, but a starter list to provoke some thoughts around what is appropriate for your organization.

Musing about the scope of IT infrastructure, it is easy to come up with broad categories such as hardware, software, networks, and documents. These are all included in the scope of configuration management, but are still too broad. Under hardware, there are workstations, servers, network equipment, telephony equipment, personal devices (PDA's, cell phones, pagers), and perhaps even process control equipment. All these categories are commonly included in the scope of configuration management. In the software realm, scope probably includes categories such as operating systems, business applications, desktop productivity software, database management systems, web application server software, transaction processing middleware, and even embedded software.

Relationships categories are not as easily identifiable. In most cases, you can define the types of relationships you want to maintain by looking at the list of configuration items. Are you keeping track of operating system software? If so, you'll want a category for describing the relationship between an operating system and a computer. If you decide to track logical network concepts like IP subnets or security zones, you will want to create a category for tracking hardware relationships to those logical networks, and perhaps even the relationships between logical networks and physical network devices. Throughout this book you'll see many other ways to leverage the exciting possibilities of relationships, and this may give you ideas of categories you want to use in your own scope.

On the other hand, some items are clearly out of the scope of your configuration management system. Incident records, change records, and similar kinds of information may be stored in the same physical database as your configuration management data, but they are not configuration items in and of themselves. Likewise, many documents such as business continuity plans and change back-out plans are not configuration items, even though they likely reference configuration items. Relationships between a printer and the workstations configured to use it are an example of an association that is probably out of scope for most configuration management systems.

Perhaps the most unclear aspect of choosing scope concerns documents. One reason documentation is a difficult category is that few solid relationships to documentation can be tracked easily. ITIL is clear that documents should be referenced in the CMDB. Documents that substantively help define the IT environment should definitely be included in scope. Some examples are the document describing how to perform change management, the list of all software installed on a standard Linux® server, and the installation guide for a custom-developed business application. But it is clearly ridiculous to store every document that describes some aspect of the IT configuration. You wouldn't, for example, store the standard installation manual for Microsoft Office, but you would most likely store a document that one of your people wrote describing how to quickly roll out Microsoft Office across your network domains. Think carefully through the issues surrounding the scope of documentation and especially the relationships you want to define for documents.

Another often-debated area of configuration management is the role of people and organizations. Some organizations choose to manage these expensive IT resources just like any other resource and thus decide that people and organizations are two of the categories which are part of the scope of configuration management. Others decide that the intricate relationships between people, organizations, and IT are best managed in a dedicated human resource system and would be too costly to also try to track in the IT configuration management system. There are advantages and disadvantages to both approaches, so the decision is never an easy one. Follow the guidelines in the next section to make the best decision for your organization.

Complex decisions clearly must be made around the scope of configuration management. Rather than proscribe exactly what should be in your CMDB, I'll provide a set of guidelines you can use as you make these decisions. By starting with the model proposed by the DMTF and following the outlined criteria, you can establish a scope that will be perfect for your organization.

Criteria Used to Determine Scope

You can use the following criteria to determine the scope of configuration management for your organization. Like all criteria, they must be used with a good knowledge of how your organization works and a dose of common sense. But used correctly, they can help guide you to a good scope for your CMDB.

Start Simple

As with most complex problems, the way to start is the simplest way possible. Simplicity of scope typically involves going after those things that can be quickly learned and easily maintained. If you already have an IT asset management system, for example, you probably have existing processes for gathering and maintaining asset data. Use the same scope for your configuration management efforts, even though in the long run asset management and configuration management serve different purposes. Simplicity might also be geographic, involving only one or two of your locations in the initial scope.

This guideline of simplicity also can be applied to the depth of your coverage. For example, you might want to include business applications that you've developed yourself in the CMDB. That's a good, simple thing to do. But undoubtedly some of these applications consist of a back-end database component, a web or other presentation component, and maybe an application layer component. Tracking each application as a single entity simplifies both the configuration item scope and the set of relationships that must be created, but your approach needs to be balanced between simplicity and the needs of the organization. One of my favorite sayings is "Keep it as simple as possible—but no simpler!"

Consider the Cost

As illustrated earlier, the scope of configuration management should be determined largely by what you can afford to manage and what you can afford to ignore. On one end of this spectrum is mainframe equipment, which is relatively expensive and changes only after very careful deliberation. In almost all cases, this is well worth tracking. On the other end of the spectrum are cell phones, which are relatively inexpensive and very difficult to keep track of. This is not to say that cell phones cannot be part of your configuration management scope—just that you would want to have a very strong reason to expend the energy and money to keep track of them.

Remember that the cost of managing a configuration item over its lifetime is almost always more than the cost of gathering information about it in the first place. What drives up the cost is the degree to which the relationships change. It is amazing that the actual CIs don't change very often, but it sometimes seems that the relationships can change daily. As you develop your scope, consider the relationship model carefully and be sure that you don't add relationships that would be nice to have but will also be very expensive (or technically impossible) to maintain.

Score Easy Victories

Much of the success of your configuration management effort will be determined by how much confidence your entire organization puts in the database. Choose your scope in order to build confidence early. Include only those items you can track with a high degree of certainty, and leave out those things you are less sure of. Adding data to your scope that just ends up being incorrect later will bring your entire project under suspicion. It is possible to institute processes and tools that improve the quality of data, but consider how effective those are likely to be and how much extra risk your project must manage to put that extra process and tooling into place. If you decide the risk is worth managing (based on other criteria here), then go ahead and include the scope; but if not, then leave out the risky parts of the scope. The entire configuration management program can be killed if data is incorrect early on, so you may not get a chance to recover later.

After you've begun to track configuration items and their relationships, you should ruthlessly eliminate other sources of that information. This may seem like strange information, but experience shows that information stored in two separate places is automatically assumed to be incorrect in both of them. Your entire organization will begin to depend on the configuration management database only if they see it has content nobody else can give them. This isn't to say you should dismantle genuinely useful systems like your asset management database or software license management servers, but as part of your scope decision you should carefully consider whether you are setting up duplicate sources for the same records. You can often score a quick victory by simply referencing those other data sources rather than replicating their full content.

Look Ahead to Value

In thinking about the scope of your efforts, consider the future value of having accurate information. Experience shows that there is a class of IT projects which fail for lack of accurate information. Look forward to projects your organization is likely to tackle in the near future, and structure your configuration management database to provide the information that will be needed. Are you going to consolidate servers? Servers should be a key category in your configuration management scope. Need to roll out the next desktop operating system? Then make sure desktop systems and their current operating system are in your configuration management system. Ultimately every element you add to the scope of the database should be driven by some business value you can gain by tracking that element.

Of course, it is impossible to predict every possible need for information in the future, but it is remarkable how often looking at past projects will reveal a pattern of missing data. Think just of the large IT projects your organization has conducted in the past two years, whether those were successful or not. How many of them would have cost less or been done faster if accurate data had been available at the onset? Thinking along this line will often reveal some very obvious additions to your scope, which will add significant value to future projects.

Reduce Your Risk

Configuration management systems fail because of erroneous data. The best scope for configuration management is one that reduces the risk of errors. It is critical to plan ahead for not only how you will gather the data on all items within your scope, but how you will manage that data. Proper management involves accounting for all changes to the configuration item, whether they are planned or unplanned. You must consider carefully what will happen as configuration items break, are retired from service, are enhanced, become obsolete, and many other things that can happen to technology. Remember that each of those events is more than a simple change to one record—all of the relationships involved need to be changed as well, and this could be extensive. The more completely you have planned for every possible event in the lifecycle of your configuration items, the lower will be your risk of erroneous data. Similarly, if there are lifecycle events that you know you'll never be able to track, you will want to think twice about attempting to manage the CIs that participate in those events. For example, maybe your management team interacts directly with a supplier to request the latest model of cellular phone whenever they like. You would have no chance of tracking which phones are in your organization or which person has which phone. If that is your situation, simply don't include cell phones in your scope.

Expand Slowly

Your initial scope will not be your final scope. This shouldn't discourage you from carefully considering your scope at the beginning of your effort to implement configuration management, but it should make you realize it doesn't need to be perfect. As your configuration management efforts mature and prove their worth, you will want to expand your scope to cover a broader range of IT infrastructure. If the value is proven, it should be easy to get additional funding to implement additional processes and tools to expand to a wider scope.

Please be aware, however, that you can jeopardize your initial success if your scope outpaces the maturity of your process. Consider again the criteria provided in this section and decide which items are prudent to allow into your scope, and which ones you're still not ready to tackle. Slow and steady growth will increase your business value and keep your risk to a manageable level.

Documenting Scope

All the thought involved in determining the scope of configuration management needs to be captured somewhere. You could simply take a piece of paper and try to write out every decision you've made and why you made it. But by far the best way to document the scope is to create something that will be needed later anyway—a category structure.

The category structure is simply a hierarchical way to organize all the elements that will be included in the scope of your configuration management efforts. Start at the top with a broad category like "IT Infrastructure" or "ABC Company IT Environment." Then break that into discrete pieces that make sense given the scope you've chosen. For most people, hardware, software, and documentation will be categories at this first level. There may be others like "networks" or "telephony." Continue down the structure, going to as much detail as you've determined you need. When you've run out of new subcategories and levels to create, you'll have two very important items—the complete scope of your configuration management system and the "authoritative" name of each kind of configuration item. This set of categories will serve as the basis for working with and reporting on your configuration management system, so it is worth taking some time to consider what the categories will be and what they will be called.

As much as possible, use terms that your organization will be familiar with. If you routinely group your servers into midrange and mainframe servers, don't get formal now and call them Complex Instruction Set and Reduced Instruction Set computers in your hierarchy. On the other hand, if there is confusion among different groups or business units in your organization, try to use a name that everyone will relate to. The name will show up in change and incident tickets, reports, and of course the configuration management database itself, so make them as usable as possible. If you've adopted the CIM, you'll find that you already have the hierarchy defined. You simply need to make sure that you keep all of the parent classes to every child that you've adopted in your model.

In your scope document, draw the categorization hierarchy using a drawing tool, and then describe each class that you intend people to use. Where confusion will be possible, give explicit instructions such as "This category is for network routers that operate at network layer 3.

For switches and other devices that operate at layer 2, use the network hub category." Most implementation projects choose to document the scope, span, and granularity together in a single document called the "Configuration Management Plan" or the "CMDB Schema."

Span

As mentioned earlier, the span of your CMDB documents which items of each class you're going to capture. The obvious question is why you wouldn't capture every item of the types you've identified. There are many reasons for choosing to capture only some of the possible range of configuration items. This section describes some of those reasons and helps you document the span of your CMDB.

Span is all about establishing boundaries, and the ways to describe span are as varied as the kinds of boundaries that can be considered. For an international organization with different regulatory compliance needs in different geographies, span can be used to include only those CIs of some specific class that are in regulated countries. An investment banking concern might decide that workstations on the trading floor are critical but those in general office space are not. Perhaps one division of your organization is going to be sold soon, so you want to exclude all the business applications from that division from your span. You might also define different spans when different outsourcing vendors support different parts of the infrastructure, or even when a single IT organization supports different "customers" with different services. These are all valid ways to establish boundaries identifying which CIs will be in the database and which will not.

Of course, the moment you introduce such boundaries, you start to have issues with relationships. You need to make a policy decision on how to handle a relationship between a configuration item within your span and one outside it. These kinds of relationships can be extremely difficult to support, but sometimes there are legitimate reasons to include them in your span. For example, you might want to include only the items at a specific geographic location in your span; however, because a wide area network line connects to that location, you should include it in the database even though it has a relationship to equipment at another location as well. When this happens, be aware that you are creating a need for special procedures to deal with the relationships. You may even need special features of your configuration management tool to handle relationships between something your CMDB knows about and something it doesn't include. Unfortunately, most of the popular tools today don't offer help with this situation.

Criteria Used to Define Span

This section describes some criteria that can help you determine the correct span of your CMDB. Like those for scope above, these are general guidelines that can be used in conjunction with your knowledge of your own organization and some common sense.

FORGETTING SPAN

I've been told in several projects to ignore the issue of span and simply gather all the data we could find. In each case, I've asked (politely of course) where I should start. The resulting direction inevitably consists of a statement of span. Even if you're going to tackle a bigger project with multiple spans, it makes sense to define the span boundaries as a tool to make project management easier.

Span Defines Projects

The definition of span can be used to help define projects. For a very large, global organization, it's nearly impossible and very risky to populate the entire CMDB as part of a single, long-running project. By partitioning the span into more manageable chunks, you can create the scope for several phases or releases of the implementation project. Geographic regions typically are a good choice for creating boundary lines, although you need to be careful of global CIs. Business applications that are used throughout the world or wide area network links between different regions are examples of global configuration items that should specifically be named in your statement of the CMDB span.

Your span does not have to define only one kind of boundary. For example, it is quite possible to define a span that includes servers at several geographic data centers and applications from one or more business units together into a single statement of span. This will almost certainly be the case if you follow the advice of Chapter 10, "Choosing and Running a Pilot Program," and start with a pilot program. For that pilot, you might need to bound the span by three or even more boundaries to get a small enough data set to make the pilot workable.

Tools Sometimes Dictate Span

The tools you choose to use sometimes dictate the span of your database. If you have an excellent tool that scans details of Windows based servers, but doesn't work on UNIX servers, you might want to exclude UNIX servers from the CMDB for a while. Once you've implemented better scanning technology, you can increase your span to include those servers. But perhaps you still don't have a good way to capture network information. This is unfortunate, but occasionally you will find yourself constrained by the tools and able to use only the span that those tools support.

Follow the Leader

When choosing the span of your database, it is important to understand the degree of risk your project sponsor will tolerate. The definition of span is the single best way to control the risk of your implementation project because it directly determines how much data you need to gather, manage, audit, and report on. Normally it is best to define the span incrementally so that you can be sure of managing a smaller set of data before trying to grow to a larger set. Your stakeholders should offer guidance in the best way to approach getting the entire enterprise.

Some items might be permanently out of your span, and some may simply be out of the span of a single project but assumed to come into the span later. These should be clearly differentiated. Policy statements should be documented to indicate which configuration items and relationships you will never incorporate and why. These policy statements will save countless future hours of confusion and renegotiation each time a separate project is begun. For those items that are simply deferred to a future project, include rationale statements in the span statement to indicate why you've chosen to defer them.

Documenting Span

There is no perfect format for documenting the span of your CMDB. Most projects I've participated in simply used a document that listed each boundary along with a rationale for placing that boundary in the span, and a consideration of the configuration items and associations that would cross the boundary as exceptions. For example, suppose you want to include executive workstations in your span, but not other workstations. In the span document, indicate your definition of an executive workstation and the reasons these are included while others are not. Also indicate whether there are exceptions, such as some other workstations to include, some relationships between included configuration items and general workstations, or some executive workstations to exclude. If there are no exceptions, simply state that no exceptions exist. The span document should be concise and understandable. Your organization may prefer to combine the scope and span information (along with granularity) into a single document.

Granularity

Scope and span determine which items you will track, whereas granularity determines what you'll track about each item. While scope describes the breadth of the configuration management effort, granularity describes the depth. Just like scope and span, granularity is determined by trading off the value of information against the cost of discovering and maintaining that information.

Granularity is best defined as the set of attributes you want to understand about each of your configuration items. As an example, let's assume you've decided that network hubs are part of the scope of configuration management for your organization. To determine granularity, you need to decide what information you will maintain about each network hub. Some obvious examples are the location of the hub, the person who is responsible for supporting the hub, and the serial number on the device. But perhaps there would be value in knowing other details, such as SNMP community string, the management IP address of the hub, and even the backplane speed. If these details are of importance to your organization, you would include them as part of your configuration management database. If you're never going to use them, it would be useless to include them and add extra cost and complexity to your project.

The three dimensions of your CMDB are described in this chapter in the order that you must define them. It would be very difficult to describe span without first understanding what the universe of all possible types of configuration items and relationships will be. Likewise, it is difficult to assign specific granularity before you know what the scope and span dimensions look like.

Granularity is typically defined for each individual category from your scope, but often the attributes that you need will be changed by the span you've agreed on. Going back to our example of the executive workstations, if your span includes all workstations, you might want to include an attribute that indicates whether the workstation belongs to an executive. Of course, if you choose to disregard all other workstations, you wouldn't need this attribute as part of the granularity definition.

Setting the granularity is by far the most complex of the three dimensions. This section will help you understand granularity better and choose the right level of configuration granularity for your organization.

Fixed or Variable Granularity

One of the key decisions to be made is whether all configuration items will have the same attributes. If you insist that all configuration items and relationships share the same set of attributes, you've chosen a fixed granularity. If you allow the category to determine which attributes are present, you're setting up a system with variable granularity. This section describes the benefits and drawbacks of each scheme.

Fixed Granularity

Whether talking about a network router or a custom-built business application, you could store the exact same set of attributes. This is called fixed granularity, and it makes your configuration management efforts much simpler. The thought is that you can define a fixed set of attributes that is wide enough so that all configuration items can be fit into this single set. Fixed granularity is most often used by organizations very comfortable with IT asset management systems and choose to convert their asset management system into a configuration management system.

The benefit of a fixed granularity system is that data collection and maintenance are greatly simplified. You can create a single spreadsheet template and fill in every configuration item as a row using the same template. Just add another template for relationships, and you have described the complete CMDB granularity. Tool implementation, reporting, and even data collection are greatly simplified using a fixed granularity.

The drawback of fixed granularity is that you must choose between two inconvenient options for things that don't fit the model. The first option is to add extra attributes and simply make them optional. For example, you could add a CPU speed attribute, and then just leave that value empty for configuration items that represent documents or software. The other option is to store detailed configuration data in another system and simply use the CMDB as an index or card catalog to point to those external sources. This can be useful if you already have all of the configuration items documented in other tools, but you want to use a centralized configuration management system to track relationships between the CIs.

There are a couple of interesting variations on fixed granularity that attempt to achieve some of the benefits of variable granularity, but without all the costs. The first option is to define a set of "extra" attribute fields that are fixed. These fields are often called "Custom1," or "Variable1," or something similar. The intent is that these fields might have different values depending on the category of the configuration item. So if the configuration item is a server, you might use the first field for the server name and the second for the main IP address of the server. If the configuration item is a software application, you might use the first field for the software version and the second field for the type of license. This represents fixed granularity because all configuration items have the same number of attributes and the same types of attributes, but it simulates variable granularity by overloading the definition of some fields. The downside of this scheme is that anyone wishing to search on or report on the configuration data will need to know the mapping of fields to categories so they know what type of data to expect in these variable fields.

Another variation of fixed granularity is the attachment of an XML document to each configuration item record. The content of the XML document can then contain additional fields and values, which represent additional attributes that are category specific. This is really just another means of representing a variable granularity in a system that doesn't natively support variable field structures. These attached XML files really represent what you would have put in as fields given another system.

Although fixed granularity seems very logical, it is seldom practical. If you're putting effort into implementing configuration management in the first place, you've already signed up for a series of challenges. Working with variable granularity is another challenge, but one worth pursuing.

Variable Granularity

What is variable granularity and why would you want to use it? This simply means that the set of information you track differs based on the type of configuration item. So, if you're tracking a PDA, you might want to have attributes about its screen size and whether it can connect to wireless networks, but those attributes wouldn't be any part of the attribute set describing a process document. Being able to describe each type of configuration item and relationship in separate terms allows much more flexibility to store information.

Variable granularity generally is defined following the hierarchy indicated in the scope definition. Consider the very simple scope described in Figure 3.1. For all the hardware devices, you've decided you want to capture the manufacturer. But documents and software don't have a manufacturer—they have a publisher instead. So manufacturer becomes an attribute only of the hardware node. By putting manufacturer there and not at both the servers and network nodes, you don't have to repeat, and you don't have to remember it if you add additional nodes (like workstations) under hardware. You can add more specific attributes, such as an SNMP community string, to leaf nodes like network. That indicates an attribute which applies only to that specific node. In defining granularity this way, you're leveraging a very powerful capability of object-oriented programming, called *inheritance*. Essentially, each category or "object" inherits all the attributes from its ancestors.

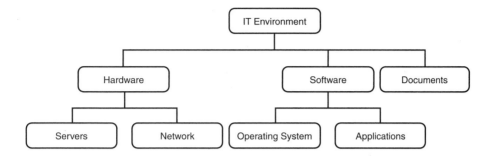

Figure 3.1   A simple scope to illustrate variable granularity.

This brings us to the most important feature of variable granularity. Attributes defined at the top impact *every* category in the CMDB. In other words, if you confined yourself to defining attributes only as this top level, you would be back to a fixed granularity. But why would you?

Although the discussion of attributes is largely around CIs, don't forget that relationships can also have attributes. In a variable granularity system, different kinds of relationships might have different attributes. For example, the relationship between a server and a network might include a "how attached" attribute, whereas the relationship between a business application and a server might have a "date deployed" attribute.

The downside of variable granularity is cost. It is more complex to define which attributes will be tracked for each category. This extra complexity will be reflected directly in the cost of data gathering. Having to stop and think about what to gather based on the type of device adds significant cost to your data gathering efforts. Variable granularity will also add to the costs of implementation, maintenance, and reporting. Clearly having more data will make your project more expensive over all.

Criteria Used to Define Granularity

You have to decide whether the extra cost of variable granularity is worth the extra value earned. The following criteria apply to either fixed or variable granularity; but as you read through them, you will most likely get a picture that variable granularity is almost always worth the extra costs. But whether you use fixed granularity or variable, these criteria can be combined with your business sense to settle on the best definition of granularity for your CMDB.

Get the Essentials

The first rule is to make sure that your granularity includes the essential elements that are critical to know about each configuration item. For many organizations, this will be the candidate list for a fixed granularity. The essentials will always include a unique identifier or name for the configuration item, the status of the item, who owns the item, where the item is located, and the category of the item. Your organization might also include other essentials, such as the organizational owner of each configuration item or the support person for each configuration item. The key is to determine which pieces of information are absolutely critical for your organization to accomplish the business goals defined for configuration management.

Remember that you must also define the attributes of relationships. Beyond the two configuration items participating in the relationship, the essential attributes might include a status indicator, a date the relationship was formed, and the name of the person or system that created the relationship.

Understand the Source

After the essentials, you begin working on what other data is available. In many cases, this involves looking at many potential sources for data. Do you have an existing asset management database? If so, this is an obvious source for data. How about IT inventory systems that automatically scan for hardware and software data? That can be an excellent source for configuration information. You will need some source for information about the people in your organization so that you can capture both owner and organizational information. Understanding which sources are available helps in determining which attributes you want to track. It makes perfect sense to track attributes that have a conveniently available source. If you can't think of how you would be able to get a data element, it might be best to leave it out of your plans. This is especially true in terms of relationships. It might be great to assign a "Date updated" attribute to the relationship between a workstation and its memory, but how will you find out the installation date of the memory on all your workstations?

Know Your Needs

When considering the level of granularity you need, consider what will be needed to convey configuration management information adequately to all of your stakeholders. If nobody needs to know whether the user is right or left handed, you won't need to gather and maintain that data element. But if your organization deals with highly classified data or government contracts, you may need to know the security classification of every configuration item. Careful consideration of your data needs will lead to the correct granularity for your efforts. If you have decided that granularity does not need to be fixed, you can then make the secondary decision concerning which set of configuration items you need any given data element to cover. It might be appropriate to know the support person for every shared printer, for example, but not necessary for each process document. Build your granularity based on what is needed by your organization.

This is another reminder to look at past projects and potential future projects to help you define the CMDB. What information would have made your recent projects more successful? Where has lack of information availability put projects in jeopardy? What upcoming projects will need specific pieces of information? Questions of this type will help you think more deeply about what attributes your configuration items and relationships should have.

Balance Knowledge and Effort

After understanding the needs of your organization, you need to balance those needs with the effort required to both initially gather and later manage the information. Some pieces of information are so important that they need to be managed at any cost. Other pieces of information are so costly to maintain that they are not worth managing. Although you may not be able to avoid the need to gather and maintain security classifications for every item, you should at least be able to understand what the cost will be to keep that information. A pharmaceutical company, for example, may have IT equipment connected to laboratory devices. Because of the oversight involved in drug testing, it may be necessary to have attributes describing those connections in great detail, even if it means a physical inspection of the interface on a regular basis.

In some cases, you can make trade-offs in precision to save cost. A perfect example is location—it might be very expensive to track each configuration item down to a specific room or grid location, but much less expensive to simply assign each item to a building. Determine whether the extra cost of adding attributes for floor, room, or grid is worthwhile. Organization can be another example where tracking to the division might be easy whereas tracking down to a department level might be very difficult and thus expensive. Use your knowledge of the organization to achieve the best balance between detailed knowledge and expensive effort, and then hold the line against "feature creep" by reminding your stakeholders that you've made the decision based on cost.

Avoid Dead Weight

The tendency in configuration management systems is to include too much detail. Just because you have scanning software that can get the speed at which your hard disks spin doesn't mean that you need to store this information in the configuration management system. Avoid choosing data items that simply add mass to the CMDB without adding value to your configuration management service. Each data source should be filtered before flowing across an automated interface into the database, and those filters should be created carefully to avoid keeping data that you haven't specified. Resist the strong temptation to include data items just because you can easily discover them. Keeping this kind of dead weight in your system leaves the impression that you're running a curiosity shop for technicians rather than a business information system.

Caution: Manual Attributes

At the opposite extreme, avoid using attributes that are too difficult to maintain because the only way to keep them is with manual effort. Of course, there will be cases where the information contained in the attribute is worth maintaining. But be aware that any time you have to gather and validate data manually, you are open to a whole set of errors that are difficult to detect. All attributes that are maintained manually should be flagged as suspect, and audits of your configuration management system should pay special attention to understanding how accurately those data items are being kept.

The procedures used to maintain the manual attributes must be flawless and reviewed frequently. The single largest cause of inaccuracy in the CMDB is attributes that are maintained by some person who is supposed to be following the right procedures. You can avoid this problem altogether by minimizing the manual attributes in your granularity definition.

Documenting Granularity

While a simple tree structure is sufficient for documenting the scope of configuration management, getting all the attributes documented requires a bit more complexity. The best way to capture your granularity decisions borrows from object-oriented programming and uses a class diagram. To create an effective granularity diagram, begin with a single box at the top, and include in this box the essential attributes that all configuration items will share. Remember that an attribute definition usually includes a type, a length or maximum value, and could include some validation criteria like a set of valid values or a minimum value. At this point, you have a simple list of attributes, and if your granularity is fixed, you are finished documenting all of the attributes.

If you have opted for variable granularity, however, your work is just beginning. Next, you list all categories that will have additional attributes beyond the essentials. If this involves many categories, you probably want to use the hierarchy that you determined in analyzing scope. For each second level box, put only the attributes that are incremental—don't repeat the common attributes in each box. Also, add only those attributes that will be common to every subcategory into this second level box. Remember the principle of inheritance. Continue to define attributes at the second level until you've finished. Move down to the next level and repeat the cycle until you've completed all attributes at all levels. A useful exercise is to double check that attributes make sense by starting at the bottom of the tree and listing all the attributes of a category by working up the tree to the top. If all of those attributes make sense for the category you're looking at, you've defined a reasonable granularity.

As an example of documenting attributes, let's consider a very simple hierarchy that has a root called configuration items with branches for hardware, software, people, documents, and intangibles. Under hardware you're going to have servers, workstations, network devices, and components. You've decided that all elements will have attributes for unique ID, name, description, status, and criticality, so those attributes are listed in the box for "Configuration Items" at the root of the tree. You next decide that hardware will also have manufacturer, model, and serial number fields, so those go in the "Hardware" box. Finally, you've decided to record physical memory, number of processors, and purpose for each server, so those attributes get listed in the "Servers" box. They key to this exercise is to make sure everyone understands that for each server entered into the CMDB, the full set of attributes is the union of all 3 boxes in the tree—so the total server has 11 different attributes, not just the 3 that are specific to the server class of CIs.

Defining the overall schema for your CMDB should be an iterative exercise. As attributes are defined and documented, you might find that it is more convenient to reorganize the hierarchy, thus changing the scope slightly. This may generate some new thoughts about span, and will certainly make you think about new relationship types. Also as new classes of CIs are defined, you might want to change the attribute list of parent classes to include more detail at a higher level of the tree. In general, you'll find that pushing attributes as high up the tree as possible will simplify both data collection and data maintenance as you go forward.

Don't be afraid to let the definition of the CMDB schema take a while. In practical terms, it can run in parallel with requirements gathering, and may take just as long. Just like requirements, scope, span, and granularity are best defined by teams of stakeholders, project team members, and sponsors. Documents should be reviewed, questioned, rewritten, and reviewed again to make sure that they are accurate and your organization is comfortable with the design that is taking form.

Having a documented schema is a major step toward implementing configuration management. In documenting requirements, you defined what would be implemented; but in working through this chapter, you have begun to define how it will be implemented. You'll recognize, however, that the schema is essentially static at this point. In the next chapter, we'll work on the process and see how the process sets the static structure in motion.

CHAPTER 4

Customizing the Configuration Management Process

In a configuration management project, you can easily focus on data, schemas, tools, and techniques, but forget the most important piece of the foundation—the process work. By process, I mean the documented set of defined inputs, workflows, and specific outputs for each activity involved in the configuration management program. The configuration management process must define how the data will be gathered, and more importantly, how it will be maintained accurately. Tools will sit idle if the process does not define when and how they are to be used. Organizations will be inefficient if they don't have a reliable process to follow. Every organization has a configuration management process of some kind, but if you don't consciously customize and document it, your organization is not likely to have an effective process.

TOOLS WITHOUT PROCESS

I haven't always been a process zealot. My career started as a technology person, so I was much more comfortable deploying tools and letting others worry about process. It's actually much easier to simply configure the latest tool and put it into place.

Of course, I kept getting frustrated when people told me the tools were too hard to use or didn't accomplish the whole job. And every time we deployed a tool, the support costs were more than double what we projected they should be.

The reason, of course, is that tools can automate only a known process. By ignoring the process, I was implementing tools without context and causing people to find their own way to make sense of what I had given them. A tool deployment will be successful only within the overall context of a business process.

Although the IT Infrastructure Library (ITIL) does provide guidance, it does not contain a complete configuration management process. Instead, it gives you a set of categories that you can use as a framework to build a process. This is more than a semantic distinction—those looking to directly implement the ITIL process will be disappointed. The outline provided by the library is extremely useful, however, because it provides the groundwork which ensures that the process definition will be complete and in line with the best practices of those who have gone before.

It is important as we work through this chapter that you realize your process work will mature along with the rest of the configuration management program. You don't need to develop a perfect process as part of your first project, but you do need to have a complete process. This is where the ITIL guidance can be extremely helpful to ensure that you haven't skipped anything others have discovered shouldn't be skipped.

This chapter describes how to use the standard framework to customize a complete configuration management process that will work for your organization. We look at some of the issues likely to come up in your process engineering efforts and describe ways to make your process fit the business goals of your organization.

The Standard ITIL Framework

Figure 4.1 depicts the standard ITIL configuration management framework. ITIL doesn't provide a beginning-to-end flow of activities, but rather a set of coordinated tasks that happen mostly at the same time. For example, you don't identify configuration items (CIs) and then move on to controlling them. Instead, you begin controlling as soon as a CI is identified, and you continue to identify new CIs as they become part of your information technology (IT) environment. Each step gets revisited as your environment changes. These steps are not specifically called a process. That would imply you could pick up the ITIL books and follow them directly. Instead, the steps tell you what elements should be in the process without specifying exactly what that process must be. The phrase often heard in service management circles is "descriptive but not proscriptive."

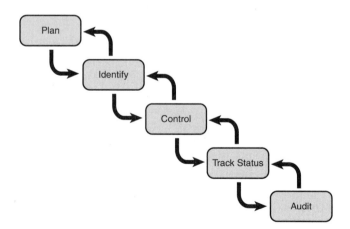

Figure 4.1   ITIL provides an outline of the configuration management process.

Planning

The first pillar in the ITIL process framework is planning. Planning always starts the configuration management process, but good planning never ends. Key elements of planning include determining your scope and granularity, customizing your process, determining your project parameters and requirements, and all the other steps described in Part I of this book. Planning should result in a document called the *configuration management plan*. You know you are ready to move past the planning phase of the process when you have version one of that document approved. You should expect that over time, however, you will be generating many follow-up versions. In all cases, be open to changes in the plan as you implement and operate your configuration management service.

Don't confuse configuration management planning with project planning. It is quite likely that you will implement configuration management in several steps or phases, each of which will require a project plan. Regardless of the number of projects that get run, however, you will have only one configuration management plan. As described in Chapter 3, "Determining Scope, Span, and Granularity," this is the document that defines the scope, span, and granularity of your Configuration Management Database (CMDB). Each subsequent project might impact the one configuration management plan, but only before the first project commences do you actually create this document. If you create an overall roadmap, indicating a set of projects that will be used to implement the complete configuration management service, it is wise to hold the milestones of that roadmap in your configuration management plan.

Planning is not a one-time activity, either. Although you certainly must have a configuration management plan early on, it should be maintained as a living document throughout the life of your overall program. Changes to span happen as new phases occur. Changes to granularity and scope can happen as new requirements are identified. You should be sure to include in your process work a process for updating the configuration management plan in an ongoing way.

Identifying Configuration Items

The second part of the configuration management process is always identification of CIs and the relationships between them. Just as you can't identify anything without a plan, you can't control what hasn't been identified yet. Depending on the data sources your organization already has at hand, this identification process could be very complex and lengthy, or just moderately complex. If you already have a strong inventory or asset management system with reliable data, that will jump-start the identification of CIs. Remember, however, that documentation, processes, and standards might well be part of your scope for configuration management and probably will not be part of an existing inventory system.

While it seems like completing one pass across your organization will complete the activities required to identify CIs, this isn't true. New technologies will continue to be acquired, new documents to be written, and whole new categories of things might be added. Identification of specific CIs will be an ongoing activity, and the processes that you define for identification should never assume they will be used only once.

Controlling Configurations

By far the most important part of the standard ITIL configuration management framework involves putting adequate controls in place. Controls are like fences that keep your data between the boundaries of accuracy you've set—the more fences you have, the better your accuracy and the more you'll work at maintaining the fences. These fences might be dictated by external regulatory groups, your organization's business rules, or just common sense. But in any event, they will provide a degree of control over what can and cannot be done with CIs.

The control part of the process is where you'll be doing the most customization because the controls that might be adequate for another organization probably won't fit yours. Defining and implementing adequate controls requires maturity, so don't worry about being perfect at the start. As your organization better understands and leverages configuration management information, your set of controls can be refined to strike the right balance between being too restrictive and too lax. The most common way to tell if your controls are adequate is by using the results of an audit process, another key element of the best practice framework.

As an example of a control mechanism that might be documented in your process work, think of the interaction of the service desk with the CMDB. You might, for example, define a control procedure that provides for the service desk to validate the workstation configuration whenever a user calls. The procedure would cover how to do that validation, and what steps to take if a discrepancy is found. Documenting controls such as this will help to keep the data in your CMDB accurate.

Status Tracking

The next area ITIL describes is tracking the status of configuration items. Most organizations that have considered the topic have some notion of the lifecycle for an asset. The lifecycle normally begins with acquisition, and goes through testing, installation, operations, maintenance, decommissioning, and disposal. Each phase represents a value in the status attribute of the CI. The set of status values you use for configuration management will be somewhat narrower than those for asset management because you're not concerned with what comes before deploying something into the production environment. You probably already have a process for promoting software into production, for example, but as part of the configuration management process set you'll want to define where in that process the CMDB gets updated with the new version. The status accounting set of process elements helps your organization understand and implement the steps needed when a CI moves from one state to another, and normally are interlocked closely with the control processes.

Versions are very important in accounting for the status of CIs. Unfortunately, this is a somewhat vague concept in the ITIL documentation. You want to document a policy that describes exactly which changes create a new version of a CI and which create a brand new item. For example, if you replace the system board of a computer, have you created a different version of that computer that can be tracked by the same CI? Or, by replacing the system board, have you created a completely different CI? Your policies dictate which case prevails for your organization.

Auditing

Inaccuracy is a death knell for a CMDB. There is no measurement quite as important for the configuration management service as the accuracy of the database. Because of the importance of accuracy, a set of procedures to audit your CMDB is critical. The procedures should document the following:

- How often audits will occur

- How the set of data being audited will be selected

- What data will be compared for the audit

- How discrepancies will be resolved

- How you will know when an audit is completed

In a sense, the audit steps are the last in the overall configuration management process because they validate that the other parts of the process are working well. But never let the audit steps be the least steps in your process, or you run the risk of executing the other steps to no purpose.

Auditing typically is done by comparing two things. One of the critical policies you need to define sets the scope for this comparison. Assume that you are tracking documents in your CMDB, and the document CI has attributes for version, author, and date of last update. In conducting a CMDB audit, you look at the actual document in a word processor and find that the author name listed in the document is different from the value in the author attribute of your CMDB. Your policy dictates whether this is an inaccuracy, and if so, what the severity of the error is.

The five pillars of the ITIL process framework are planning, identification, control, tracking, and auditing. If your desire is to implement configuration management that is in accord with the best practices defined by ITIL, you need to document processes in each of these areas. The rest of this chapter describes specific issues to consider in building out your processes.

Common Process Customizations

As we've seen, there really is no "out-of-the-box" ITIL process. Everyone must build a process, and the library offers advice on what areas the process should cover. But building the process can be confusing because configuration management represents a new way of thinking for many people and because the configuration management discipline intersects with so many other process areas. The following paragraphs describe some of the facets of the process and the most common procedures that need to be considered and documented.

Top Down Process

Good process engineers normally work from the top level of detail down to the bottom. They start with a single flow that describes the entire set of process steps, albeit at a very high level. Then each nontrivial step is defined in a more detailed flow, which may also include steps that are still too high level to be practical. The exercise continues until each process step at the lowest level can be accomplished by a single person in a reasonable amount of time.

At a top level, the process includes the five areas provided by ITIL and described in the previous section. It isn't necessary, however, to follow the ITIL guidance slavishly. If your organization is just beginning to explore and deploy configuration management, it might make more sense for your high-level process to combine control and status tracking into one top-level process. These two areas are so intertwined that the distinctions might wait until later. You also might want to use different names in some of the areas to relate better to your organization. For example, many organizations use "configuration discovery" instead of configuration identification. At the very minimum, you need to create a single top-level process document that captures the end-to-end scope of your configuration management process.

Planning Procedures

Inside the planning set of processes, there are many lower-level procedures that must be defined for your organization. While defining the schema may seem like a one-time event, you want to document a procedure that can be used for considering changes to the schema. These procedures should include both adding content and retiring pieces of the schema that are no longer used. The planning process set should also include policies that document naming conventions and other data standards because consistency of data greatly enhances accuracy. At a minimum, you should document how CIs will be uniquely identified. It also makes sense to include a general change-control mechanism for changing policies, standards, and procedures in the future. The following list indicates some of the procedures you should document as part of this first process area:

Potential Procedures to Document for Planning

Manage configuration management plan changes

Naming standard for configuration items

Standard values for key attributes

Procedures for CI Identification

If your organization already has inventory management practices in place for your IT environment, you already have most of the procedures defined for identifying configurations. If not, it is critical to define how data will be collected, and especially how disparate sources will be reconciled. One of the most difficult pieces in inventory management or configuration management is to marry the correct demographic data, such as user name, location, organizational ownership, and asset tag number, with the technical data, such as CPU speed, installed software, and network address. Consider carefully where each piece of data is coming from and how to match it up with data from other sources. Don't forget to document how disputes will be handled when different systems store contradictory data.

The most challenging procedures in configuration identification are not identifying the actual CIs, but in discovering and documenting the relationships between those CIs. How will you capture which applications run on which servers or which servers sit on which network segments? Your procedures should document who is responsible for discovery of each type of relationship, and how those relationships will be captured and maintained.

Potential Procedures for Identification of Configuration Items

Identifying computer workstations

Importing data from a scanning tool

Preparing for and conducting a wall-to-wall inventory at a site

Conducting a data center inventory

Registering application CIs as part of the development cycle

Creating a policy for registering documents as configuration items

Establishing relationships in the workstation space

Establishing relationships in the data center space

Establishing relationships in the network space

Procedures for Control of CIs

By far the majority of your process customizations will occur in the area of controlling CIs. This is where the integration with change management comes into play in determining when the CMDB gets updates as the result of each enterprise change. But you will quickly discover that control is a matter of considering every exception. Most organizations begin with the notion that every CMDB update must happen as a result of an enterprise change record. Unfortunately, there is some level of change, either explicitly documented or tacitly understood, that your organization doesn't choose to capture in a request for change.

For example, many implementations of configuration management choose to associate a person with each hardware device as the owner or administrator of that device. When that person leaves the organization, the association needs to be updated, but seldom is an enterprise change record used. To cover situations where enterprise change doesn't reach, you need to define procedures for administrative updates of the CMDB. You also might want to consider special controls for project work where hundreds of configurations are being changed as part of a coordinated roll out. If your organization is medium to large size, you also need procedures for "discovered" configurations—things that have been running in production for a while, but which someone just noticed are not part of the CMDB. The control procedures will be the most volatile set for most beginning configuration management programs.

Potential Control Procedures

Integration of configuration management with change control

Administrative updates to the CMDB

CMDB usage in a compliance audit

Standards of access to CMDB data

Discovery of unregistered configuration items

Handling registration errors in configuration data

Status Tracking Procedures

Status accounting procedures are perhaps the most simple. Here you document the set of statuses that are possible and define procedures for transitions from one status to another. For example, what is the effect on your CMDB when an application moves from development to test and from test to production? Do you choose to ignore the development and test environments because they are not part of your production environment? If so, you can simplify your status accounting for applications, but you need a more robust procedure for promoting that application into production. What about decommissioning servers? You need to define which statuses are "terminal" in the sense that you expect CIs in that status to no longer participate in enterprise changes or incidents. CIs in a terminal status normally can be archived after some defined retention period, and those procedures must be defined in this category.

Potential Procedures to Track CI Status

Definition of CI lifecycle

Procedure for managing relationships at each lifecycle change

Managing versions of a CI

Recording and using CI history

Audit Procedures

In the audit and validation category are all those procedures about how to verify the accuracy of the CMDB. This could include cross checks between the inventory discovery tools and the CMDB. It might include a physical inventory of some part of your organization compared against the CMDB representation of that same group. The procedures for audit should include how a sample set is selected, how people will be notified of the audit and their responsibilities, how audit data is to be collected, what criteria will be used to conduct the audit, how discrepancies in the data will be identified and recorded, how those discrepancies will be resolved, and how the results of the audit will be published. In addition to formal audits, there is great opportunity to validate configuration data within other process areas as that data is needed. For example, service desk agents could ask callers to read the asset tag on their workstation while the agent validates that the tag is the same as found in the CMDB. Release managers could validate that the architecture of an application is consistent with the CMDB representation of that application. All these procedures should be customized as part of the configuration management effort.

Potential Procedures for Auditing the CMDB

Frequency of CMDB audits

How to select an auditable sample

Criteria to be used to determine sample accuracy

Handling discrepancies discovered in audits

Reporting on audit outcomes

Return audits and handling of repeated failures

Modifying the Process to Fit Business Goals

While working methodically through the process customizations that must be done, it is very easy to forget the purpose of the customizations. Remember that the entire purpose of configuration management is to help the business make better decisions. With this in mind, let's consider some possible goals of the business and how you can accommodate those goals by modifications to the configuration management process. Of course, which of these you actually use will depend heavily on the requirements you documented for your project.

Perhaps your organization is interested in deciding whether to continue building custom applications or to invest in an off-the-shelf solution such as SAP or Siebel. To help make those kinds of decisions, you want to focus your procedure work on areas that will help make better decisions about business applications. Your planning procedure should consider where in the development cycle the architecture of the application will be captured as a set of configuration items. In the identification procedures, you want to carefully consider the linkage between your source code control system (often called the software configuration management system) and your ITIL-based configuration management tool. You should plan on accounting for the status changes between versions and how to handle major releases and maintenance releases. Your auditing procedures can have special emphasis on ensuring that the proper relationships are maintained between business applications and their component pieces. All of these customizations will help answer questions about the cost and capability of current applications to help make better investment decisions.

By focusing specifically on the areas of the process that most impact application development, you will be able to gather data on the business applications and their entry into production. By mixing this with project management data from the development projects, you should get a very clear picture of the impact that development of your own applications is having on the overall IT environment.

On the other hand, perhaps your organization is interested in ensuring availability of your infrastructure and eliminating single points of failure. Then your planning procedures are likely to include how to get accurate data from network and server discovery tools into the CMDB. You definitely want to customize controls that tie service continuity testing results to CMDB accuracy. To focus on eliminating points of failure, you want your audit system to frequently validate the technical, discovered data about your environment to its representation in the CMDB. This kind of process focus will give your organization the information it needs to make better availability plans and to respond to outages that detract from overall availability.

Perhaps your organization is worried about software licensing and wants to make sure that you haven't purchased too few (or too many) licenses for your needs. To accomplish this business goal, you can customize the configuration management procedures to focus on ways to help make these decisions. Your procedures for identifying configurations should include great detail on keeping track of each individual license, while your procedures for control should show the strong tie between purchase and deployment of licenses and include details about what to do about downloaded software. Your audit procedures should focus on comparing the software loads of servers and workstations with the configurations that have been recorded in the CMDB. By doing so, you can control the actual licenses used in your environment so that you can compare them with data from asset management on the purchases that have been made.

There are probably a hundred such scenarios. Each scenario shows how you choose to focus your process customizations on areas that are of interest to your business. The key lesson here is that although it's a noble idea to build a general process that will cover all of configuration management equally well, the reality is that projects get funded if they meet business goals. You can help to achieve the goals of your sponsor and stakeholders with the emphasis you place in your process efforts.

Of course, it would be rare to implement your configuration management service focusing on just a single business need. In most cases, you will have multiple points of emphasis to help guide your process customization. Your requirement set should help guide you to the process areas that need the most customization. If you don't have enough requirements to indicate which process areas need the most work, go back and interview more business leaders and update your requirements appropriately. Don't stop working on getting more process definition (and requirements, if needed) until you see a strong indication that you are going to meet business needs and not just have a process because ITIL says you should have one.

The Appropriate Level of Process Detail

Interestingly enough, one of the most difficult parts of process customization is deciding when to stop. Stopping too early will leave your configuration management team confused and without sufficient direction or consistency to perform their jobs well. But the opposite extreme is also possible—too much process and procedure detail can be stifling and cause your team too much "busywork" and limit their creativity and skill. Experience shows that defining the process to the lowest possible level of detail wastes money and discourages the IT professionals who must follow those processes. This section considers this important question of "how much is too much."

One rule of thumb for process customization is that you need to leave room for tool user guides. If your procedure says things like "fill in field A," "press button B," or "scroll to tab C," then you've gotten too detailed. You should rewrite the procedure to be more business related with instruction like "fill out the CMDB update form." Try to keep the procedures at the level of business activities without getting into exactly how those activities would be accomplished with a specific tool. A good test is to ask how much the procedures would have to change if you switched to a different tool set. If you find that the procedure would need to be mostly rewritten, it is probably too detailed. The difference between procedures and tool user guides may seem irrelevant, particularly if the same people in your project team are responsible for writing both kinds of documentation. But the more you can isolate the tools from the procedures, the more ready you'll be when you change tools, or even upgrade to the next release. By keeping the procedures separate, you also allow improvements to be made to the process and procedures without having to rewrite a lot of tedious tool-oriented documentation.

The guiding principle at the other end of the spectrum is that each procedure should get consistent results despite who is executing it. If the procedure leaves room for different outputs from different people, it is too vague or general. The entire purpose of documenting a procedure is to ensure that the best practices and corporate knowledge that your most skilled people apply to their work can be used by the newest members of the team. If you find that two different people can do their best to follow the procedure, but end up at different places, you have not yet finished customization in that area. Further detail should be added to the procedure to ensure consistent outputs are defined and that the steps in the procedure lead regularly to those outputs. It should never be left to the imagination of your staff to decide what the outcome of a procedure should be, or you will have disconnects between the end of one procedure step and the beginning of the next, leading to inefficiencies in work and inconsistencies in the resulting data.

One more general rule is that procedures aren't finished if they are too costly to implement. Consider, for example, a control procedure which dictates that every configuration database update requires a separate request for change. This might seem like a good level of detail until you try to implement the procedure and realize the volume of Requests for Change (RFCs) demanded will quickly overwhelm the change management process. Reworking change management to accommodate this detailed configuration management would most likely prove to be costly. A more detailed configuration management procedure might help determine the correct times to match up with an RFC and when it is appropriate to make an administrative update to the CMDB without a corresponding change record. Process customization shouldn't end if some of the process or procedure steps are too costly to implement. Instead, keep working on finding different, more efficient ways of doing things until the implementation and execution of the process are optimized.

The best way to understand when the configuration management procedures are finished is to evaluate the business value of the procedures. When the set of procedures is sufficient to get the work accomplished, and detailed enough to accomplish all tasks consistently, stop refining them. Further refinement will cost more money to accomplish without really adding more value to the service you can provide. Remember that process improvements are always possible, but not every improvement will turn out to add significant value. As the organization matures in its understanding and execution of configuration management, you'll be in a much better position to determine which process customizations will add more value.

Of course, the process work is much like every other part of the configuration management project—it will get perfected through a series of projects as your organization matures. Keep track of process versions, and make additional improvements as business needs dictate. Changes should never be made just for change sake, but when significant new business value can be added, don't be afraid to produce a new version of the processes and procedures. This is another reason to keep the process documentation separate from the tool documentation. Not every project will need to improve both at once.

By following the ITIL framework of planning, identification, control, tracking, and auditing, you can ensure that your configuration management process will be complete. By driving down to the appropriate level of detail, you can be sure your process work will be effective. In achieving a complete and effective process, you have the information you need to educate your organization and begin managing your configuration items and relationships. Although process work is not usually the favorite activity for IT people, it should not be omitted or slighted in any way. The process truly allows the organization to be successful—without it, no one will be able to accomplish their role effectively.

CHAPTER 5

Planning for Data Population

In Chapter 3, "Determining Scope, Span, and Granularity," we looked at the outline of the Configuration Management Database (CMDB) by understanding scope, span, and granularity. Now it is time to fill in the outline. This chapter helps you plan for the actual population of the CMDB with data from a wide variety of sources.

There are two major steps to populating the CMDB. The first involves getting data from as many places as you can find it. Using data that already exists in some electronic format, such as a database or spreadsheet, is ideal. If you have to physically collect the data through an inventory exercise by deploying a discovery tool of some kind, the cost in terms of resources and schedule time will be much higher. The first part of this chapter describes the plans you need to make in order to collect data successfully.

The second major step in populating a database involves organizing the data in the appropriate way. Although many people think of the CMDB as a single logical database, that doesn't necessarily have to reflect the physical storage of your data. We'll introduce the concept of database federation to better understand the different models that can be used to house the data you've collected. Figure 5.1 shows the two major steps and the subtasks involved in each one, and serves as a visual outline of this chapter.

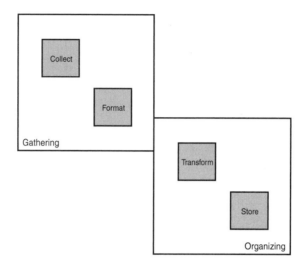

Figure 5.1   Your plan should include tasks for gathering and organizing data in the CMDB.

Gathering Data for the CMDB

When word gets out that a CMDB is being built, almost everyone will have data they feel should be included. The list of potential sources for data is as varied as the organizations that can benefit from a CMDB. Although specific sources will vary for every organization, the following sections describe the most likely types of data you'll encounter.

Note that there is room for disagreement about almost all of these data sources. People, for example, are not included in every world-class CMDB. Many times an organization will decide for privacy reasons or simplicity of implementation that people do not get treated as individual configuration items (CIs). The discussion in the following sections hopefully will help you reach a decision about whether each particular source of data will benefit your implementation. Figure 5.2 shows the variety of data sources that might be used.

Your project plan will include a similar set of steps to collect each kind of data identified in the following sections. Start with a series of meetings with the owners of the data to understand what they have, and more importantly, what they don't have that you need. If the data is owned and managed by a part of the organization different from that sponsoring your project team, you will most likely need more detailed technical team meetings to iron out what formatting can happen before the data is sent, how the data will actually be transferred, and what processing must happen after the data is received. Finally, your project plan should include some set of tasks for confirming that the data was received without transmission errors.

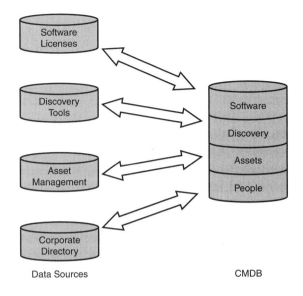

Data Sources   CMDB

Figure 5.2   There are many different sources that can provide data for the CMDB.

People Data

Now that you understand the general landscape better, it is time to consider the various sources of data that will mostly be used to populate the CMDB. We'll consider data about people first. People data is an important ingredient for several classes of business decisions. For example, if you don't have people CIs related to business application CIs, it will be impossible to calculate how many users are impacted by an outage of an application. If you don't have information about people and their relationships to workstations, it will be hard to quickly determine the failing component when a user notifies the service desk about a workstation incident. People information, and specifically the relationships between people and organizations, can also be used to form the basis for chargeback systems. Before deciding not to include people as configuration items in your database, you should carefully consider whether you'll still be able to make the decisions necessary according to your project scope.

But where is the data about people likely to come from? The most common source would be an automated human resource or payroll system, which most likely has data about every person in your organization. The challenge with these systems is that privacy and other confidentiality issues must be addressed. The rules for data access might vary by country or even by state. Your choice of which fields you can access might be limited by corporate policy or even the law. These restrictions often have already been resolved by other projects, and a suitable extract is available that contains just the nonconfidential data about people. If you find resistance to your use of the corporate HR system, but you have no other source for people data, you might propose that the HR team build an extract process for your use.

Some organizations have corporate systems such as Active Directory or LDAP directories, which can be a perfect source of people data. These directories are meant to be accessible electronically and can often be integrated easily with your configuration management tools. If your organization has a regularly updated telephone book or group address list structure, talk to the people who maintain these and ask how they get their data about people. You're likely to learn exactly what you need to understand in order to get people data for your configuration management effort.

For smaller organizations, people data might be obtained from organization charts or other paper-based documentation. If this is your only source of data, you might want to consider a "people inventory" to make sure the documents are up to date. To do so, you simply pick the management structure from the latest organization charts you can find, and then go talk to each manager to gather the data you need about their people. Along the way you can make sure everyone knows about the value of the CMDB you're building—starting with the fact that it will serve as a corporate directory, and nobody will have to come bother them again!

One important question is how much detail should be maintained about people? This question is somewhat related to where the people data will come from. If you're using a corporate wide directory structure based on LDAP, your actual configuration items might contain no more than a pointer to the directory system where all of the details can be readily found. If you have paper documentation, on the other hand, it might make sense to include other details, such as phone numbers and work locations, as attributes because those aren't being maintained anywhere else. Privacy and confidentiality also should be carefully considered. For example, it would be considered improper by most organizations to hold an employee's home telephone number in the CMDB, even if you have access to the data and there is no other place to store it. Remember that the CMDB is for making decisions—you want to avoid storing data that requires you to put security filters in place. The key is to not duplicate so much data into the CMDB that you significantly increase your risk of the CMDB data getting out of synch with the original source.

As with other volatile data sources, people data sources demand stringent processes for how updates will be managed. The best case is that your configuration management tool allows for real-time integration with your directory servers, and data is updated immediately when the directory changes. Short of that perfect situation, the best practice is to send all changes from the source data to the CMDB every night in a scheduled job. Sending more than the changed data can cause processing to become unwieldy if there are many people in the organization. Unless your organization has exceptionally few changes or is very small, directory data should be updated at least once daily. Of course, if you've had to walk around talking with managers to obtain people data, you were smart enough to leave them instructions on how to notify your configuration management team of changes. A summary of the various sources of people data and the advantages and disadvantages for each is included in Table 5.1.

Table 5.1   Summary of Sources for People Data

People Data Source	Advantages	Disadvantages
HR or payroll system	Easy to access Very accurate data	Privacy issues Confidentiality issues
LDAP or Active Directory	Already filtered Always up to date	Access only via programming
Manager survey	Always available	Costly to obtain Difficult to maintain

Asset Databases as a Data Source

The most common set of data to bring into a CMDB comes from an asset management system. An asset management system typically contains a register of hardware and software packages that your organization has purchased. Many organizations have had an asset repository long before they heard of IT Infrastructure Library (ITIL) or considered configuration management as an important discipline. Even where there isn't a corporate asset management repository, there are likely to be informal lists that individuals have kept in order to accomplish their jobs. Ask the server administration team for a list of servers and you'll likely get a spreadsheet that contains most of the server information you need. Ask the desk-side support team how they know which PCs need refreshing, and you might find a small database containing the workstations and which operating systems they run. Application support teams most likely have lists of which applications they support. All of these can be considered data sources under the asset management category.

The most important thing to remember in using an asset database is that it is not a CMDB, nor should it be. Asset management is concerned with your financial responsibilities—what the organization owns, what is being leased, the purchase value, the remaining lease payments, the current depreciated value, and the tax basis for that depreciation are all key asset management questions. Configuration management, on the other hand, is concerned with questions of operational capability rather than ownership.

Several examples can help clarify the difference in data between asset management and configuration management. First, consider a block of five thousand licenses of a standard office tools suite. You might have deployed only three thousand of these licenses thus far, and have two thousand in reserve. Your asset management database should clearly show all five thousand that you've purchased, whereas your configuration management database is likely to show only the three thousand that are part of your operational environment. Conversely, consider what happens if you hire an outsourcing company or even a large number of subcontractors who bring their own personal workstation equipment with them. These PCs are not owned by your organization, so you most likely won't keep them in your asset management database. However, if you allow the machines to connect to your production network, they certainly are part of your operational environment and should be tracked in the CMDB. Everything you own, whether it is in production or not, should be in the asset database. Everything you deploy, whether you own it or not, should be recorded in the CMDB.

Beyond the question of which assets will become configuration items in the CMDB, you must also wrestle with the appropriate separation of attributes or data fields between the two disciplines. Many organizations have practiced asset management for a while without having the notion of configuration management. Those organizations will find it especially difficult to sort out the operational information about assets from the financial information, because running with a single database means having to mix the two together. There are really four kinds of information about any asset: generic, financial, operational, and relational. The generic information consists of fields such as name, description, importance to the business, and location. Financial information normally involves monetary values such as lease residual, tax basis, and purchase cost. Operational information is most important to the configuration management team and involves measures of capacity, reliability, or serviceability in some way. Fields that have measurements associated with them, such as gigabits per second or megabytes of storage, involve operational data. Relational information includes anything designed to position the asset, such as location, organizational affiliations, and component information.

Unfortunately, much of the data you find in the typical asset management database spans more than one category. Most assets have at least one defined owner, for example. But is this the person who should be called when the device fails, indicating the operational owner? Or is this the person who should be called if you want to purchase another device to augment capacity, indicating the financial owner? Location is another great example of a data element that spans both financial and operational domains. You'll become very interested in the location of a server when its lease expires, so it is definitely financial data. On the other hand, someone putting a new memory SIMM in that server understands that location is critical operational data. The bottom line is that many fields will need to be duplicated in both the asset management database and the CMDB. Table 5.2 summarizes the differences between asset management and configuration management so that you can better decide which attributes of the asset data you want to bring into the configuration management database.

After you consider both the rows (which assets) and the columns (which attributes) from the asset database, there is one question left to ask. How clean is the data? If your organization is very comfortable with the quality of the asset database, consider yourself fortunate. While it may seem obvious, there is a great temptation to scoop up any available data to quickly populate a CMDB. If you haven't checked the quality of your data sources, your project could be facing a cleanup effort bigger than you anticipated.

Table 5.2   Comparison of Asset Management to Configuration Management

Asset Management	Configuration Management
Concerned with finances	Concerned with operations
Scope is everything you own	Scope is everything you deploy
Only incidental relationships	All operational relationships
Interfaces to purchasing and leasing	Interfaces to ITIL processes
Maintains data for taxes	Maintains data for troubleshooting
Lifecycle from purchase to disposal	Lifecycle from deploy to retirement

Discovery Tools as Data Sources

Discovery tools are a great source of configuration management data. These tools generally use some small agent code to scan a computer or network device and pull out the technical data about that device. This kind of technical data is a gold mine of operational information. Discovery tools are a critical piece of almost every successful configuration management project, but some planning is required to get the most out of this data source.

When thinking about discovery tools, the first thing to understand is that you don't have to use all the data available to you. Most tools discover esoteric bits of information that have no significant operational value. For example, one tool tells you the number of milliseconds that a keyboard key must be held down before it repeats. Another tool reports the number of files currently on a disk drive. One popular discovery tool even indicates how much memory is currently in use on a workstation.

Although this information is interesting in certain situations, it doesn't belong in a CMDB. Something like the keyboard repeat rate is not important in managing change or resolving incidents and can be disregarded. Information about the current state of a machine is often useful but is so dynamic that it should be gathered when needed rather than stored permanently in the CMDB. Total physical memory installed is probably worth managing, but the amount used at any specific time is interesting only to someone directly troubleshooting a problem; there are better ways to find out than by looking in a CMDB.

Therefore, the first part of getting useful configuration management data from a discovery tool is to fully understand what data that tool will gather and reject data that is not going to be manageable. Don't get lulled into thinking that more data is always better. Accuracy trumps quantity every time. Use only the data that will significantly help your organization make better decisions and which has a high probability of being accurate at all times.

The second thing to consider about discovery tools is how to map the data they provide into something you can recognize. More precisely, you need to consider how to marry the discovery data with demographic data the tool doesn't gather for you. You can accomplish this goal in many clever ways, and most involve some type of manual intervention on each device to be discovered. For example, the IBM Tivoli® Configuration Manager can be configured to prompt the workstation user for a user name, location, fixed asset tag number, and other external information, and then leave that information on a file in the workstation's file system. Either you need to train the entire user community to respond to the inventory prompts (and enter accurate data), or you need to send an information technology (IT) person to every desktop to enter the data the first time on the user's behalf.

Another possibility for the marriage of inventory and demographic data is to get the demographic data from sources like a corporate directory and exploit a single value shared between the demographic source and the inventory source. In some cases, discovery tools will read the serial number that the device manufacturer has put into the system's Read Only Memory (ROM). If you also happen to have device serial numbers recorded as part of a user's asset record in the corporate directory, you could create a linkage between everything known about the user and everything gained from the inventory tool. This kind of linkage requires some careful planning because it is not a one-time-only interface, but must be reused each time inventory scans are executed.

The challenge of marrying discovered data to demographic data is one of the most significant pieces of asset management or configuration management. The previous examples indicate scenarios that apply to devices with a single user, and the problem only gets worse when you consider devices with many users, such as servers or network printers, or devices that typically don't have any users, such as network routers. In almost all cases, these devices require human intervention to combine the demographic data with data from a discovery tool. The best you can do is to make sure that after the data has been tied together, the bond is not broken through any subsequent change management activity.

Software License Data

Among possible data sources, software licensing data is perhaps the most controversial. Some would argue that software licenses are more about financial ownership than operational capability, so they belong in the realm of asset management and not configuration management. Others would say that only from operational knowledge do we get the full picture of everything needed to manage software licenses appropriately. Understanding both sides of this issue will help you determine whether to use software license data as a source to feed your configuration management system.

In order to fully understand your licensed software environment, you need three pieces of information: what licenses your organization has rights to use, which software packages are installed where, and which licenses are actually in use. The rights to use a license normally come from a specific purchase, and that data is accessible from your asset management or procurement records. Information about which software packages are installed should be part of your configuration management information. The third piece—what is actually being used—is what causes the controversy. Data about actual usage normally is obtained only from specific technical license management tools, and most organizations generally aren't sure what to do with this kind of information. It is too fleeting to put into one of the longer-term data storage locations, such as the CMDB or the asset management repository, but it is not useful without the data from those two places.

There are two possible solutions to this dilemma. You can move software installation data from the CMDB into the asset repository, and then use that asset management system in conjunction with the technical license management tool to fully manage your license compliance. Alternatively, you can take the information about license purchases from the asset system and import license information in your CMDB to enable you to make a connection between the CMDB and the license usage data. Both can be equally effective, and the choice of which direction to go is dictated by the strength of your asset management tool, the integration capabilities of your license management tool, and the requirements for managing license information.

There are two models for storing software information as configuration data, and the choice of which model to use is dependent on the presence or absence of licensing information. These models are displayed in Figure 5.3. In the first and simplest model, each commercial software product is stored one time as a configuration item for each version. So Microsoft Project Standard 2003 becomes a single configuration item and Microsoft Project Professional 2003 becomes a separate configuration item. These two CIs have relationships of the type "installed on" to each workstation on which a copy of that specific version is installed. You can capture license information in a second relationship type, "licensed on." Using this model, you have relatively few software CIs with large numbers of relationships to each CI.

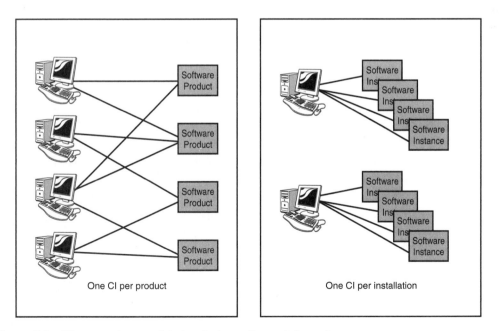

One CI per product   One CI per installation

Figure 5.3 There are two models for storing software information.

The advantage of this simple model is in maintenance, because the rollout of a new product just requires a single addition of a configuration item. When you upgrade the version of a software product, you simply break the old relationship to show that the old product is uninstalled, and then form a relationship to the new product's CI to show the new version is installed. Looking at a list of relationships for a single CI can immediately show how many copies of a software product are installed in your environment.

The downside of the simple software model is a lack of history. Relationship history typically is not maintained as well as configuration item history. For example, if a problem arises and you want to know what version of Oracle was running on your database server last month, it can be extremely difficult to determine without some sort of snapshot of the CMDB from last month. The relationship that was there last month may not be the same as the relationship you find today, and most systems don't allow you to see a history of what relationships a CI have held in the past. Another deficiency of the simple software model can occur if your CMDB tool has difficulty in managing a single CI with thousands of relationships. Not all tools can accommodate this model well.

The second model for capture of software products in the CMDB is to have a separate configuration item for each instance of a product. This is very parallel to hardware, where each router in your environment is represented by a separate CI in the CMDB. If you have twelve hundred copies of Open Office at your site, you should have twelve hundred separate CIs to represent them. Under this model, a license becomes a different CI type, but each license becomes a configuration item of its own. A simple relationship type of "uses" can then exist between the installed software CI and the license CI to show that a license is used. Any license CI that has "uses" relationships to more than one software package might be a license compliance issue, and any license without any relationships represents a spare license that can either be used without further purchases or returned to eliminate cost.

We think of this model as more complex because the number of configuration items that are tracked is exponentially larger than for the simple software model. The benefit of tracking all these extra items is richness of information. Each software product is tracked individually, including its history and current status. You can relate a set of change records and even incident records to a discrete installation of a software product. In the simple model, for example, you might be able to see that nine hundred incidents were associated with the single CI for Lotus Notes® last year. Using the more complex model, you might see that eight hundred of those incidents were recorded against just a set of six Lotus Notes servers in product development and the rest were scattered throughout the enterprise. This richness of detail allows you to explore replacing a few servers rather than a much more expensive project to replace Lotus Notes® with another groupware product.

Of course, the downside of the more complex software model is complexity. Managing software as a huge number of configuration items will require development of specific software processes, training of dedicated staff to do just configuration management of software products, and may drive the development or customization of specific features in your configuration management tools to make it feasible to manage all of the configuration items. For example, most CMDB tools don't provide a simple way to copy a CI to create another almost identical CI. But if you choose to manage software with this complex model, you'll find it difficult to live without this feature.

The model you choose for managing software products will dictate what kind of information you get back. The simple model will do an adequate job of tracking what is installed, and with the addition of licensing, information from a procurement source can track whether you have installed more than you're legally allowed to have. The more complex model will give you a full history of each software product and even a status of each license if you choose to import license data. The simple model will be easier to implement and less costly to maintain, but at the risk of providing less information to make key business decisions. The complex model, while more costly, offers a more detailed picture of your operational environment. It's important to make the decision carefully because shifting from one model to the other would be very difficult and costly.

Other Kinds of Data to Include

Some types of data are considered so integral to the understanding of every configuration item that they are sometimes mistakenly tracked as attributes rather than separate configuration items. This section covers some of the more frequently misconstrued data types and the sources you can use to populate them.

Almost every configuration management service needs to track the organizational affinity of each configuration item. It is extremely tempting to think that each CI should have an attribute labeled "department" or "division." It is a common mistake to think that configuration data will fall into neat boxes where each item is uniquely related to exactly one part of the organization. But on deeper reflection, you'll soon stumble across shared servers, core routers, and documents that span the enterprise. What would you populate for the "department" or "division" for those items? This is why it makes much more sense to store your organizational structures as configuration items. Each department, region, country, division, sector, or product line should be stored as a separate configuration item in the CMDB. When infrastructure items such as servers or LAN switches are shared, they can be related to as many of these organizations as needed. You can even create multiple relationship types for "funded by," "managed by," and "used by" types of relationships to facilitate better detail than would be possible in simple attributes. The organization data to populate these configuration items most likely will come from the same location as information about people, and can even be maintained in the same way as people data.

Another type of information commonly stored incorrectly as an attribute is location. Until you try to populate an actual database, it is easy to believe that some configuration items will have a specific country, city, province, building, floor, and room, while others won't. The natural thought would be to make each of these attributes of certain types of CI, but not to have them as attributes for the categories that aren't location specific. While this seems logical, the better practice is to keep your locations as configuration items. The most common way to do this is to build a location structure using each specific location, such as country, city, and building, as a separate CI and then use "contains" relationships to link these together. For example, you would have a "Netherlands" CI and an "Amsterdam" CI related to indicate that the Netherlands contains Amsterdam. In a similar way, you can define the geography all the way down to specific room numbers or floor grid locations where these are important.

The benefit of this structure is the flexibility to relate any configuration item to any level of location. For example, a firewall device could be related to a specific grid location in the machine room where it is installed, while a document describing the organization's privacy policy could be related to the specific country or countries to which it applies. This hierarchical approach to building out the locations allows for terrific flexibility, and because locations are not likely to change very frequently, maintenance of the complex structure is not overly expensive.

A less common type of information captured in some CMDBs relates to compliance tracking. With the advent of the Basel II accord, the U.S. Sarbanes-Oxley Act, and increasing pressure on import and export controls, many organizations need to track the compliance of their hardware and software with various regulations. The first thought often is to add a flag to the CI to indicate, for example, whether that CI needs to be considered for import regulations. Again, a much more flexible approach is to add each regulation your organization faces as a CI unto itself. Relationships between those compliance CIs and the hardware and software CIs in your system will allow for more flexible tracking of which pieces of hardware and software are related to which regulations.

Formatting Gathered Data

After you've considered all the potential sources of data and planned which ones you will leverage, don't forget to include some tasks in your plan for actually formatting the data appropriately. Although it may be possible to control the format somewhat by the means you use to extract data from various sources, it is inevitable that you'll need to modify the format slightly to match your CMDB schema. Whether something so simple as changing the case of a text string or as complex as building intermediate matching tables, you need to consider what kind of formatting each set of data requires in order to best fit into your CMDB.

Figure 5.4 describes the two general steps involved in formatting data regardless of the source. It is easiest to think of the steps as two different filters that modify the data to make it more pure for population into the CMDB. The first filter is primarily a technical one and is generally easy to implement. Actions such as changing the case of text, validating that dates fall within acceptable ranges, culling out numbers that are outside of desired ranges, and making sure key fields have unique values are all actions that take place as part of the validation filter. Anything that a machine can easily check can be considered part of this first stage of data formatting. The results of the first filter will be some records that can be modified automatically and others which will be marked as "suspect" and will have to be examined by a person in order to be formatted correctly. The specific set of tasks that need to be accomplished to set up and execute the validation rules for each incoming data set should be clearly defined in your project plan.

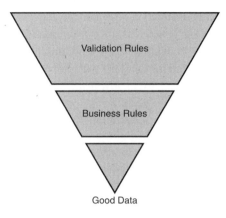

Figure 5.4 Formatting data from multiple sources involves passing through both technical and business filters.

The second filter to be applied involves business decisions. For example, when importing asset data, there is most likely a field or set of fields that describes the category of the asset. Of course, the values in those fields will not match the set of categories you defined in the scope of your CMDB. You must define a business rule that formats the categories from the asset system into the proper categories for the configuration system. In general, you will discover this pattern each time you move data from a field with a discrete set of values in one system into a field with a different set of values in your CMDB. This is not a trivial task, and you should be careful to allow plenty of time in the project plan for this kind of data formatting.

Organizing Data in the CMDB

Getting data out of the many sources you find it in is the most difficult part of populating a CMDB. Next comes the easier part—planning how you will actually put the data into your still pristine database. This section describes how data will get transformed to fit the scope and granularity requirements of your plan. Finally, we look at different physical models for storing data to understand what impact those models will have on the plans you're making.

The Importance of Naming Conventions

Whenever configuration management is a topic of discussion, the issue of naming conventions inevitably arises. Everyone agrees that naming conventions are absolutely critical, but there the agreement ends. It is imperative that you define naming conventions for all of your data early in the planning process, but of less importance is what those conventions actually are. You won't be able to properly transform the data you need to put into the database until you've established good rules for naming data elements.

What sorts of things need to have naming conventions? First and foremost, each type of CI must have some sort of naming standard. You will probably have one way to identify servers, another way to identify applications, and yet another way to name all the documentation that will be saved as CIs. Having some documented way to name instances of each category will allow the identification of configuration items to proceed smoothly, but it is hardly the end of naming.

As a special case of naming conventions, there are many discrete value lists that can make recording and searching configuration data easier. Some important lists that you will undoubtedly have are the list of all the possible statuses, the list that identifies the criticality of any configuration item, the list of manufacturers for any hardware items, and the list of organizations that might be owners of CIs. In each case, there should be some documented way to add values to the list so those values have consistency with the values that are already in the list.

So what is the best naming convention? That is highly dependent on your organization's needs, but here are some general guidelines to think about. First, do you favor human readable names or computer-generated names? Many asset inventory tools automatically generate numbers and assign them to the things the tool discovers, but the names end up looking like "SFW001231" instead of having easy-to-identify names like "BEA Weblogic." In many cases, your plans for collecting data will determine the best naming conventions for that data. If you have an existing system that tracks all of your in-house developed business applications, the logical naming convention for applications would be to use the unique identifier from that system. On the other hand, if you are going to get data from a wall-to-wall inventory of hardware, it might make sense to incorporate the external asset tag into the naming scheme.

One very important point is that names are much harder to change than they are to create initially. Never use a variable that might change as part of the name of a configuration item, or you will have misleading data in your CMDB as changes occur. It would be foolish to name a server "Payroll Server" because you might later want to redeploy that server to a different use, and the name would have to be changed. Many people like the idea that hardware should be named with the manufacturer name, the model number, and the serial number as this uniquely identifies the device not only for your organization, but for the world. This is an example of a naming convention that is becoming almost a defacto standard. Unfortunately, such standards don't exist for software, documentation, locations, and many other categories of configuration items you'll need. Again, having a standard for each category is far more important than what those standards actually are.

If your organization doesn't already have good naming conventions, be sure to include steps in your project plan to draft a standard, review it widely with your stakeholders, and then adopt it. This is the first step toward transforming your data into something that can be pushed into the CMDB.

Normalizing and Integrating Data Sources

The next step in transformation is to bring these disparate sources of data together to form a single CMDB. The problem will be broken down into two separate elements—normalizing data and integrating data.

You normalize data that has similar meaning but different ways of expressing that meaning. For example, an asset database might contain information about the people who have financial responsibility for each asset. The corporate directory contains information about people who work for the company. When bringing data from these two systems together in the CMDB, you must somehow match up the people information from asset management to the people information from the corporate directory. In a perfect world, each person would have a unique identifier, such as an employee number, and that number would be the same in both systems. In a less than perfect world, you need to choose the most desirable common data field and build a conversion table to match the data together. The worst case scenario for the asset data and the corporate directory is that while the directory has a unique identifier for each person, the asset data just contains the user's name. In this case, you would have to electronically match up those records where the employee name is unique in your organization, and manually investigate the cases where two or more employees have the same name.

Formatting the data helps some with the problem of normalization, but completely normalizing data cannot be done until after all available sources are brought together. After all the data is linked together by the best possible common fields, it is time to plan for integrating the data. Integration involves taking all the best parts of the data to include into the CMDB. Going back to the example of the asset data and the corporate directory, you will most likely choose to include serial numbers, manufacturers, and descriptions of hardware from the asset database, and choose phone numbers, email addresses, and preferred contact methods from the directory. Match the information you need to the items that fit your planned granularity to create a specific plan for integration of data.

It is important to have a strong integration plan because the integration will not be a one-time event. As the data in the asset database, the corporate directory, the discovery tools, and all the other data sources changes, you want to reflect those changes through some kind of automated process into the CMDB. Chapter 9, "Populating the Configuration Management Database," provides more information on the actual integration, but without adequate planning, the activities described there will be much more difficult.

While it might seem that these details can be deferred to actual execution, formatting and transforming data is where many projects fail. Experience shows that you cannot be too detailed about exactly what needs to be done. Many project plans simply create a single task called "format data" and enter a rough guess of a week or two. If you want to have a successful plan, however, you should break down the steps into the discrete details that need to be done with each data set, and then get estimates from people who are actually going to do the work. Don't get concerned if formatting and transforming data end up taking months. These are the most important steps in the plan for ensuring you'll end up with an accurate and usable CMDB.

Federated Data Models

Finally, a word about the physical storage of data. One of the key buzzwords in configuration management is *federation*. Although federation is a technical term from the database field, it is used in configuration management to indicate grouping data from several different sources. This grouping can be as simple as moving data from each source into the same single place, or as complex as an indexing scheme that leaves the data stored in its original source but provides access to it from the CMDB. In this section, we describe possible models for storing the data so that you can determine which model to build your plans around.

Let's consider the simplest case of federation. Suppose you have an asset database full of hardware and software information and an LDAP directory that holds information about the people in your organization. Building loader programs that move the asset information and the people information together into a single relational database would be the simplest form of federation. All that is required to accomplish this level of federation is some common field that can be used to link the two sources and a schema that accommodates all the data elements from each source. A database administrator would recognize this architectural pattern as simple batch loading of data, as illustrated in Figure 5.5. This is the model that most configuration management tools today support. The idea is that they help you build loader programs which handle much of the formatting and transforming of data as it is moved from the source through the intermediate files and eventually loaded into the CMDB.

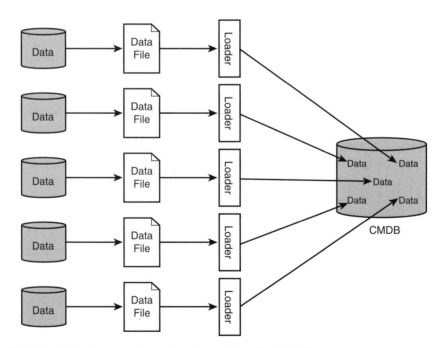

Figure 5.5   Batch loaders can input data physically to the CMDB.

The more complex case allows for data to remain resident in many different locations but provides a single interface that can query and possibly even update that data. This interface copies the data to the CMDB as updates are made, and if built as a two-way bridge, could update sources when the CMDB gets updated. This requires fairly sophisticated programming but enables a decentralized model for maintaining the data. This pattern is called a data bridge. Those just beginning the configuration management journey should be advised to avoid this more complex and risk-prone model, but it is included here for the sake of completeness as Figure 5.6. At the time of this writing, no commercial products implement this model, although you can use standard database and configuration management software as a base for your organization to program this type of system.

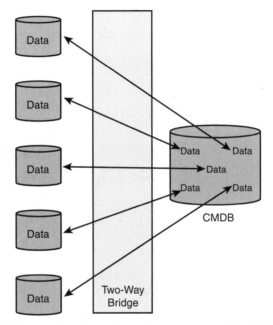

Figure 5.6   It is possible to simulate federation using a two-way data bridge.

The third model is actually what database gurus would call a federated database (see Figure 5.7). The key difference in this model is that data never gets transferred physically to the CMDB database. Instead, the CMDB simply maintains pointers to the data much as a card catalog in a library maintains pointers to books. This is by far the most sophisticated model, and one that demands both a special configuration management tool and a special database management system. The clear advantage of this model is that the formatting and transforming of data are completely programmed as rules for federation, and after those rules are established, your data is updated at the source rather than in the CMDB.

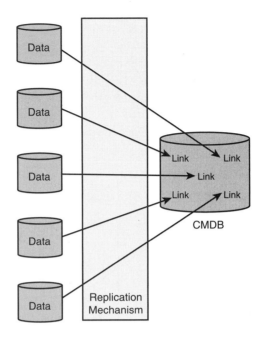

Figure 5.7   True federation leaves data at its source, but references it with pointers.

Which method should you use to store your data? The choice usually is driven by the tools you select. In most cases, the physical storage mechanism that the tool chooses will not be a significant differentiator among your various choices. After you perform the tool trade study described in Chapter 7, "Choosing the Right Tools," you should decide to store data in the way that is easiest for the tool you've chosen. This section should help you in two ways, however. When you read the vendor's literature and hear that a tool's major feature is that it supports data federation, you will know to ask which model the tool supports. Also, having more information about the various methods of data storage should help you put detailed tasks into your project plan to build the right kind of database, whether that is building loaders for the batch method or the advanced programming of a configuration management bridge.

You've now seen all the components that should go into planning for data population. Identifying data sources, gathering the data from them, formatting that data for use, transforming the data into your CMDB schema, and then actually putting the data into the correct physical model should all be represented by a series of tasks in the plan. We revisit data in Chapter 9 and include many more details on how to actually execute these steps. Unlike a development project where running code and an empty database satisfy the objectives, implementing configuration management is mostly about putting data into the final CMDB.

CHAPTER 6

Putting Together a Useful Project Plan

Thus far we've looked at parts of an overall configuration management project. We've seen how to gather and analyze requirements, how to document the scope, granularity, and span of your Configuration Management Database (CMDB), how to customize the configuration management process, and what you need to understand to plan for data population. But thus far we haven't actually *done* anything. Now it is time to put all of this knowledge together into that most tangible of documents—a project plan.

Never get fooled into thinking a project plan is the same as a project schedule. The specific tasks, resources, and dates that make up a schedule are only a small part of a complete project plan. Each organization has slightly different requirements, but normally the overall plan is comprised of a communications plan, some sort of plan for supporting the system, and some kind of budget. You also want to document the outstanding issues that you know the team will face, and create a way to describe the architecture or design of the service you're planning. Although this isn't a book about project planning, this chapter at least examines the typical deliverables that make up a complete project plan and gives you some perspective on how these can be critical to a successful configuration management deployment. Expert project managers should still find enough content here to help hone the configuration management project plan.

In general, project planning should be about synthesizing the information from Chapters 2 through 5. We begin by reexamining scope, requirements, process, and data population from a project planning perspective. In the second part of the chapter, we pull together the other deliverables needed for a full plan. Figure 6.1 shows a visual outline of the chapter.

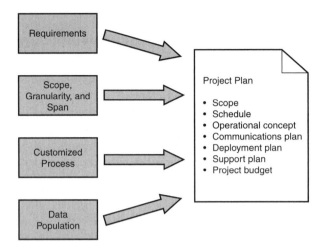

Figure 6.1   The project plan brings all the elements of planning together and adds important plan documents.

Documenting the Project Tasks

The first step in building a project plan is to gather together all the tasks that must be accomplished. For configuration management, the list consists of requirement tasks, scope definition tasks, process customization tasks, and data population tasks. The following sections serve as a reminder of the tasks involved with each of these activities and give some hints about the duration of the tasks and the dependencies between them. The intention of these sections is to give you a solid base for building a realistic project schedule.

Planning for Scope, Granularity, and Span

The first thing that should go into your project plan is the scope and granularity that you documented in Chapter 3, "Determining Scope, Span, and Granularity." Setting the scope and granularity comes even before defining and analyzing the requirements because without a solid scope, it will be very difficult to structure your requirements gathering sessions. Those early requirements gathering sessions with your stakeholders must be based on some already derived work, and the scope documentation is a perfect starting point. Just be careful that you don't set the expectation that scope is completely finished—at this stage, it is really just a working model that will be shaped through the requirements gathering. Upon understanding even the basic concept of configuration management, most people will be eager to start talking about scope, so this is the first part of the plan.

Begin by defining the set of steps necessary to get a solid scope. You can go about this exercise in essentially two ways. You can start with a pre-existing scope document, such as the Desktop Management Task Force's (DMTF) Common Information Model (CIM). This model defines a set of objects that encompass a typical information technology (IT) environment. The model is very rich and extensible, and it's probably much more detailed than you want for your initial implementation. So, the best way to use the model is to understand its use, and then begin to choose pieces of it that you will implement in the scope of your project. This is the "subtractive" method of defining scope. Typical tasks that you would add to your project plan when adopting this method might be "analyze CIM model," "work through the application subset," and "review proposal for system subset." Eventually you should work through all the subsets of the overall model and determine which you will keep in your scope.

The "additive" model for building a scope is to begin with looking around your organization, using any convenient framework you may already have. Perhaps your support teams are broken into a network group, a distributed server team, a mainframe operations team, an application development team, and a workstation support team. That's a framework you can start with. Meet independently with each team and quiz them on the key objects they deal with every day, and then use what you learn to define the scope of configuration management that will serve that team. If not from your organization structure, you might also find a useful framework from the categories used to classify incidents in your asset management tool or from the set of asset types in your asset management system. The two methods for getting at CMDB scope are depicted in Figure 6.2.

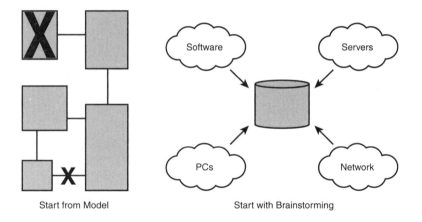

Start from Model   Start with Brainstorming

Figure 6.2 One way to build a schema is to subtract from an existing model; another way is to add based on brainstorming sessions.

Regardless of the approach, your discussions on scope will frequently lead to conversations about span. Your project tasks should encourage this interplay and make time for it to occur. Rather than a sequential relationship between scope, granularity, and span, make these tasks overlapping, where span and granularity cannot complete before scope does. This will represent a much more realistic plan, although the total time taken for developing your complete schema will not necessarily be shorter. The iterative nature of the discussions will, however, allow you to create intermediate milestones. For example, you could create a task called "define scope for network equipment," another called "define span of network equipment," and a third called "define granularity of routers. This allows better project management than a single task for creating the network part of the schema.

After you have a framework, you repeat a cycle of interviewing people who are experts in each space, documenting what you've heard, sharing it with the domain experts for confirmation, and then reviewing it with your stakeholder team to make sure the framework will meet the defined requirements. Using the additive approach to setting scope will typically take longer because this cycle will need to be repeated several times in each area of the framework as questions are raised and thinking becomes more mature. The strength of this additive approach is that you will have a greater assurance that your scope will meet the needs of your entire organization because you've built is by consensus.

Whichever approach you choose for determining scope should then be followed by a set of tasks for gaining agreement on granularity. The best method here is interviewing the people who have the data (normally the support teams) and the people who will use the data (your stakeholders). Through a series of interviews and documents, you should help these two groups come to consensus on the right level of granularity, using the rules of thumb documented in Chapter 3. From a project point of view, these tasks for getting to granularity can be run in parallel with the start of getting requirements, assuming you have enough staff to do both things at once.

Of course, in all your discussions about scope, span, and granularity, you should never lose sight of the requirements you've defined. You should certainly include the tasks needed to define your scope, but those tasks should be interlocked with the tasks needed to meet the requirements as described in the next section.

Planning to Meet Requirements

The majority of tasks in your project plan should be directly related to the requirements you have committed to meet. In Chapter 2, "Gathering and Analyzing Requirements," we learned that requirements need to be prioritized because it might not be possible to complete all of them in a single project. Now it is time to revisit that idea. Most successful configuration management programs are implemented in a series of discrete steps or phases rather than as one single project, so you should be thinking in your project plans about what those pieces might be.

Here are some general guidelines for breaking up a configuration management program into workable pieces. If your organization is not starting from the very beginning, some of these phases may be less applicable, or could already be accomplished. For everyone else, the first phase will probably include some way to prove the value of configuration management to your organization. This might be called a "pilot" or a "proof of concept," but the idea is to implement enough of the organization, the process, and the tools to prove the value is real. In most cases, this will involve choosing a small set of IT decisions that have significant value and organizing a miniature configuration management system to help make just those decisions. If you're struggling to determine the correct hardware refresh cycles, for example, you might choose to implement configuration management for Sun servers as a first phase. Implementing all the processes and tools to manage these servers, including tracking incidents and changes associated with the servers, you can demonstrate the value of configuration management in deciding the larger issues of refresh management. This first phase, or pilot, is described in more detail in Chapter 10, "Choosing and Running a Pilot Program."

Depending on the successes and difficulties of the first phase, the second phase broadens the program to a wider set of data. Following the preceding Sun server example, you may want phase two of your program to achieve configuration management for all servers, and perhaps even for applications that reside on those servers. If the first phase was a tremendous success, or if your organization is small, you might want to tackle all servers, applications, and network components in the second phase. Again, the guiding principle should be value gained for effort expended. Each phase should demonstrate value and make the project sponsors eager to support and fund the following stages. Each phase will accomplish a piece of the overall span of your database until everything included in the total span is part of the CMDB.

Plan as many phases as are necessary to completely populate all of data envisioned in your scope, granularity, and span. Each population stage should feature enough new data to help support significant IT decisions, but not so much that the phase lasts more than six months. The rule for any IT project—and configuration management in particular—is that the value of a project decreases as the time to achieve that value increases. Smaller segments that show more specific value are better than larger chunks with more general (and hard to quantify) value.

Providing a firm estimate on the size of every situation isn't possible, but Table 6.1 offers a general guideline to determine whether your estimate of time to populate your database has the right order of magnitude.

Table 6.1 Magnitude Sizing for Populating a CMDB

Influence	Modifier	Rationale
Base for any population	Two months	The simplest possible population of a database requires at least two months.
Complexity	Add one month for every 100,000 CIs	More complex databases take significantly longer to populate.
Asset management	Add two months if you have no asset management Subtract one month if you have a strong, reliable asset management service	The practices and skills of managing assets are similar to those needed for configuration management, so if your organization has this discipline, you benefit.
Number of locations	Add one month for every ten countries past the first one	Geographically dispersed assets make the job more difficult, even if you centralize the team.

After the population of your database is complete, you might think the phases of implementation are over—but you would be mistaken. As more data gets populated, you will undoubtedly find ways that the processes defined in the first phase can be streamlined or improved. You're likely to find some better way to organize the people involved, and you're certain to receive suggestions for improving your tools. All of these modifications should be gathered up through the population phases, and only the most critical implemented. After the database is populated, it is time to kick off another major phase to complete as many of the "latent" requirements as possible. Knowing up front that this second round of organization, process, and tools changes is coming will help you to keep the intervening phases focused on populating the data, thus reducing their risk significantly.

It is crucial that you plan the life of your program in advance. All the phases should be known and understood from the onset. This allows you to plan which requirements are going to be implemented where. It is much more palatable for a stakeholder to hear that their requirement will be implemented in phase four than to hear it didn't make the cut to get implemented in the first phase. It is also much easier to manage expectations around a series of incremental values than a single, large value statement. Note that it is also possible to satisfy a requirement only partially in an early phase, and then complete it in a later phase.

Each phase becomes a project of its own, with a separate schedule, a specific set of requirements to be achieve, a finite scope, and the entire rigor of project management and execution that your organization normally uses. Although all phases should be known at the beginning, you only need to plan and execute them one at a time. If the value is not proving to be adequate, you can embark on a new course by adding or removing phases as necessary. This significantly decreases the risk of implementing the overall configuration management program.

After you define the "big picture" in terms of the number of phases and their approximate content, you can begin the detailed work for the first phase. This is where you capture the actual project tasks and resources needed to meet the requirements specific to this initial phase. Simply parse through the requirements with the technical team, asking repeatedly "What will it take to get this done?" until the team agrees that you've captured all the tasks. Remember that you need only the details for the phase you're currently planning. Future phases will be planned in detail in their own time.

Planning to Customize the Process

Configuration management is much more than just meeting a set of requirements, however well they are written. You also need to include in your project plan all the steps needed to set up and execute the configuration management service. This includes defining and refining the process down to the level that people can actually execute it day to day. This section describes the general set of steps you need to customize a configuration management process.

Process work should be done using an iterative model. Begin with the top-level configuration management defined in a single document. This document should include a top-level picture that most likely will look something like the one at the beginning of Chapter 4, "Customizing the Configuration Management Process," where the whole process is captured in one diagram. In addition, your process document should include the relationships you envision between the configuration management process and any other operational processes, such as incident management, change management, and availability management. This high-level document is also a great place to document the enterprise policies regarding configuration management.

After documenting, reviewing, reworking, and finalizing the high-level process, you can begin working on the next level down, which many organizations call procedures. Take each of the process blocks and determine how they break down. For example, you most likely have a high-level block for controlling configuration items (CIs). Within this block, you might want to define a procedure for updating the CMDB, a procedure for batch loads of many CIs at a time, a procedure for updating relationships as the result of change records, and a procedure for archiving CIs after they have been retired. In defining and documenting procedures at this level, you might need additional policies, or even some minor changes, to the higher-level process. Go back and change those documents, review them, and when they are updated, continue at the procedure level.

In very large or very complex organizations, you might need additional levels of procedure work to further elaborate on the high level of procedures. Review Chapter 4 for a description of when to stop. Be sure to include tasks in your project plan to work at as many levels as needed.

After the procedures are reviewed and in good shape, have the actual people who must execute them look them over to determine whether they need more information to be able to execute. Many times you'll discover that specific, detailed instructions are needed to fill in some gaps in the procedures, or to define how multiple procedures blend together into a single job description. These work instructions should be specific to the tools, techniques, policies, and procedures you want people to follow. If your staff is new, or is brand new to the discipline of configuration management, you will most likely need to define more work instructions at a deeper level of detail. For staff that has some experience or a better understanding, fewer work instructions will be needed.

Document all tasks that will be involved in this iterative approach to customizing the process, as shown in Figure 6.3. Remember to include review time, rework time, and plenty of time to gain the approvals you'll need at the higher levels. Some of these tasks might intersect with the tasks to meet your requirements, but in other cases, these will be new tasks that must be accommodated in the overall project plan. If your organization is familiar with doing process engineering activities, you should have some experience to draw on to make your estimates. If not, you should be aware that process work always takes longer than you expect.

Planning Integration of All Data Sources

After getting all the requirements planned and the process work covered, it is time to consider the additional tasks required for integration of the data. As described in Chapter 5, "Planning for Data Population," pulling data from multiple places into the CMDB requires integrating that data together. You should go through a similar set of tasks for each data source, so the tasks are considered in order here rather than separately for each type of data.

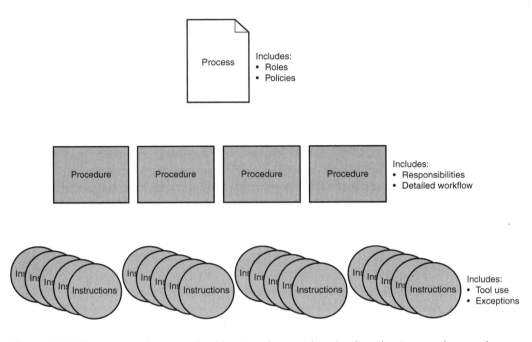

Figure 6.3   The process is customized in a top-down style using iteration to rework upper layers as details emerge.

To integrate data into the CMDB, you need a map of that data. These maps go by the names "database schema," "entity relationship diagram (ERD)," or perhaps "data dictionary." You need to know the number, types, lengths, valid values, and description of each data element in the potential source. Where accurate maps already exist, this task can be straightforward. If you discover that no suitable maps exist, this task can take quite a bit of effort as you reverse-engineer a system to discover what data it manages. Don't ignore the possibility that the data you're mapping might have relationships that can be converted either directly or indirectly into relationships in your CMDB.

After you have the data map, the next step is to analyze the data in light of what you need in the CMDB. Match up fields to understand where the data will be placed. For fields that are of different lengths, determine whether you need to pad or truncate the incoming data to fit your CMDB model. If the external data source has a specific set of defined values, match those to the possible values in your CMDB model. For example, perhaps you're dealing with an asset management system that has status values of "on order," "in storage," "deployed," and "retired." Your CMDB allows status values of "production," "redeploy," and "retired." You need to form a mapping from the four values to the three values, which might include a rule which says that any asset with the status of "on order" is not brought forward to the CMDB. Complete the detailed design of exactly how the data will come into the CMDB.

The third activity is to actually create the import mechanism. Will you be loading the data with a SQL input facility? If so, write and test the SQL. Will you be pulling the data from one system, putting it into a spreadsheet, and then importing the spreadsheet into the CMDB? Whatever your means of moving data, the third set of tasks should define those things necessary to build the "road" on which the data will travel. Building and testing this transport mechanism enables the data to flow, either one time or repeatedly if that is necessary.

After the roadmap has been drawn, the trip planned and the road paved, it is time to actually make the journey. Transfer the data into your CMDB, starting with a small part. Test to make certain that the data you've sent has been stored just as you want it in the target database. When the tests show that the data movement is successful, repeat the process with all the data from your data source.

The project plan should include the preceding four steps for every data source you need to integrate into the CMDB. These tasks will encompass all the work needed to integrate the various data sources described in Chapter 5. Include all the detail in the plan for each different data source to ensure careful tracking of this vital part of the plan.

Putting All the Pieces Together

By now you should have a fairly long list of tasks. Your working set should include a set of tasks to define the scope, granularity, and span, all the tasks needed to meet the requirements, all the tasks needed to customize the process, plus all the tasks necessary to integrate the data. Add to these tasks any others necessary for project administration in your organization, such as hiring and training staff, communicating status regularly, producing project required deliverables, and any other tasks that your standards require.

While the list of tasks might seem like it is fodder only for the project schedule, this long list of tasks gives you all the raw materials to actually put together a useful project plan. For example, if you have a task calling for documentation of a CMDB audit procedure, it should remind you that part of your communications plan should include a briefing of your corporate audit or QA group so that they understand their role in auditing your processes. Likewise, a task calling for gathering software license information might lead you to document a project risk that software license information might not be available. Think carefully through each of the tasks and imagine any possible obstacles and ways you can reduce those obstacles. That will lead you to all the information needed for a complete plan. This section describes how to finish that plan.

Scope

The first piece of any good project plan describes the scope of the project in a clear, concise, and unambiguous way. For a configuration management plan, the scope should include the set of requirements that you intend to achieve, the procedures you intend to document, and the set of data sources that will be integrated. Architectural concepts, such as a system context diagram or a high-level use case diagram, are often appropriate in a scope document. Depending on your organization's policies, the scope document might be an exhaustive, detailed description of everything you're doing, or an executive-level overview of just the key deliverables and milestones for your project.

The scope should be understandable by everyone on your implementation team. The scope will serve as a guideline many times when in the midst of low-level details people ask what they really are supposed to achieve. Compare the full set of tasks you've documented with the scope and make sure that all tasks are necessary per your scope. You might need to change the scope document, or perhaps you documented tasks that don't actually need to be done. Make sure the scope document is agreed by all of your sponsors and at least understood by all the other stakeholders. Nothing can torpedo a project faster than someone coming in at the end to question whether your scope was valid in the first place.

Schedule

Along with understanding the scope of the project, your list of tasks will also help you develop a reasonable project schedule. If your organization has little experience with configuration management, it might be difficult to get good estimates to schedule the project. To compensate, we recommend both a "top-down" schedule and a "bottom-up" schedule be built.

To build the top-down schedule, have someone at the top of the project do an estimate for every major block of work to be done. Perhaps this will be your sponsor or the project architect. For each major block, allocate what seems like a reasonable amount of time to complete that work. For example, it might seem reasonable that it will take three weeks to gather, analyze, and document a good set of requirements for the project. It might seem like six weeks is enough to analyze, map, develop, and import all the data you need from various sources. Continue doing those kinds of estimates for each major part of the work, and you'll have a "top-down" schedule. Normally, a schedule developed this way will represent the absolute shortest time in which a project can be accomplished.

To build the "bottom-up" schedule, you need to assign each task to the person who actually has to do it. Determine your project resources and begin allocating tasks to those resources. Now ask each person to estimate the amount of time it will take to complete the tasks assigned to them. You'll find that people who have done this kind of work before (if you have any on your staff) will give fairly close estimates and everyone else will overestimate the time needed. Put all of these times together, taking into consideration that certain tasks can be accomplished in parallel, but no one can work more than the normal hours per week. Blending all the estimates together will create a "bottom-up" schedule, representing the longest possible time it could take to accomplish the project.

To get to the actual schedule, take the "top down" and the "bottom up" and reconcile them (see Figure 6.4). This takes some practice and knowledge of the people who did the estimating. Determine which tasks are likely to be on your critical path and spend the most time refining the estimates for those tasks. This reconciliation will reveal the best possible schedule for the implementation.

No schedule is really complete without an accompanying budget or cost case. From the task list and estimates, you should be able to develop the labor costs for your project. Other costs like hardware and software should already be known from previous planning steps. Put all this together into a budget for your project, which can be included in the schedule, or maybe a separate document depending on the expectations of your sponsors.

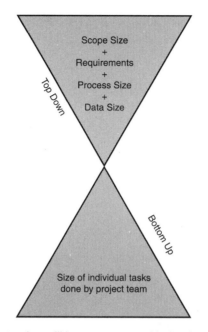

Figure 6.4 The most accurate plan will incorporate two kinds of estimates.

High-Level Design

In addition to a scope and schedule, your project plan should also include some technical description of what will actually be built. Many organizations call this an architecture document or high-level design. This operational concept should include organizations involved, technology to be used, and a brief description of how things will operate after steady state is achieved. In most methodologies, the operational concept or architecture will lead to a high-level design, and possibly a lower-level design. This kind of information provides some confidence that the technical team has thought deeply about the issues of configuration management as part of the planning phase of the project.

The design is based primarily on the requirements document. That is, the requirements describe what is to be accomplished by the project, and the operational concept or architecture document describes how it will be accomplished. The operational concept need not be very detailed early in planning, but before the full plan is settled and implementation begins, a clear and precise design should be available. Don't assume the design just includes tools, or should be drawn up by a software architect alone. The design should adequately describe which processes will be defined, what organizations will be created or modified to support the configuration management service, where hardware or networks will be augmented to support the CMDB, and data rules and validations that will be in place to facilitate accuracy. A good, solid design serves as a guardrail to the project team, helping them avoid making critical decisions independently later in the project.

Communications Plan

Finally, no project plan is complete without a communications plan. In general, we use a model that starts with the project team at the center, with the sponsors, the directly impacted stakeholders, the interested stakeholders, and the rest of the organization in concentric rings around that center. For each ring, decide and document how often you will communicate to them and what method will be used. Include any regular meetings to be held, training sessions to be scheduled, and news sources such as web pages or newsletters to be developed. The communications plan should tell everyone where to look for continuing information on the configuration management project.

Baseline the Plan

After your key project documents are all assembled, it is critical that you gain the approval of your sponsors, and then baseline the plan. By baseline, we mean that you establish a control mechanism for making changes to the documents, and insist that every change go through the mechanism you've described. If your organization is accustomed to this, you already know the benefits. If not, you will quickly learn that having control over the changes in your project plan documents can save hundreds of hours of rework and discussion about what you're really intending to do.

After the plan has been approved and is under change control, take a moment to celebrate with the team. You've completed the hard part by putting together a careful plan. Now all you need to do is implement!

PART II

Implementing Configuration Management

97

CHAPTER 7

Choosing the Right Tools

A significant step in deploying configuration management is selecting and implementing the best possible tools. The requirements documented during planning will determine the best tool for your situation. This chapter describes the three categories of tools available, and then considers some of the key tool characteristics that make certain tools more attractive than others for your particular situation. At the end of the chapter is a description of a simple method for evaluating configuration management tools and choosing the one that best meets your needs.

Types of Configuration Management Tools

Configuration management tools basically come in three different flavors: tools to discover configurations in the environment, tools that are dedicated to creating a Configuration Management Database (CMDB), and suites of service management tools that include some level of configuration management capability. These are recounted graphically in Figure 7.1, which serves as the visual outline for this chapter. This section summarizes the key distinctions and differences among these tools.

Discovery Tools

Discovery tools are the most varied. There are specific point solutions that will discover only Cisco routers, Novell directory structures, or other very specific domains. The strength of point solutions is their capability to completely capture their target environment with the highest possible accuracy. Because of their narrow focus, and because the publishers of these tools are often in significant business relationships with the suppliers of the components they discover, point solutions are often the first tools capable of identifying the latest infrastructure components. If your organization lives on the leading edge of technology, this may be a significant factor in the choice of which discovery tools you use.

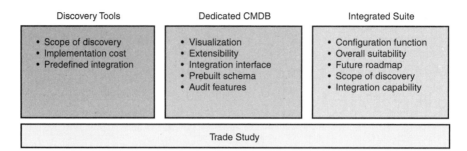

Figure 7.1   The criteria for choosing tools differ based on which type of tool is being considered.

The weakness of point tools is that they cover only a narrow piece of the overall environment. To get complete coverage across the entire space often requires a hodge-podge of tools and a significant amount of integration effort to get data from all the point solutions into a single integrated CMDB. More tools to purchase and more integrations to perform generally leads to a higher cost of initial implementation and ongoing maintenance. In many cases, you won't be able to upgrade one or more of your other tools without a corresponding upgrade in the discovery solution. In other words, the extra functionality of the point tools comes with extra expense.

More generalized discovery tools attempt to gather a broader range of information, but sometimes do so with less detail than point tools. Solutions such as Microsoft SMS, CA Unicenter Asset Management, Opsware, or IBM Tivoli Configuration Manager will all discover across a wider range of hardware and software than the point solutions. These more generalized tools can often provide all the discovery functions that an organization would need, especially when their lower level of detail is sufficient.

Point solutions and general discovery tools are not mutually exclusive, however. Sometimes the best strategy is to use a general solution to cover most of the enterprise, and then to select one or two point solutions in areas where a greater level of detail or a higher focus demand more specific tools. For example, if your organization is heavily dependent on using Novell for file and printer sharing services and corporate directory services, you might deploy the Tivoli Configuration Management product to accomplish most discovery needs, but then also deploy Novell Zenworks to get the best possible level of detail in your Novell environment. An example of a working set of discovery tools is shown in Figure 7.2.

Dedicated CMDB Tools

After all the discovery data has been collected, you need a place to store it. That is where a dedicated CMDB product comes into play. Compared with discovery tools, which have been around for a decade or more, most of the players in the dedicated CMDB market are fairly new. Companies like nLayers and SolidCore define offerings that typically include both a back end database structure and a set of tools for populating that database with relevant configuration information.

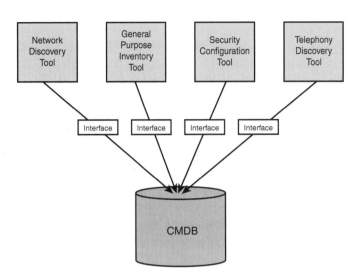

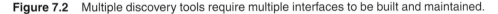

Figure 7.2   Multiple discovery tools require multiple interfaces to be built and maintained.

The major benefit of a standalone CMDB tool is ease of initial deployment. Vendors of these tools are very adept at creating a customized deployment plan that can get you up and running in a matter of weeks. Unfortunately, this strength is also a weakness—the tool that you have up and running is not very customized to your organization and may not meet all the needs of your organization. All too frequently, someone creates a CMDB deployment project as a shortcut to fully implement IT Infrastructure Library (ITIL) configuration management, thinking the appropriate tool is all that's needed. Although the choice of tools is important, the plan is much more critical. Hopefully, this book will convince you there is more to configuration management than simply installing the right tool.

That isn't to say, however, that a dedicated CMDB tool can't meet your needs. These dedicated tools offer rich functionality in terms of visualization of your data, discrepancy tracking, integration to a wide variety of discovery tools, and extensibility as revisions to standard models are available. Because the vendors focus on configuration management rather than trying to accomplish more of the ITIL space, they often produce the strongest configuration management tools. Of course, the same advice applies to dedicated CMDB tools as to very specific discovery tools—the cost will be higher because you have to create the integrations to incident management, change management, and other ITIL disciplines. An example of a complete systems management tools environment is shown in Figure 7.3. You can see that the dedicated CMDB product offers a convenient way to tie together all of the discovery tools into one interface, but still requires extra care in interfacing to the rest of the systems management tools.

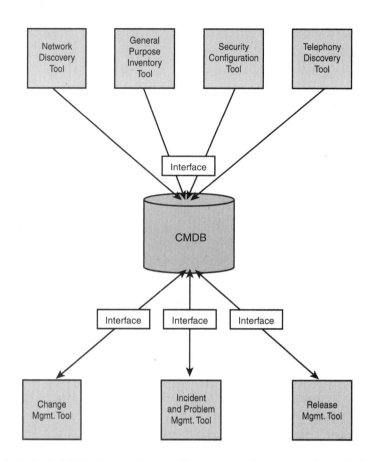

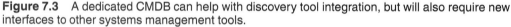

Figure 7.3   A dedicated CMDB can help with discovery tool integration, but will also require new interfaces to other systems management tools.

Integrated Service Management Suites

The third class of configuration management tools is perhaps the most intriguing. These are the integrated product suites that include configuration management tools with other service management tools. Tools such as Remedy from BMC, Service Center from HP, and IBM's Change and Configuration Management Database are examples of products that include functions to not just hold configuration management data, but to provide controls around the information technology (IT) environment that integrate with configuration data.

The benefit of an integrated suite is fairly obvious—you don't have to build custom code of any kind to form the important links between change records and configuration items, or between incident records and configuration items. The tools already understand those relationships. Another huge benefit is that one of these suites can form the backbone for a complete systems management effort—you won't have to integrate together a bunch of point solutions and deal with support from separate vendors. This can significantly lower the total cost of implementing a complete ITIL solution.

The downside of the integrated suite approach to tools is that none of them are perfect. There is always some aspect in which a standalone CMDB tool is stronger than the integrated suite. You get a total package that offers a bit of everything, but you give up on the best of many things. For example, you might get a very strong change management system, but give up the visualization capabilities of a dedicated CMDB tool. Figure 7.4 shows a typical implementation of an integrated suite, interfacing with discovery tools but otherwise self-contained.

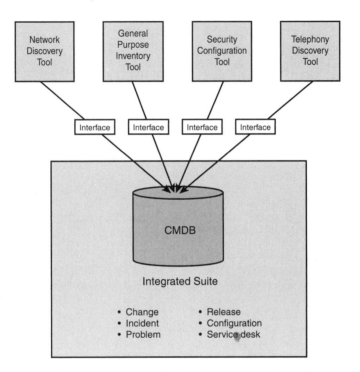

Figure 7.4   An integrated systems management suite can make integration simpler.

Tool Attributes

Now that you understand the three different kinds of tools and how they fit into the overall configuration management tool set, it's time to dig deeper and learn exactly what capabilities to consider in making your tools selections. This section looks at some broad categories and tries to help you understand the terms you're likely to run into when reading marketing literature. I'll try to stay vendor-neutral for two reasons. Foremost, the capabilities that each vendor provides will change as they race to provide ever better configuration management tools. Second, I'll give you a very concrete method in the next section to help you determine which vendor and exactly which product is right for you—so my opinion won't have to count for very much.

Integration Capabilities

Feature	Description	Benefits
Data import	Bring data into the tool from a variety of outside sources.	Reduce cost of data population Provide reliable way to update CMDB in the future
Import transformations	Change data as it is being brought in, such as changing case or truncating.	Improved data quality Correlation of multiple data sources
Import preview	See the effects of the import before it happens.	Improved data quality
Reconciliation engine	Change source data to avoid import problems.	Improved import reliability Lower cost of population
Import scripting	Define scripts that conditionally import records based on values in record or existing CMDB.	Lower cost of population Improved data quality
Prebuilt integrations	Integrations already defined for key discovery tools or systems management products.	Reduced cost of implementation
Application programming interface	Create code that calls functions of the tool from other programs.	Opportunities for tighter integration and lower operational cost

One of the primary things you need from a configuration management tool is the capability to integrate well. Integration can happen at many levels. Some tools simply have an interface you can use to import data from sources as wide ranging as comma-separated value (CSV) files to relational databases. Other tools provide an application programming interface that allows you to access the features and functions of the tool from external programs. Still other tools allow user interface integration by running as Java™ applets that can be easily integrated as a window in compatible Java software.

The most basic integration feature allows data to be imported into the CMDB. This feature is absolutely essential because you will always find one or more data sources that cannot be linked in any other way. Almost all tools offer a basic import feature, but the better tools go way beyond basic import. Look for the variety of formats that can be handled, including the capability to pick up data from text files, data from spreadsheet files, and connections to ODBC data sources. Also look for richness of features around how you define the import. Most tools offer some way to map the external data source fields to the specific data elements of your CMDB schema. Some will also offer customizable transformations, such as changing the case of incoming text data, reformatting date fields, or determining how to truncate data when the external data field is longer than your schema can support.

A key part of any import process is gaining an understanding of what happened, possibly even before it happens. Some configuration management tools offer ways to compare external data sets to your current CMDB, along with a report of what will happen when you actually import the data. In some cases, the report even gives you the ability to add controls that determine which records will get imported, and whether incoming data will overwrite existing data or just fill in elements that don't already have values. This can be extremely useful if the data you need to import isn't very clean. You can use the report to help adjust the external data source before actually running the import, greatly increasing the accuracy of your CMDB after the import. If you have a lot of data sources with suspect data, you might want to consider this import preview feature as essential to the tools you choose.

Some configuration management tools will give you a great deal of control over exactly how data sets get merged together. These tools help reconcile the differences between the incoming data and the existing data, giving you much more than just a preview of the results. You can define scripts that allow you to manipulate the results. For example, you could define a script that will take a proposed configuration item (CI) update from an external data source, look up the value of the CI owner field in a table, and choose whether to import the record based on who the proposed owner is. This kind of detailed control of the import process is helpful for very complex implementations, but the full power won't necessarily be used by everyone. If you've thought carefully through the issues raised in Chapter 5, "Planning for Data Population," you will know whether these features will be important.

Another feature that many will find desirable is preexisting import definitions. Many CMDB tools have the capability to integrate with one or more discovery tools with a minimum of customization. This kind of integration exists because the vendors involved in the CMDB and discovery tool have cooperated to make both tools easier to deploy by building a working integration model between them. You need only deploy the model they've built. Of course, any tweaks to the data model of either the CMDB or the discovery tool can quickly spoil the predefined integration because those fields won't be as the software publishers expected to find them. Normally, however, this kind of prebuilt integration is excellent if it is offered between two of the tools that you have selected anyway. It isn't normally compelling enough to be a main reason for choosing a tool, however.

Beyond data integration lies program integration. While it is a great thing to be able to consolidate data from different sources into a single CMDB, it is another thing altogether to be able to execute configuration management functions from the change or incident management screens. With an integrated systems management suite, this function comes as part of the package. With a dedicated CMDB, however, the ability to call selected functions of the tool without having to use the native login capability can be critical.

As an example, consider an organization using a dedicated CMDB tool along with a separate service desk tool that handles incident management. For each incident, the service desk agents would like to name the failing CI. With the manual method, the service desk agents could keep the CMDB tool open in a window on their workstation. For each call, they could use the CMDB search capability to find the right CI, and then copy the identifier from the dedicated CMDB tool and paste it into the appropriate field in the incident record.

If the CMDB tool allows program-to-program integration, however, some code could be written that would automatically search the CMDB based on some other data elements of the incident record—for example, the contact person and categorization of the incident. Our hypothetical code could then take the results of the search and put the corresponding identifier back into the correct field in the incident, and perhaps even consider server and network redundancy issues to identify the correct component. This automation could potentially save 30 or even 45 seconds on every incident call; this is a significant savings for desks handling hundreds of incidents per day.

If your organization would like to achieve this kind of tight integration but you don't want to use a suite that already has it built in, you should strongly consider looking for configuration management tools that support programming APIs or at least native web services protocols as part of their function set.

Visualization Capabilities

Feature	Description	Benefits
Search by attribute	Find configuration items based on any attribute of the item.	Can retrieve CMDB data
Search by relationship	Find configuration items based on their relationships to other items.	Can retrieve much wider array of data Ability to leverage relationship data
Combination search	Find configuration items based on both attributes and relationships.	Speeds data retrieval
Configure results display	Modify the way results display, including columns width, sort order, and filters.	Usability Speeds data retrieval
Display relationships in table	Can see relationships in a table format.	Simplifies reporting
Graphic relationship display	Can see relationship information in a graphic.	Quicker visualization of relationships

Sadly, although there seem to be many tools with great import capabilities, very few tools focus on the most-often used part of configuration management—the user interface. This is most likely because many vendors started out in the asset management space, where visualization of data is not very critical. Nobody really wanted to look at dry listings of lease residuals and hardware depreciation values, so the user interface wasn't a major selling point. This section describes some of the more desirable features for visualizing configuration data, but be fore-warned that it will be difficult to find any tools that provide all of these features.

It is interesting to note that a new category of IT and business service visualization software has grown up around this gap in CMDB visualization tools. In this scenario, the CMDB feeds an external tool that provides visualization of the data. If you really need the high-end features of a dedicated visualization system, then the capabilities of your CMDB program in this area may not be as important to you.

The most basic feature in a user interface is the capability to search for a configuration item. A basic search on any of the main attributes of a CI is common, but there the commonality ends. Some tools allow you to search on custom attributes that you've added to the data schema, but not all will. Some of the things you may think are "standard" in search utilities may or may not be included in the CMDB searching tools. Can you use wildcard searches? Can you search based on a range in a numeric or date field, such as workstations that have more than 512 megabytes of memory but less than 2 gigabytes? Sometimes case sensitivity is desired and some-times not—find out whether the tools you're considering provide the ability to search either way. Part of searching has to do with what languages the data can be stored in. It is surprising how many vendors fail to consider the possibility that data could be stored in languages other than English. The CMDB tool sometimes passes this responsibility off to the underlying database management system, so be sure to ask what features of display are dependent on the database and which are supplemented by the configuration management tool.

If you think very long about configuration management, you'll realize that searching based on CIs is only half the story. There will be many times when you want to search through sets of relationships—either all the relationships in the database or all the relationships where a specific CI is involved. For example, you may want to quickly find all cases where an application does not have a relationship to any server. That would be a very strange operational setup and is probably an error. Surprisingly, many configuration management tools don't have the capability to perform even this simple query. Similarly, once you've found a specific router, you might want to search all the IP subnets connected to it to find out which ones are fast Ethernet based. This is a more complex query using a combination of configuration item characteristics and relationship types, and there are very few tools that allow this kind of search without significant customization.

The optimum CMDB search tool allows advanced queries using Boolean logic across both the CIs and the relationships. To discover useful data requires this capability to chain together both relationships and attributes in a single search string. Because many tools don't have this capability, many organizations have resorted to putting attributes in place of relationships. For example, many people would like to know all of the firewalls at a specific location that have an old level of the firewall rule set. In a pure CMDB sense, this would involve searching across the firewall-type CIs that have relationships to a location CI and to a specific rule set CI. Because the tools won't allow this kind of search, many people opt to make location an attribute of all hard-ware CIs and rule set version an attribute of firewall. Although this makes the query easier, the

challenge now becomes whether you add street address, contact phone number, and other attributes to the hardware class that normally would have been part of the location type of CIs. You lose
significant data trying to accommodate a tool set with less features than you need.

After you've searched for data, the job is not finished. Displaying results and allowing further refinement of results are expected in modern tool sets. Most CMDB tools allow you to display a basic results list of the configuration items you've chosen. Some tools allow you to sort the
results list in various ways, resize the columns displayed, or even choose which columns will or
will not display. Few tools allow you to further refine the list based on additional search criteria,
and thus far we haven't seen one that will allow you to refine the search list based on which CIs
have relationships. Because even a small-sized organization can generate thousands of CIs, it is
often critical to be able to filter the results list in order to quickly drill down to the one or two
needed items.

Another way to extend the visualization capabilities that may be lacking in a configuration
management tool is by augmenting it with a dedicated reporting tool such as Cognos, Crystal
Reports, or Actuate. These powerful business intelligence tools can add significant features to
otherwise inadequate CMDB tools.

Beyond searching, the visualization capabilities of a tool must extend to somehow displaying relationship data. It would not be unusual for a single server to have relationships to six or
seven business applications, an operating system, a middleware product, a location, and eight or
more business entities. The server in this example quickly gets to twenty relationships even in a
very simple model. Even after the search capability has eliminated all other configuration items,
it's still necessary to sort through the relationships on just a single CI.

Most configuration tools provide the ability to view relationships either as a table or as
a graphic. Some provide both ways to view relationship data. A table view has the advantage
of being able to sort by relationship type and can display more data on the attributes of a relationship, such as the related CI, the date the relationship was established, and the type of the
relationship. The graphical view of relationships looks better in tool demonstrations and in
the executive suite. Both kinds of visualization have their place. The ability to filter relationships
is much more important than the actual way relationship data is displayed onscreen. Look for
tools that allow you to select the types of relationships to display, or, better yet, to define the characteristics of the related CIs that will be displayed. For example, an ideal tool would be one that
allows you to find a single CI, and then display all relationships, and even filter those relationships based on the criticality or state of the related CI. This would allow navigation using criteria
that are likely to be important to most organizations.

Figure 7.5 shows a screen shot from BMC Atrium, showing one possible way of displaying
relationship data graphically.

Although visualization is one of the most used parts of the system, the capability to store
data remains at the heart of the CMDB. When shopping for a configuration management tool, it is
important to consider the tool's capability to handle all the data you're likely to need. Chapter 5
touched on integration capabilities, but this section describes exactly which attributes to look for
in a tool you consider deploying.

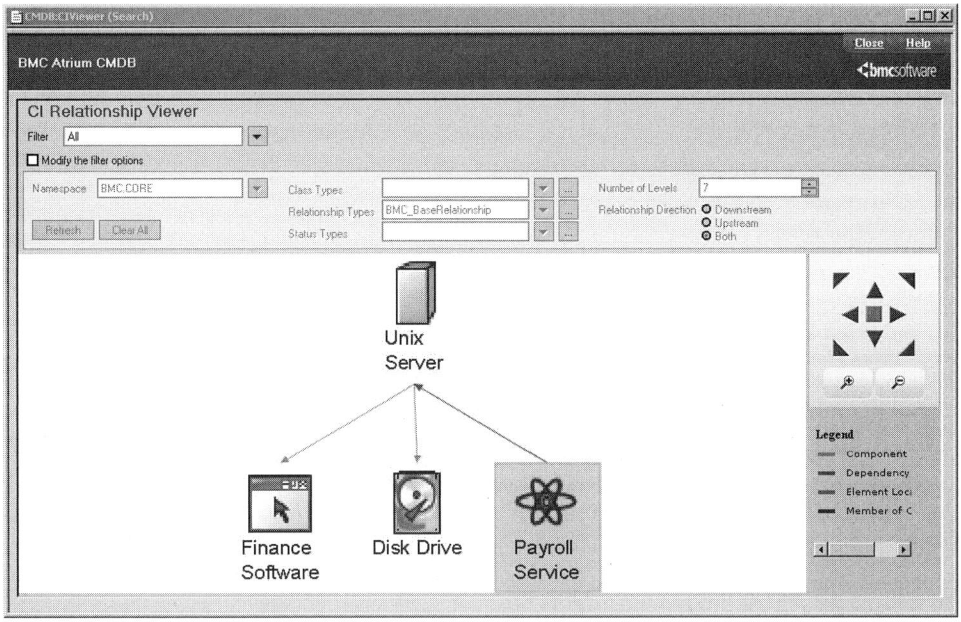

Figure 7.5   Relationship data can be easier to understand when viewed graphically.

Federation Capabilities

Feature	Description	Benefits
Import tools	Bring CI and relationship records from outside data sources and store them in the CMDB.	Avoid costly programming
Wide range of formats	Read data from text files, LDAP directories, XML documents, spreadsheets. and databases.	Can retrieve much wider array of data Avoid costly programming
Fast input	Data can be stored quickly.	Reduces risk of data corruption during long imports
"Shadow records"	Federation by proprietary method of interacting with source systems.	Instantly up-to-date data Avoids migration issues
Federated database support	True federation outside of CMDB tooling.	Reduces setup cost

The hot buzzword in database technology is *federation*. To a database purist, this means the ability to leave data physically stored in many different locations, but to query and view the data from a common system. In regard to configuration management implementations, federation loosely means somehow bringing together data from many different places to make it available as a single CMDB. The single source might be a purely logical construct, such as a search engine that can find data wherever it lives (think Google), or it might be a more traditional relational database system with a whole series of interfaces that import data periodically from other sources. In either event, it is fashionable to call this a "federated" database; and given this loose definition, almost every configuration management implementation is going to use to a federated database.

While exploring configuration management tools, be very specific about what kind of federation you intend to use. At the very least, any tool should be capable of "import federation," which means that you can import data from other sources into the tool. If this is your objective, you need to find a configuration management tool to make your job easier. If you can move data directly from your data sources without having to write programming on the sending end, you'll be much better off. For example, if all the data about people is in an LDAP database, you'll want to find a CMDB tool that can read LDAP. Otherwise, you have to write some code to read from LDAP and put the data into a format your tool can consume. Each small programming effort that you must do will add exponentially to the overall support cost of your configuration management service, so you want to avoid programming whenever possible.

Also be sure to ask questions about the capacity of the input utilities in each tool. The ability to input one configuration item every second isn't very helpful if you know you have an asset database with more than one hundred thousand items that need to be imported. Consider how many records will need to be imported and how often, and then use those numbers to determine whether the import utility will be able to meet your needs. Almost all configuration management tools come with an import utility, but not all of them perform at the same level for the biggest jobs. Hopefully you've documented some requirements around capacity and performance in your requirement set. This is the time to compare potential software tools against the needs you uncovered. It might take some digging to discover the capacity from the software vendor, but it is definitely worth finding out before making a commitment.

If you know you need more than basic import of data, the next level possible is "shadow records." In this model, used by several of the tool suppliers, the configuration management tool keeps what amounts to a card catalog of other places where data is kept. For most general queries, the tool just provides the ability to search these indices. If details need to be viewed, the actual data can be retrieved from the other sources by following the links stored in the CMDB. In this way, the external systems can be changing the data regularly and the CMDB will always get the latest version of the data by doing a real-time query.

The ability to support shadow records normally requires that the configuration management tool know access details for each of your data stores, and that those data stores support active query capabilities. So if you have some data in an unstructured text file, for example, that data won't be able to participate in the federation, while data that is stored in a relational database can participate. Another drawback of this indexing approach is that actual viewing of the data is much slower than if the data were stored in the CMDB tool itself. For this reason, many implementations mix direct import of data and shadow records, using direct import for sources that can't be indexed or that are frequently viewed in detail, while using shadow records for CIs that are not used as frequently.

Finally, the purest possible federation approach is one that actually uses an underlying database technology to achieve the federation. Increasingly, the major suppliers are providing tools that virtualize the database by understanding how to access data from a wide variety of sources. Thus, an application such as a CMDB tool that is written to work with any relational database middleware can run in a federated mode without actually knowing it. The CMDB simply defines the table structure it wants, and the Database Analyst (DBA) uses the underlying technology to get the records from many different systems and sources into what looks like a single table.

Of course, federating at the database has the same restrictions as shadowing records in the configuration management tool. You don't get great performance when pulling up data that isn't stored locally because you have to contend with network performance issues. Also the federated database management systems are limited to only certain kinds of data they can support. We would expect, however, that these issues will be solved more quickly and more expertly by the database suppliers than they will by the configuration management tool vendors. For the same reason that nobody implements their own data storage code inside their application today, those implementing database virtualization capabilities inside a configuration management application will look out of date not too far into the future. It is best to allow the middleware to take over this space.

Extensibility of the Tools

Feature	Description	Benefits
Add new categories to scope	Add a new type of configuration item to be tracked.	Can customize the model
Add new relationship types to scope	Add a new type of relationship to be tracked.	Can customize the model
Add new attributes	Add attributes to both new and existing configuration item types and relationship types.	Can customize the model
Remove model elements	Remove CI and relationship types and remove attributes from both CI and relationship types.	Can customize the model
Effective model maintenance	Doing maintenance on the model is both easy and fast.	Lower cost of implementation
Add new fields to interface	New attributes added to the model can be added to the user interface.	Integrity between model and screens

Feature	Description	Benefits
Search on added attributes	Users can search on newly added attributes.	Functionality can be incrementally added
Rearrange the interface	The screen can be rearranged to match optimal process flow.	Productivity gain
Powerful interface designer	The interface can be changed extensively in many ways.	Closer match between process and tool
Simple interface designer	The interface can be changed easily without programming.	Lower cost of implementation

One of the things you'll quickly find in looking at configuration management tools is that none of them completely fit your needs. This is why all tool vendors allow their tools to be changed in some ways. Of course, some of the tools are more extensible than others. This section describes the ways you might want to modify the tools and helps you determine which extensibility features you can expect to choose from.

The most common modifications will be to the data model. Each organization will have its own definition of scope and granularity, and that definition must be captured in the tool set. Look for a tool that makes updating the schema easy. Some of the more crude tools out there will require you to directly change the underlying database using whatever tools the database middleware supports, but most tools will offer some sort of interface which will not only change the underlying database, but also update the search screens, detail views, and other user interface elements to immediately recognize any modifications to the model.

Remember that making modifications should also include the ability to remove some of the CI types or any attributes of any of those types. Most vendors provide a standard data model, often based on recommendations from industry groups or standards bodies. Although these models offer a quick way to get started, they aren't likely to line up perfectly with the way your organization has decided to manage configurations. Leaving unused data elements in place can cause confusion in reporting and querying, and extra work in configuring the user interface to move these elements out of the way. Look for not only the ability to add to the data model, but also to remove some of the elements the vendor delivers with the tool.

Most of the work of customizing the tool's data model is done during the first stages of implementation. However, don't let that fool you into thinking that performance of these administrative interfaces isn't important. In one project, we used a tool that took more than four hours to add a single data element to the model. Because we didn't anticipate this extraordinary amount of time to make even simple changes, we ended up having to rework our entire deployment plan. The bottom line is that you should not only ask whether it is possible to change the data model, but ask what mechanism is used to do so and how well that mechanism has been tested.

In addition to configuring the data model, you will most likely want to modify the user interface of any configuration tool. Whether it is integrating the tool's authentication mechanism with your corporate LDAP structure, adding a few fields, or defining entirely new kinds of searches, every organization has needs that go beyond what the tool vendor has imagined. Tools with good extensibility characteristics should allow for adding new data elements to the interface and for rearranging the interface to accommodate the needs of the organization. The integrated suites will often provide a workflow engine that can be customized to correspond to more closely automate the control processes that you've defined. Users can be allowed to edit certain fields only when the CI is in the proper state. This kind of workflow can be very helpful in organizations without a lot of deep knowledge of configuration management because the tools will help enforce business policy.

If many user interface modifications will be necessary, be sure to choose a tool set that will allow them to be done in an inexpensive way. Some tools tend to offer lots of power, but make it available only to programmers who have learned the tool's proprietary language. Other tools offer very simple administrative interfaces to make Graphical User Interface (GUI) changes, but only allow limited things to be changed. The amount of power and capability you purchase will depend on how closely the "out-of-the-box" interface meets your needs as defined by the requirements.

The third area of extensibility is integration. As mentioned several times already, you will need some degree of flexibility in how to move data into (and sometimes out of) the CMDB. Some configuration management tools offer a very high level of control over each data element and how they move into and out of the database. Normally, this high level of control will cost more because of the skills needed to understand and use the more complex tools. In other cases, the configuration management tool offers very little control because the import process has been designed to be easy to configure and operate. This approach costs less to implement and maintain, but may not match as perfectly with the requirements of your project. In the next section, you learn a methodology that can be helpful in determining which end of this spectrum is best for your organization.

Performing a Tools Trade Study

Many vendors market tools they say will do some or the entire configuration management job. It is important to realize that the only perfect tool is one which you haven't purchased yet—immediately after that, you'll start to find the flaws. Because of the proprietary nature of the data structures used by configuration management tools, you're going to be stuck with your selection for a very long time. This section describes how to make a choice between your many alternatives.

At a high level, the technique for choosing between various competing alternatives is not new to anyone. We determine a workable set of desirable characteristics, assign a relative weight to each characteristic, and then compare all the alternatives by assigning a score for each alternative to each characteristic. The results, visible in Figure 7.6, are a matrix of scores. Totaling these scores will show the degree to which each alternative fits your needs.

Configuration Management Tool Trade Study

Need	Importance	Tool 1		Tool 2		Tool 3		Tool 4	
		Raw Score	Weighted Score	Raw Score	Weighted Score	Raw Score	Weighted Score	Raw Score	Weighted Score
Characteristic 1									
Characteristic 2									
Characteristic 3									
Characteristic 4									
Characteristic 5									

To choose the best configuration management tool, start by deciding which characteristics or attributes of a tool are important to you. You can use the categories in this chapter (integration, visualization, federation. and extensibility) as your guide to select the characteristics against which you'll evaluate each potential tool. Maybe you're a big user of a particular IT inventory tool and you want to make sure to select a configuration management tool that offers a prebuilt integration to your inventory tool. Perhaps you have a requirement for a graphical relationship viewer, so this becomes an important characteristic to you. One important document to consider is your set of requirements because if you can meet requirements by simply choosing the correct tool, this is almost always less expensive than having to customize the tool. Conversely, if you choose a tool that cannot meet a requirement no matter how you configure it, you are adding a risk to your deployment.

After all the desirable characteristics are known, it is time to prioritize them. Assign each characteristic a weighting. I like to use a five-point scale, where five means that we absolutely must have that feature and one means it would be nice, but we can live without it. Three-point scales tend to not differentiate enough, whereas ten-point scales are overly complex. Assign each characteristic a weighting to say how important it will be in your tool selection process.

After you have weighted characteristics, it is time to score each potential tool. In most cases, you want to use two different passes. In the first pass, take every tool that you can find and evaluate it using just the marketing literature provided by the software vendor. This can often be done using a web site or publicly available literature without having to engage the actual marketing team. The advantage of this quick first phase is that you won't ignore tools which potentially might be useful, but you won't spend a lot of time talking to sales teams who don't have what you need. Evaluate each characteristic by assigning it a score (again, I like a scale of one to five) based on how well it meets the characteristic. Five might mean the tool automates this feature and requires virtually no effort on your part, and one might mean that you could write some custom code to make the tool meet the characteristic.

After providing an individual score for each characteristic, multiply the score by the weighting factor. This provides a weighted score, which gives you a good idea of how well the tool will meet your needs in that particular area. If you continue this work across all characteristics, and then add together all of the weighted scores, you get a single raw number to indicate the overall "score" of a tool. This number isn't particularly important by itself, but can be compared to the score of other tools to help you assess which ones are stronger candidates for your organization's use.

After the first pass, choose the top two or three candidates for a deeper assessment. This is the time you bring in the vendors and allow them to demonstrate their tools for you. When possible, ask the vendor to demonstrate against your set of characteristics, using the weighting you assigned to determine which things are most important for you to see in a demonstration. In some cases, you will want to get an evaluation copy of their software so that you can conduct an even deeper "hands on" evaluation.

For these deeper evaluations, you may find a need to expand on the basic evaluation matrix you used in the first pass. Normally, this would involve breaking down a single characteristic into multiple rows which indicate different aspects of that one characteristic. For example, on your original matrix you might have had "graphical view of relationships" as a characteristic. In working through your first pass, you noticed that some tools just offered a graphical view, others provided color coding to show relationship types, and yet others provided filtering on the graphical view. These could be broken into three separate characteristics, all under the heading of "graphical view."

Most likely, there will be some attributes of the tools that don't fit neatly into the matrix. Cost is certainly one of these. Although you can use a trade study matrix to evaluate functional attributes, your overall choice of tools should use the raw scores from the trades study as only one decision point. Speed of implementation, reputation of the vendor, references from others who have successfully implemented, and cost of implementation should also be taken into account.

CHAPTER 8

Implementing the Process

Regardless of how well you advertise your configuration management plans and how many people get involved with the selection of the configuration management tools, nothing will seem real until you start to deploy the process. Exactly at this point the organization will begin to understand that configuration management will truly happen, and anyone with unresolved issues will come forward to get them resolved.

The best way to handle unforeseen issues is through the careful planning you've done in the first part of this book. But the best plans will be helpful only if you execute them well. This involves getting the right people on board, communicating effectively, empowering people with good instructions, training the complete team, and then measuring the effectiveness of the entire process. Staffing is a necessary prerequisite for all other activities, and communication should be ongoing throughout your implementation. The other tasks can be accomplished in parallel to some extent. This arrangement is depicted in Figure 8.1 as the visual outline for this chapter. This chapter will help you to implement the process and prepare to resolve some of those issues.

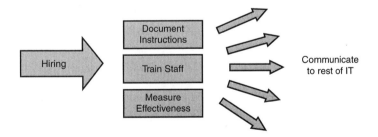

Figure 8.1   There are several steps to consider when implementing the configuration management process.

Staffing for Configuration Management

In order to implement a process, you must have people who will execute that process. In some organizations configuration management will simply be another duty assigned to an already over-worked staff. In other organizations, you will be faced with staffing a configuration management team from the ground up, hiring people to fill all of the roles you've defined. In either case, staffing the team is critical because regardless of how good the tool is or how completely the processes are defined, the people will have to do the job. The effectiveness of your configuration management program can never be better than the effectiveness of your staff.

Begin staffing by asking how many people you will need. Roles are described in great detail in Chapter 12, "Building a Configuration Management Team," but for now simply realize there will be a variety of roles to be filled. For very small organizations, perhaps all roles could be accomplished by a single highly-skilled person. In a very large organization, you might need multiple people to fill each defined role, and perhaps even some leadership or management roles to organize the staff. Figure 8.2 depicts the difference between a small configuration management organization and a large one.

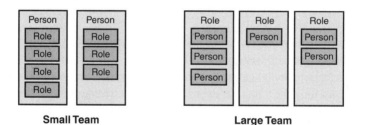

Small Team   **Large Team**

Figure 8.2   There are key differences in staffing a large team or a small team.

You can estimate how many people will be needed by looking at your process documents, understanding the responsibilities of each role, and making estimates of the time required for each responsibility. Remember that nobody actually has eight hours of every day available because there will be obligatory meetings, mandatory HR tasks, email and phone messages, and all the other things that can steal people's time. For dedicated personnel, you can assume six or seven hours of each day will be spent doing the things you've identified in the process. If you're using staff with duties outside of configuration management, adjust accordingly.

After you know how many people you are seeking, it's time to calculate what the skill level of the people should be. The general rule is that the fewer people you have, the greater their skill must be. If you have a large team, 1 or 2 experts can provide enough knowledge to fuel 10 or 12 less-skilled team members. In a 2- or 3-person team, however, there is no room for a weaker link—everyone must have a good, overall knowledge of configuration management and be able to make decisions that are in the best interest of the organization.

Be especially careful in hiring to distinguish people who can get things started and people who can keep things going. The mindset needed to define processes, select new tools, and imple-ment the service will not be the same as the mindset of someone who can audit for data accuracy, follow the process attentively, and make day-to-day decisions about the configuration management service. Both "big picture" people and detail-oriented people are important, and neither should be neglected in your staffing. People who are good at implementing configuration management generally are not as good at the day-to-day management of configuration data.

Finding people with experience in configuration management is obviously ideal, but hiring people with more general skills is also a possibility. You should look for people who have experience in a wide variety of information technology (IT) roles because they will best understand the far-reaching uses of configuration data. You should find people who pay close attention to detail and have experience in large data management activities, such as IT asset management or inventory efforts. People with a process bias are helpful because they can define the value of the process and help make incremental improvements even as they are executing the process. Again, if you are planning a large staff, you will have opportunities to find people with only one of these skills; but if you're hiring a small team, you need to find people who blend several of these attributes.

I've found that mixes of experience are also helpful on a team. Teams staffed with only experienced people will have too many opinions on key issues and tend to not come to consensus as quickly, whereas teams without any experienced members will need too much direction and "hand holding" to be effective. A team with one or two key leaders that have extensive experience and several other team members with new, fresh ideas is generally best. Like so many other areas, seek diversity in building your team so that strengths and weaknesses can be balanced out. Not just experience, but a wide range of experiences is helpful.

Be sure to consider that newly hired staff will need some time to get acquainted with the culture of your organization and the general responsibilities of their jobs, so don't plan on immediate productivity if you have to get people from outside your organization.

Communicating the Process to the IT Organization

In order to successfully roll out the configuration management process, you need the cooperation of the IT community. The configuration management service touches so many different aspects of IT that it would be impossible to implement it without broad support from across all parts of the IT organization. Change managers must agree to update the Configuration Management Database (CMDB) at the end of every change. Service desk agents must be willing to determine the failing component in light of configuration data. Capacity planners should define plans for specific configuration items (CIs). IT finance managers should consider the cost of services by analyzing the CIs used in the service. Literally every part of the IT group is impacted by the introduction of the configuration management process.

Note that I'm not talking here about communicating to the entire organization. An overall communication plan is described in Chapter 11, "Communication and Enterprise Roll Out," but communication to the IT organization needs to be accomplished first. Without getting the buy-in from IT, the rest of the communication will be seriously undermined, so be sure to treat the IT organization as a separate communication effort. In cases where a new organization or new staff is added, you need to be especially careful to define the boundaries and avoid any hint of stepping on others' territories. You want to form a strong partnership at the outset so that the storms and lulls natural to every project won't shake the communication foundation you're trying to build.

For your communication with the IT organization, you want to prepare several things. As a standard project deliverable, you probably already have design or architecture documents detailing the tools to be deployed. Use those, plus the procedure documents and the requirement documents as raw materials to put together an IT-oriented marketing presentation. Depending on the starting point of your audience, sell the benefits of configuration management in general, and specifically for the various parts of your IT organization. Experience shows that IT people in general like projects that promise improvements to efficiency and accuracy of their work. But IT people also want to understand the service completely, so be prepared to talk in depth about the process, the tools, and the overall service to be offered. Remember that your goal is not just to educate your peers, but to make them advocates for you as they interface throughout the wider organization later.

Deliver your message anywhere you can find IT people gathered together. Perhaps you can get 15 minutes on the agenda of the CIOs staff meeting. Maybe 10 minutes at the end of a Change Advisory Board (CAB) meeting. For larger IT shops, you might get need to bring your presentation to each director and ask permission to go to each of their various department meetings. Use internal web sites or collaboration team rooms to post your presentation, complete with speaker's notes, so people can understand configuration management at their own pace. The more ways you can get the message broadcast to the IT organization, the easier will be your communication chore later when you address groups outside of IT. A sample communications plan for addressing IT is included as Table 8.1.

Table 8.1   Sample IT Communications Matrix

Message	Audience	Venue	Key Emphases
Overview	All IT	IT all hands meeting (15 minute slot)	Place in ITIL Value to IT
High-level process	IT directors	CIO staff meeting	Seek approval
Tool selection	Ops staff	Called meeting	Functions Install plan
Implementation plan	Project managers	PM weekly meeting	Overall plan Risks Integration
Staffing plan	HR	Called meeting	Skills Roles Experience
Data schema	Information Architects	Data council	Structure Shared elements

Creating and Documenting Work Procedures

When you are communicating to the IT organization, you will undoubtedly get many questions. Some of them you will have anticipated in your communication plan, but many of them will be brand new and will represent specific details you haven't thought of yet. Use those questions as a basis to understand where your process work needs more detail. Rather than being frustrated that everyone can't understand the elegant plan in your mind, use this opportunity to really think deeply about how configuration management will be integrated within your IT organization.

Conversely, some of the things that you communicate to the IT organization will be perfectly clear and will generate no questions. You don't want to waste effort by documenting additional work procedures in those areas. If people already have a general understanding of what they need to accomplish, you'll only annoy them by detailing exactly how they must accomplish that work.

Tie any needed additional work instructions into the overall process and procedure framework, which you began in Chapter 4, "Customizing the Configuration Management Process." You can either choose to update those documents directly, or you can create new work instruction documents and simply reference them in the appropriate places in the procedure documents. For example, suppose you discover a need for a more detailed work instruction on exactly how to compare the CMDB version of a CI to the same item in your inventory discovery tool. The instruction would include how to log on to each system, how to extract relevant data into a spreadsheet, how to compare the items, and what to do with any discrepancies found. That could be significant content to add to the procedure documents, so you might decide to put this into its own document and simply make a note in the procedure document indicating where the specific steps can be found.

Either way, be sure the work instructions are detailed enough to answer the questions raised by the IT organization, and that they help enhance the process rather than obscuring it. Ideally, the work instructions should be a set of specific steps that help people know how to use tools to accomplish the processes. Chapter 4 advised you to make the procedures independent of the tools, but you need to be more specific in instructions. Good instructions describe functions of the tools and how to accomplish those functions. Don't simply duplicate the text of a tool's user guide, however. For example, your configuration management tool user's guide will most likely already tell someone how to run the import tool to pull in new data. Your work instruction should provide more detail about where to find the source data, what the naming convention of log files should be, and how to check for and handle errors in the import. None of these details could possibly be covered by the user's guide.

This work instruction step is the final time you will engage with the process architects, so use this time well. Be sure to clarify cross-organizational boundaries, especially when subcontractor, consultants, or outsourcing partners are involved in the process. It is especially important to provide clear instructions on relationships and how they will be handled as changes occur in the environment. Think about retired CIs and how you will clear them out of the database, if that is desirable. Use the entire IT organization to help you drive down to the lowest possible level of detail. Although this might seem excessive at first, it is literally impossible to put too much detailed thought into the work instructions. Anything that could be a question for any current or future person involved in the service should be considered and documented. Obviously, you'll want to schedule plenty of time for this activity in your overall project plan.

Building Training Materials

After all work instructions are documented clearly, you should have a mountain of data from which you build training materials. This is a good thing, because one of the primary rules in building training is to never create anything new. Everything in your training package should be able to be derived from the information and documentation you've already amassed. Certainly you will want to train people on the scope, granularity, and span to be expected in the configuration data. You'll want to use the process documents and work instructions specifically to teach people how to effectively do the configuration management job. Some general background on the requirements will be necessary, and of course you'll want to train people to use the tools that you've selected. All of this information should be part of the overall training package.

Training materials should be organized by the audience you intend to train. Sponsors and interested stakeholders should receive general training highlighting how the requirements are satisfied and the benefits of configuration management for the organization. People who need to use related processes such as change management, incident management, and problem management should be trained in how to obtain and leverage the information they need to make their processes more effective. People responsible for working directly with the CIs, such as network administrators or desktop support teams, should be taught the importance of the data and how to maintain the data through their day-to-day interactions. Each group down the line should have specific training materials prepared so that they have the knowledge to fully participate in the configuration management service.

This isn't to say, however, that each group must have completely different materials. Training materials normally take the form of a set of specific scenarios that walk through the various aspects of the service, from updating the configuration management plan through the entire process to dealing with CMDB audits. Each scenario needs to be described in great detail, including any applicable work instructions. After that is accomplished, you can present the full scenario with all pieces to someone who needs to execute that scenario regularly. You can reuse most of the material but take out the detailed work instructions for someone who just needs a good understanding of the process. Then you can take out even more material but still present the same scenario as part of a general overview training session. As shown in Figure 8.3, the same material is used at different levels for different audiences.

And just as the audiences are diverse, so are the training methods. Some groups can be trained by presenting a simple set of slides in a teleconference. Others might need a longer, face-to-face session. Perhaps some will benefit from an organized classroom session where they can have the tools in front of them and work through practical exercises. Others might be able to use self-paced online modules to understand the material best. Be creative in determining which materials will have the most benefit to your organization, and remember that while there is a big push for education at implementation time, there will be an ongoing need to train new employees as they come into your organization or change to new roles.

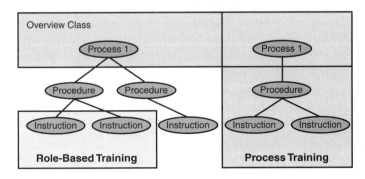

Figure 8.3   The same training material can be used for multiple audiences.

The materials you prepare should be built in such a way that they can be easily maintained. As processes change or new releases of the tool are built, you can update existing education rather than starting over. As the organization matures in its knowledge and use of configuration management, you may want to add new education topics to cover more advanced issues. As lessons are learned and corrected, new information should be gathered in the education materials to benefit the entire organization.

In many ways, educating users and deploying the process are synonymous. In essence, you're telling people about a new way of behaving and showing them what you expect from them. Be sure to be organized in your delivery of education to all of your various groups. Plan for all the normal business contingencies which dictate that not everyone will be able to attend your planned sessions or complete a self-study in a timely manner. Keep accurate logs of who has been educated and what version of the education they receive. It will be important to understand what gaps are left after the initial education roll out is completed so that you can fill those gaps as needed.

Many organizations find it useful to certify people in the key configuration management roles. This involves creating a set of criteria and measuring whether the person meets the criteria to adequately perform the role. This can be as simple as a test administered after education is finished, or as complex as having someone experienced in the role follow the new trainee around for several days and observe them doing the job. In addition, you might use external certifications, such as ITIL Practitioner or a Six Sigma certification. For roles such as the quality manager, it is a very good idea to ensure the person is comfortable with the role before the deployment team just expects they will do it well. This could be a formal certification effort, or you might simply talk with the person to determine whether they know the job.

Understanding and Improving Process Compliance

This brings us to the whole question of whether the process implementation is successful. Because the process deployment is the first visible sign that configuration management is taken seriously, you should be prepared to evaluate the deployment. Poor perceptions of the quality of the deployment will result in lower expectations of the overall configuration management process. Lower expectations cause people to try less to follow the process, which will ultimately result in the failure of your configuration management service. The good news is that you can avoid this cycle. Table 8.2 summarizes different ways you can demonstrate your configuration management process.

Table 8.2   Methods of Assessing Process Effectiveness

Technique	Advantages	Disadvantages
Certification	Easy to conduct Nonthreatening People focused	Not always accurate
Surveys	Easy to conduct Predicts future behavior	Participation may be inadequate Represents opinion rather than fact
Measurement	Very accurate Consistent Objective	Can be expensive to implement
Audit	Very accurate Highly visible	Always expensive Can be threatening Can't practically cover everything

But how do you know whether the process deployment has been successful? One way is to certify people in the key roles and assume certified people will make the overall effort successful. Another way is to evaluate your education efforts by asking all participants to complete an end of course survey. When well designed, a survey can indicate both the understanding of your teams and their confidence that the new process will work in the real world. We've all seen too many IT projects that looked good on paper but failed because the teams needed to implement them didn't understand the importance or the relevance to their daily duties. Surveys can tap into the psyche of the organization and be an accurate predictor of that phenomenon while there is still time to correct it. Thus surveys can help to evaluate how well the process is working, either directly after implementation or later when the process has been running for a while.

Process implementation is also the perfect time to build in measurements that will allow you to know how faithfully the processes are being followed. Some organizations might go so far as to tie the measurements to the compensation of the key people involved in executing the process. Experience shows the measurements instituted at the same time as new procedures are far more effective than those added later. Process compliance measurements typically will cover the entire spectrum of process activities defined in Chapter 4. You might want to calculate, for example, the number of proposed changes to the scope and granularity across a given span, as this can be an indirect way to validate that your people are thinking deeply about the value of the data. You could also measure CIs captured from one area to those captured in a parallel area. For example, if your organization has multiple data centers where servers are managed, is the number of CIs discovered and documented from each of those centers proportional to the relative size of the centers? This can be a good indication of how well the configuration identification procedures are being followed.

You probably already have measurements defined around the control points in the process, but early implementation is a good time to use these measurements as assessments rather than controls. That is, you should take a measurement, such as the number of change records without adequate configuration information, as an opportunity to speak at department meetings and reinforce training. Make it clear the expectation is that these inadequacies will decrease very quickly, and anyone not understanding the control point should ask for additional training. Measuring should never be about punishment but about improving the process and the systems that support it.

In addition to process measurements, you can also assess the impact of the process deployment by doing occasional compliance checks. Simply pick a piece of the process that you want to focus on, and track a set of executions across that part of the process. For example, because data audits are so important in the early stages, have a quality assurance person shadow the auditors while they conduct a data audit. Talk with the auditors about how they choose the scope of the audit, watch them as they send out audit notifications, work with them as the audit results come back, help them compare the results against expectations, and generally follow the whole course of the audit. This is an excellent way to assess how well the process is being followed. This same technique can be used in every aspect of your implemented process and should continue to be used occasionally well after implementation.

As mentioned earlier, the implementation of the process is the time that configuration management will become real to your organization. Issues beyond those described in this chapter will most likely arise. By focusing on the overall goals of your configuration management service and by being as flexible as possible, you should be able to resolve these issues and move forward to a successful implementation.

CHAPTER 9

Populating the Configuration Management Database

When most organizations first begin thinking about configuration management, their top concern is putting data into a database. Hopefully by now you realize this shouldn't be your first concern, but data population is still a critical topic. This chapter provides the details on how to execute the data population plan you created in Chapter 5, "Planning for Data Population."

You can use two different approaches to populate a Configuration Management Database (CMDB): a waterfall or a trickle. The waterfall approach is to gather as much data as possible from throughout the environment and then integrate that data to assemble a complete configuration management picture. This approach could be characterized as more active and direct, but it results in a torrent of data that can sometimes be overwhelming.

Another possible approach is to create integration points in each of the key operational process areas that are likely to deal with configuration data. By executing normal operations with these new integration points, data about configuration items (CIs) trickles into the CMDB as those items change or cause incidents. This is a far less risky approach, but one that delays the benefits of having a complete configuration management picture.

As in most real-world projects, a combination approach is likely the best. Most organizations find that waiting until all the data trickles in through execution of the processes is too slow, and dumping all data into the databases without first establishing close process integration makes the value of the data suspect. This chapter examines both approaches to populating the data so that you can determine to what degree each approach is valuable for your situation. The visual outline in Figure 9.1 shows this approach.

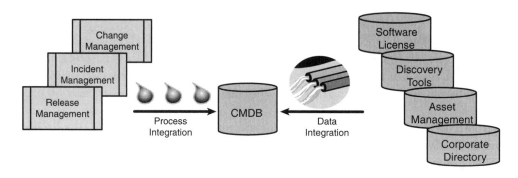

Figure 9.1   Populating data can be done with a trickle or a flood.

Data Integration

The fastest way to populate a CMDB is to get data that already exists in other places and reorganize it to fit the schema you've planned. This method will bring a torrent of data into your database. When adopting this approach, you need to ask yourself where you want the *master* copy of the data to reside. Many organizations call this the "source of truth." By source of truth, we mean the primary place where data is created and edited, as opposed to a copy of the data that exists for the sake of searching.

If you are unsure of the quality of data in your sources—or even worse, sure that it is inaccurate—you will most likely want to make the new CMDB your single source of truth. On the other hand, if you already have strong data sources with effective processes for keeping those up to date, but want to be able to effectively search all those sources and form relationships among data that is currently held in different places, you will want to form a CMDB—but leave the source of truth with the original data sources.

As described in Chapter 5, the term for a CMDB that consolidates data but leaves the source of truth in the original sources in federation. When you decide to create a new source of truth in your CMDB, you are building it by import. Because this decision between federation and import has significant implications in how to populate the database, we will examine each separately.

Distributed Sources of Truth

The topic of federation comes up frequently when talking about the CMDB. We've already decided in Chapter 5 that database purists and tools vendors often use different definitions of federation. For working purposes, we'll define federation as any technical approach that maintains the source of truth outside the CMDB.

But this begs the question of what is meant by "source of truth." What we mean in this context is that the data is updated and managed by processes whose chief aim is to keep it accurate somewhere outside the central CMDB. As an example, most organizations have a human resources system or corporate directory that is electronically maintained. Processes such as hiring, employee promotion, organizational changes, and employee retirement are linked into this directory, so all the changes in employee information and status are recorded first in the HR system or directory system. Therefore, the HR system or directory system is the source of truth, while the CMDB which holds a copy of this information is known as a federated data source.

One key observation about federated data is that you should assume it is being maintained elsewhere, and your configuration management process will need to validate it only by comparing what you have in your database against the source of truth. This is a relatively easy comparison if you disregard the timing issues created by your choice of technology to move the data from the source to the CMDB.

Consider, on the other hand, the processes around installing, moving, and changing the PCs in an enterprise. These processes are often built in such a way that each such action is recorded as an event in an integrated system, and the final step in the process is to update the CMDB. In such a case, the CMDB becomes the source of truth because no other database would have the complete picture of where the PCs are.

Why is this distinction so important for populating a CMDB? It is critical because it affects the timing and accuracy of the data you can populate. When the source of truth resides outside the CMDB, you might want to build a structure that allows instant or at least very frequent updates. You might, for example, have a corporate locations database that tracks the sites, buildings, floors, and even office numbers where your organization operates. Clearly this is data that will be extremely useful in the CMDB, so you decide to make it a federated data source. But if you pull this information into your database only once a week, there is a significant risk of needing to record a new CI from the location before the location itself gets into your CMDB.

Another reason it is important to understand which data sources will need to be federated is because in most cases these will be the first sources you can populate in your database. As you discover in the next section, the data you enter directly into the CMDB will be much more difficult to maintain, so you'll most likely save it until the processes you've rolled out are more mature. Table 9.1 summarizes the differences between federated data sources that will be directly entered in the CMDB.

Table 9.1   Comparing Federation to Direct Entry

Federated Data	Direct Entry
Distributed sources of truth	Single source of truth
Maintained outside CMDB	Maintained inside CMDB
Processes update other databases	Processes update CMDB
Accuracy managed at each source	Accuracy managed centrally

Building a New Source of Truth

Federation is a great approach to use when you have trusted data sources and solid processes that maintain those data sources. Of course, with both trusted sources and reliable processes, you could probably build a CMDB without much more help. For the real world, where processes are not followed consistently and data is unreliable, you are often faced with creating a new source of truth. This method of populating data is often referred to as *direct entry*, although this is a bit of a misnomer because the data doesn't necessarily have to be entered manually item by item.

Direct entry is used when you don't need to respect the source of the data, or when that source is going to change frequently. Suppose your organization has three different data centers, and over the years the administrators in those centers have been keeping track of what servers they have, using a variety of spreadsheets and personal databases. Each data center might have a different policy for how to record information about servers, and even with a consistent policy, the accuracy of the data recorded might be in doubt.

This would be a classic example where you would want to inventory each data center using a consistent approach to recording the data about the servers, network device, software, and other items of interest. Perhaps you would use a discovery tool for the job to make sure you capture the technical details accurately. As you can imagine, performing an inventory is expensive and time consuming, so it may not be the first part of your CMDB population effort to get funded—but in some cases it cannot be avoided due to the value of the information that can be gained. This is a case where direct entry would actually involve running some sort of loading program to take information from the discovery tool and load it into the CMDB.

You'll find that the maturity of your existing data management processes will determine the amount of direct entry that must be done. If you already have strong processes and systems for managing data and are relatively confident in the data managed, you'll be most likely want to have a CMDB that is a simple federation of those strong data sources. On the other hand, if your organization is not used to a disciplined approach to keeping accurate data, you'll most likely need to introduce that kind of approach by creating a new source of truth.

Data Correlation and Reconciliation

The biggest challenge for populating a database through data integration is not in finding enough data, but in dealing with too much data. When data is mixed together, there are often conflicts that must be dealt with. This section describes some of the more common ways of dealing with data conflicts when populating your CMDB.

One of the most common data issues is data that means the same thing but is represented differently. For example, suppose you want to maintain information about the manufacturer of every piece of hardware in your database. When integrating data, you have two different sources of data about server hardware, perhaps from different discovery tools deployed in different data centers. The first source might code some set of servers with a manufacturer code of "IBM." The second source could be different servers with a manufacturer code of "Int Bus Machines." This is a classic example of data that is semantically the same, but syntactically different, and requires reconciliation of the data by normalizing it into a common format.

When you find this issue, the solution is never easy. First, someone needs to understand the scope and complexity of the issue. This involves visual inspection of a significant portion of the data records from each source, including any discovery tools that generate data. Following the previous example, someone would pull the manufacturer codes for every record from both sources into a spreadsheet, and then sort to find all the possible codes. Eliminating duplicates results in a list of unique manufacturer codes. This list is then scanned visually to see the items that mean the same thing, but are spelled or abbreviated differently. For each such grouping, a single syntax is adopted.

After common syntax is defined, the next question becomes how to actually get the data consolidated. In some cases, it is possible to adjust the data in the actual sources—this is most desirable when the source of truth is going to be maintained outside the CMDB. If this is possible, a project should be started to update the data that already exists, and update any necessary processes to begin using that newly updated data.

Another possibility is to leave the values in existing sources alone, but make a transformation while data is in transit. This involves creating a reference table that contains the original value as found in the source data and the desired value when the record has been stored in the CMDB. The data transfer mechanism is then configured to look up the values in the table and store the new value whenever it sees the old value. The obvious downside is that this transformation must happen each time the data is transferred, which will make large transfers rather slow and can hurt performance on the receiving CMDB. To deal with large amounts of data where the source cannot be reconciled directly, you normally need to create a staging database on a separate server from the CMDB. In this way, you can do all data transformation without affecting your production CMDB, and then do a simple transfer of the reconciled data. Figure 9.2 demonstrates an example of data reconciliation with transformation directly into the CMDB.

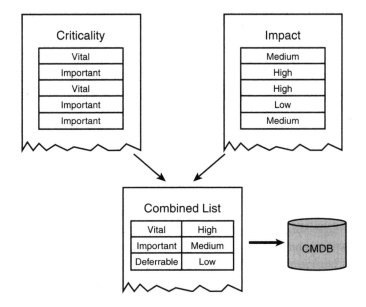

Figure 9.2 Sometimes reconciled data is pushed into the CMDB with a reference table.

Another common issue in data integration projects is correlation. This occurs most frequently when trying to relate two pieces of information without a common key between them. For example, you might have location data from a human resource system, where the key to each record is a mostly random location code that is automatically generated by the HR system. That location data is likely to have useful information, such as street address, city, and country, for each location. On the other hand, your workstation information from an asset management system might have locations listed only as a building, floor, and room number. In your CMDB schema, you would like to put these pieces together so you can know the building, floor, and city for each workstation, but there is no common key that will let you match a location from the asset system to a location from the HR system.

The first possible solution to the correlation challenge is to find a common bit of information and make it a correlating key. In the example, perhaps the asset system also has street address. Although it certainly wouldn't be an ideal key, you might be able to match a significant number of locations by comparing the street address from each system to form a reference table.

When no common data exists at all, the next option is finding a third data source that contains information common to the first two. In our example, there might be an existing facilities management database that has both the location code from the HR system and the building numbers from the asset system. This new data source could be used as a bridge to create a cross reference from the HR system to the asset system.

Finally, if no suitable correlated data source can be found, you will be forced to manually correlate the data sources. Like with data reconciliation, the best tool for this kind of manual data scrubbing is a spreadsheet. Put the room, floor, and building combinations on one tab and the HR location codes with cities on another tab. Then create a third tab where you match them up by finding people who know the locations well enough to tell you which buildings are at which HR location codes. This can be very long and painstaking work, so be sure you really need the correlated data before you undertake this kind of effort.

Although you have a choice of where to put reconciled data, there really is no choice with correlated data. You will ultimately end up with a cross-reference table that must be used on the CMDB side of the equation. If you have large data sources with lots of different elements that need to be correlated, you will most certainly need a staging database outside of the production CMDB. Fortunately, many of the available CMDB tools offer strong support for both data reconciliation and data correlation, including managing staging type data sets.

Process Integration

Populating the CMDB by integrating together existing data sources is a great way to get started. It cannot be the whole story, however, because if the processes aren't integrated, the data will quickly grow out of date and thus be inaccurate. You might think you can simply rerun the data integrations on a monthly or even a weekly basis to keep the data accurate, but that is by far the worst possible way to make sure your CMDB stays up to date.

Instead, data is kept accurate by insisting that the operational processes update the data when appropriate. One of the critical aspects of being IT Infrastructure Library (ITIL) aligned is that all processes interact with one another, and data generated by one process area can be used by another. Because configuration management is central to so many ITIL disciplines, you might assume that it gets updated from many different directions—but you would be wrong. In fact, the only discipline that should update the CMDB is change management. All other areas invoke change management when they want to alter the production environment in some way.

Of course, that isn't to say that process integration is simple. In fact, those processes that are going to use data from the CMDB need to be integrated every bit as much as change management, which is going to update the CMDB. As stated in Chapter 1, "Overview of Configuration Management," this isn't a book about ITIL or the other process areas, but this section will review several key linkages that should be put into place early in your project. These linkages keep data accurate if you chose to populate the database using data integration and help increase the rate at which data is populated if process integration is your primary means to trickle data into the CMDB.

Relationship with Change Management

Because change management is intricately linked with configuration management, you should definitely spend significant time thinking about how you will relate these two processes for your organization. The first step in linking change management with configuration management is to insist that every change record be described in terms of which configuration items are changing.

Although this is a simple concept to understand, it can be tremendously difficult to put into practice. The first question you're likely to encounter is whether you really mean *every* change record. Consider, for example, the case of a network router that needs to be rebooted. This simple change isn't likely to cause any modifications to your CMDB, but must be recorded as a change in order to facilitate communication to all the affected parties. While there might be a temptation to cite this as an example of a change that doesn't need to have configuration data associated with it, you're probably going to name the specific router in the change record anyway. It should be possible in the change description to note that an update of the configuration database won't be necessary, but it is still extremely helpful in reviewing the change to know exactly what will be changing.

After you have instituted the organizational discipline of describing every change record in terms of configuration items, you'll wonder how you ever lived without it. But be aware that there will be a bit of a "chicken and egg" problem at the beginning. You want every change record to contain at least one accurate configuration item reference, but while still populating the CMDB, those references might not be available. If you're populating your database by data integration as described earlier in this chapter, you need to establish some milestones based on data sources. For example, if you have a population plan that calls for all server data to be completely populated by August 14, you need to publish that date to the entire information technology (IT) organization so that they can begin accurately coding change records on that date. Before then, changes can either be populated with a "dummy" value, or the CI can be an optional part of the change record, which can be left empty.

If you are using primarily process integration to populate the CMDB, you need to define a streamlined procedure that allows anyone proposing a change to designate new items to be quickly put into the CMDB. Going back to our earlier example, this means that the person proposing the reboot of the router will need to send in the configuration information about the router, and someone from your configuration management organization will populate that data. The change record then can be created to indicate that the router will be changed, and it will exist in the CMDB from that point forward. Obviously, the entire organization will need to be warned of the extra step, and some leeway will need to be made for emergency change situations where populating configuration data may not be feasible.

Integrating the change process to configuration management should happen in two places. When a change is being requested, the requester should consider which CIs are being changed, as previously described. At the end of the process, after all activity for the change has completed, the configuration management team should update the CMDB to reflect any change to the affected CIs. By ensuring the correct interlocks between processes and possibly tools in these two points, you will make tremendous progress toward keeping accurate configuration data.

Relating Incidents to Configuration Items

Although change management is the only process that updates the CMDB, it is certainly not the only process which should be integrated with your configuration management process. The second process you want to integrate is incident management. In ITIL terms, incident management involves restoring services whenever they are temporarily unavailable or degraded. One of the key aspects of incident management involves determining exactly which service is down and what IT components are used to provide that service. This is where configuration management plays a key role.

Without a configuration management capability, technicians are either familiar enough with the environment to intuitively understand which components might be the culprit, or they must run various tests and scans to understand the environment. Senior technicians always seem to be able to lay their finger on the problem quickly, and less senior technicians seem to stumble around wasting valuable time while the users don't get the service they need. The goal of configuration management is to take the knowledge out of the heads of the senior people and make it accessible to everyone so that incidents can be resolved more quickly and with a more consistent process.

Of course, incident management suffers from the same "chicken and egg" problem that change management does. It is relatively easy to tie each incident to a failing CI when your full CMDB is populated. However, during the sometimes long interval when the database is only partially populated, there will be times when the failing component has not yet been recorded as a CI. Although it is logical to stop the entry of a change record waiting for a CI to be recorded, this is never a good idea with incident management. Instead, I recommend that the incident management process simply be changed to record as much detail as possible about what is found wrong. For example, the service desk might be asked to at least capture the type and location of a suspected failing workstation. Similarly, you might ask an application support team to at least record the name and primary database server for each failing application so that the configuration management team can document the CI more easily.

Then the configuration management team can be tasked temporarily with reviewing every resolved incident record to pull out and record the CIs that failed. Just as with change management, this will gradually increase the accuracy of your configuration data. Over time, enough CIs will be populated so that the incident management technicians will find it easier to simply provide the identifier of a CI rather than a full technical description of the failing component. The configuration management team will also find that many of the details they had to record before are now already in the CMDB.

Some people inevitably will ask whether the technicians should send updates to the CMDB as they resolve incidents. The response from ITIL is that any change to the environment should flow through the change management process. For example, suppose a server has crashed because a power supply failed. In order to restore service as quickly as possible, a new power supply is plugged in and the server is brought back up. In order to fully document the situation, the technician should create a request for change with the server and possibly the power supply as CIs. Because the work is already done, this will most likely follow an emergency path through the change management process, but any CMDB updates at the end will still end up coming from the change management process and not from incident management.

Capturing Configuration Data from Release Management

One of the situations that comes up frequently in configuration management is the dilemma around when something should actually be recorded as a new CI in the enterprise. For some items such as PC software and mobile devices, the acquisition cycle can be fairly quick and straightforward. Other items such as custom-developed software or mainframes can have slow and complex cycles. Bridging the gap between the acquisition cycle and the deployment of IT components into production is the ITIL process called release management.

Release management deals with the introduction of new hardware or software to the existing IT environment, and is the proper place to discuss the recording of brand new CIs. As part of each release plan, a series of individual changes will be defined. As part of the overall release policy, a specific mention should be made of exactly when the new CIs should be recorded in the CMDB. For something complex like a new release of your enterprise resource planning software, different CIs might be introduced at different times. For something more monolithic, such as a mainframe, all the CIs might be recorded together at the completion of the total release.

One of the most difficult decisions affecting new CIs involves your custom-developed business applications. Software development organizations have a discipline of their own, called configuration management, which involves breaking their work into individual modules so it can be assigned to programmers for development and unit testing. These units are recorded in a source code control system, and the control and management of these modules—including how they flow through the build process to become a total application—is referred to as software configuration management.

Having the same name for these two different disciplines is confusing enough, but the real issue is that the two must somehow intersect. The individual modules from the source code control system will get compiled or built into an application. The task for configuration management is to determine whether the separate modules are CIs, the entire application is a single CI, or whether some intermediate level is used. After the correct level is decided, process and technical interfaces then can be developed between the source code control system and the configuration management system. Be sure to include the right integration to capture the new software applications as they get promoted into your production environment.

Integrating Data across Processes

Some people get carried away with integrating processes. They form so many complex relationships between processes that the underlying systems get confusing data. As a simple example, consider the triangle that occurs between incident management, problem management, and configuration management. As described earlier, it makes terrific sense to relate your incident management process to configuration management to describe what components are actually causing service degradation. It also seems eminently reasonable to associate a CI with a problem investigation to understand exactly which component is associated with the root cause of the problem. But problems are also associated with incidents because most problem investigations stem from a service outage.

The issue that can arise comes when these three processes are automated by systems looking to link their data to one another. The incident ticket has one or more CI identifiers associated to it. The incident ticket can also have a problem record tied to it. So if you tie one or more CIs to the problem record, you have a possibility for a data mismatch. It isn't necessarily wrong, but it is quite possible that the CI tied to the incident and the CI tied to the problem might be different. This kind of "data triangle" should be avoided wherever possible, or at least studied thoroughly by the process teams to understand whether inconsistent data will be allowed.

Change, incident, and release management are not the only processes that can be integrated with configuration management. They are, however, the primary processes that most people will use to begin populating the CMDB and keep the data within it accurate. As your organization matures, you'll be able to intersect the capacity, availability, and even financial management processes to improve the accuracy of the database, as well. Whether you use these process integrations only to maintain a database that was populated by data integration, or you use them to populate the data in a steady trickle, you should spend significant effort to make sure the integrations are optimized for your organization.

I started this chapter by saying that most people first think of putting data into a database. The rest of the statement is that the first thought should actually be how you're going to maintain the data after it is already populated. The means of maintaining data (process integration) will be much more important than the means of populating the data (data integration) over the full life of the configuration management program.

CHAPTER 10

Choosing and Running a Pilot Program

If configuration management is new to your organization, you should establish a pilot program to test the waters. If your organization has tried and failed at configuration management, you should establish a pilot program to help regain lost confidence. As a matter of fact, the only time that a pilot program doesn't make sense is if you've already been successful and have an effective configuration management service today. For the rest of us, choosing and running a good pilot program is a great way to find out how much configuration management can benefit your organization.

So what is a pilot program and why is it so important? First, it is important to understand that by *pilot*, I do not mean *test*. A pilot is a full production implementation of configuration management on a smaller scale. All of the people executing the steps should be the people who will have those jobs for the long term. All processes should be the ones you intend to use when you do full-scale configuration management. The tools should be fully installed and verified before you start the pilot. The only thing different between a pilot program and full-scale production is that you will have a narrow focus and very close scrutiny.

The pilot program offers an opportunity to validate your execution capability in a short-term way. It should be treated as a separate project inside the larger project of implementing configuration management. As a separate project, it will have a planning phase, a measurements baseline, an execution, and then an evaluation phase. These short phases are wrapped in all the normal disciplines of project management, as shown in the visual outline of this chapter in Figure 10.1.

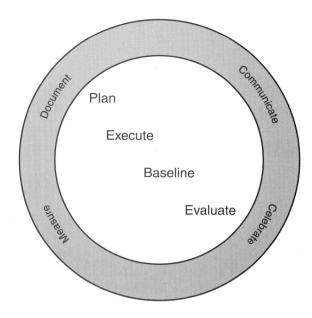

Figure 10.1   A pilot is a small-scale project with a full lifecycle.

Reasons to Perform a Pilot

There are many benefits from performing a pilot for any kind of information technology (IT) work. For configuration management, there are very few risks to balance against these benefits. You should always plan to do a pilot, especially if configuration management is a new discipline to your organization. This section gives you the reasons why a pilot is almost always a good idea. Figure 10.2 provides an overview of the key reasons, which include

- Validating the processes work for your organization
- Exercising a new configuration management organization
- Practicing with the Key Process Indicators (KPIs)
- Building momentum for the long deployment ahead

Validate Organization	Validate Process	Validate Metrics
Build Confidence		

Figure 10.2   The pilot builds overall confidence in configuration management.

One of the best reasons to perform a pilot is to make sure you have the correct processes defined. Tools are fairly easy to test, and many organizations have well-defined procedures for unit test, system test, integration test, and user acceptance test. There are also organized ways to plan the tests, execute the tests, and record defects against tools that are found as a result of tests.

Processes, on the other hand, pose a whole different set of issues. Most organizations are not very good at testing the process work they have done, and those that have tried tend to use their development methodologies and wonder why the testing of processes isn't very effective. To fully validate that the processes are working well requires several executions of the process in a setting that is as close to reality as possible. Fortunately, a pilot program offers this opportunity.

As I said, a pilot is not the place to conduct testing. You aren't really testing the process during the pilot. Testing would involve consciously causing every possible process decision box to be executed and every branch of each procedure to be executed in a sequential order. A pilot simply puts the processes into production, which will inevitably lead to the most common branches and flows being executed multiple times. Some less-common scenarios might never be encountered during the pilot phase at all, but that is acceptable as long as the processes work in the real world. Although a pilot isn't a test of the processes, it is a great way to overcome whatever weaknesses might have occurred during the test phase.

If processes are difficult to test, organization structures are even more so. Unfortunately, experience shows that most IT project fail exactly because the organization isn't able to execute the process effectively. Thorough testing of the organization would involve verifying that each responsibility is adequately assigned to a role, each person clearly understands the role(s) they've been asked to perform, and that each person is fully qualified and trained to execute the roles they've been assigned. This kind of thorough testing is seldom completed, usually because of time pressures or because nobody really knows what all the roles and responsibilities are going to be until after the project has started.

So a second great reason to perform a pilot is to validate that the organization is ready to meet the overall needs of your configuration management service. Like the process validation described earlier, this is not a test but a way of overcoming the normal weakness of not having a prior test of the organization. If configuration management is new to your organization, and especially if you've created a new team or department responsible for configuration management, it will be important to emphasize that this is not an employment test. If the organization does not work, it isn't because the people are defective, but because there has been insufficient definition of the roles, insufficient training, or perhaps too many responsibilities for one role to handle.

Processes and organization are difficult to test before production, and measurements are impossible. Until you actually start executing the process against production data, you cannot really capture any of the metrics associated with configuration management. Two classes of measurements are available:

- Those associated with the entire configuration management service
- Those used to track just the success or failure of the pilot

We'll talk about this latter group a bit later in this chapter, but for now let's focus on those measurements that will report the day-to-day and month-to-month health of the configuration management service.

A critical part of the pilot effort should be making sure that all measurements are in place and working from the beginning. How do you know if a measurement is working? You know the measurement is working by comparing the data collected against the soft evidence of perceptions about that part of the service. For example, you might be counting the number of incidents that get resolved more quickly because of configuration management data. The reports after a week of the pilot show that only two incidents were marked as having been solved more quickly; but when you interview a server administrator, she can very quickly recall three or four times when going to the configuration management data really helped her resolve an issue more quickly. Your only conclusion would be that the measure isn't working—either because it is too difficult to record the data needed, or because somewhere in the process the data is getting confused.

Chapter 14, "Measuring and Improving CMDB Accuracy," is devoted to helping you create and use good measurements. This is a very important topic, especially if you are implementing configuration management in a series of phases or releases, because getting future funding will depend on showing the value of the service you're building. Use the pilot to really understand and refine the metrics you gather.

At the end of it all, a pilot is really about increasing confidence. For yourself and the configuration management implementation team, the pilot will help you validate the planning you've put into the process, the organization, and the measurements. For your sponsors, the pilot is the first chance to see if their investment in the project will yield returns. For the skeptical people who are sitting on the sidelines wondering if there actually is any value to this whole IT Infrastructure Library (ITIL) journey, the pilot will show that the first steps are positive and the rest of the journey is possible.

In the rest of this chapter, we'll talk about how to make your pilot successful so that you can build this kind of confidence. And just in case your best laid plans don't work out, read the last section on what happens when pilots fail.

Choosing the Right Pilot

Now that you know all the reasons why you perform a pilot, it is time to think about what shape that pilot will take. It sounds simple to start up a pilot, but when you think about it more deeply, you'll find there are many ways to go about it. In this section, we consider how to choose the right shape for your pilot program.

One easy way to select a pilot is by using geography. You might decide that the pilot will perform configuration management within your headquarters building, within a specific site that your organization operates, or perhaps even within a designated country if you are part of a very large organization. The common factor is that it will be relatively easy to establish the boundary of the pilot based on geographic borders.

A geographically based pilot is a great choice for many. You'll want to review the points about setting span from Chapter 3, "Determining Scope, Span, and Granularity," because in essence all you're doing when choosing a pilot is determining the span of the first part of your total effort. The set of configuration items (CIs) and relationships in the pilot will be selected as much for political reasons as it is for technology reasons. You might get extra support from your CIO if you choose a geography that includes corporate headquarters. Or, perhaps you need to solidify your relationship with the research division, so you choose the geography with the largest research site. You'll certainly want to choose a pilot that gives you the highest possible chance of overall success, and that is not always the one that is technically easiest.

One issue that will quickly arise with a geographical pilot is what to do with those CIs that span multiple geographies. These could be something physical, such as a wide area network line with one end in your chosen geography and the other end in a different geography. The issue will need to be decided for logical entities such as a business application used by people all over the company. Each of these items will need to be dealt with in defining the exact coverage for your pilot.

If your organization is managed very hierarchically, with strong distinctions between business units, divisions, or even departments, it might make sense to choose a pilot based on business organizations. You could do configuration management for just one division, or perhaps even a single department. This is slightly more complex to do than a geographic pilot. You need to make everyone aware that if an incident or change affects the selected organization, then configuration data should be collected, used, and tracked.

For example, suppose you've chosen to pilot configuration management with just the research division. You need to notify the service desk, on-site technicians, server administrators, change management review boards, and anyone else who might come in contact with research about the pilot choice. All those groups will need to behave differently if their work is on behalf of research. That can be a complex communication and training challenge, but might be worthwhile if the political advantage of working with research is big enough.

Just like with a geographical pilot, there are seams or cracks in an organization pilot that must be considered. These normally will be in the form of shared infrastructure. Again, consider that pesky wide area network line. Odds are good that it is shared by many different organizations, so you need to decide whether it is in or out of scope for an organization-based pilot program.

A third dimension you can use in choosing a pilot is technology. Perhaps you want configuration management for only servers, only workstations, or even just the mainframe equipment as a pilot program. A technology-driven pilot is the easiest to understand and contain because it fits nicely with the structure you've already named for the scope of your overall effort. Simply pick some of the categories from your scope documentation, and manage those while disregarding others.

The three dimensions of geography, organization, and technology can be combined in interesting ways to identify the scope that is best for your organization. You might choose servers in the Dayton data center, or all equipment supporting marketing in Singapore. The set of three axes and an example of choosing the right scope among them is shown in Figure 10.3.

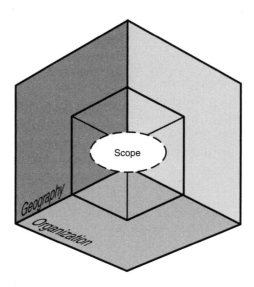

Figure 10.3   Choosing a good pilot involves navigating in three dimensions.

Be sure to carefully document the pilot scope. Nothing is worse than having mistaken expectations at the beginning of the pilot, because it is almost impossible to recover if you are planning to build one thing and others expect you to build something else. The scope document should be very concrete and give examples of what will be included and what will be excluded. This document should be carefully reviewed and widely published after it is approved by your sponsor.

Measuring Your Pilot Project

As soon as a suitable scope is chosen, you should begin thinking about the definition of success for your pilot. Because your goal is to build confidence, you will want to be able to demonstrate success in the most quantitative terms possible. Although positive feelings and happy IT people will definitely help, it is solid, uncontestable numbers that will really convince your team and your sponsors that your configuration management effort has gotten off to a good start with the pilot.

Note that the pilot does not need to have the same set of measurements as the overall configuration management service. The pilot has a shorter term and thus must be measured in weeks rather than months. Data accuracy, for example, is a long-term measure that normally takes months to establish. While accuracy should never be neglected, it isn't normally the kind of measure that will demonstrate success of a pilot.

Focus instead on the benefits your organization is hoping to get from configuration management. If you're hoping to see less failed changes, create a measurement related to how the availability of configuration data affects your success rate. If the goal is to improve your compliance posture, choose your pilot accordingly and create a measure around how configuration data helps improve compliance. The measurements you choose should be able to be measured at least a couple of times during your pilot and should demonstrate conclusively that your pilot is trending toward the promised benefits. You shouldn't expect that the pilot will completely overcome the startup costs of an immature organization, but you should run the pilot program at least long enough to see a trend toward improvement.

Don't get overly ambitious with measurements. Three or four solid numbers can be enough to demonstrate the success of a pilot, whereas 30 or 40 different measurements will only confuse everyone about what the real goals are. And while strong numbers will prove your case, don't forget to gather the "soft" benefits as well. Specifically solicit comments from people who have benefited from the pilot, and use those "sound bites" to decorate your measurements presentation. Although they aren't as powerful as the numbers, if the comments you get are positive, they will build confidence more quickly.

Ultimately, your measurements should be used as acceptance criteria for the pilot. Suppose you establish a measurement for reduced incident resolution time based on having configuration data. You could say that pilot is successfully concluded when you see more than 80 percent of the in-scope incidents being resolved at least two minutes faster. These kinds of very specific and measurable criteria are what will take the controversy out of the success (or failure) of the pilot.

While you probably won't be publishing all of the measures for the full configuration management program during the pilot, this is a good time to at least establish baselines for the critical measures going into the future. Going back to accuracy, just because you can't measure it several times and see a trend during pilot doesn't mean you shouldn't at least measure it to establish a baseline for the future. This is a part of validating the overall measurements—a key reason why you are performing the pilot in the first place.

Running an Effective Pilot

A key thing to remember while actually executing your pilot is that you will be under a microscope. Every success and failure will reflect on not only the pilot, but will indicate to your sponsors and the wider organization what they can expect from the entire configuration management service. If this seems like a lot of pressure to put on a single project, you have the right impression. Success of the pilot is a critical component for going forward and can lay the foundation for the entire future effort.

In order to manage this level of visibility, you should start your pilot project slowly and publicly. Celebrate small victories, such as capturing your first configuration item, helping to resolve your first incident with configuration information, or getting past the first execution of any of your processes. These small successes will communicate to everyone that the effort is valuable and that you will achieve the larger goals of the pilot.

While the pilot is executing, be sure to actively look for ways to improve. A quick adjustment to a process or a fast change to the Configuration Management Database (CMDB) schema when done in pilot might be able to save thousands of dollars or hundreds of hours in the future. Although you shouldn't just change for the sake of making changes, the pilot is a time for some degree of experimentation and adaptation. Take advantage of the lessons you're learning while learning them.

To make a change during the pilot, you should have an abbreviated control mechanism. This change control should include a communication mechanism to ensure everyone knows about the change, some evaluation criteria to allow rapid assessment of the change, and a tracking mechanism so you can measure the results of the change. You don't need fancy tools to track changes in this informal way—email for communication and a spreadsheet for tracking are suitable.

During the pilot, just like during the full production configuration management service, you should be looking constantly for ways to check the accuracy of data. If there is any hint of incorrect or incomplete data, be aggressive in getting it corrected or completed. If the data in the fledgling CMDB is perceived as less than completely useful, your sponsors will get the impression that this is just another failed IT project that had good intentions but ultimately doesn't deliver on its promises. Nothing will kill the spirit and momentum you're trying to build in the pilot phase faster than the perception that your data has quality issues.

But how do you avoid quality issues in the data? During pilot, you should have the luxury of double checking nearly everything. Because the set of data you're managing is intentionally small, you should be able to add extra steps to validate it frequently. Make that extra effort to ensure the success of the pilot and a solid foundation for your CMDB.

INTENSE FOCUS ON DATA

In one pilot, our customer was insistent that it was *impossible* to keep data accurate. In order to prove them wrong, we intentionally set a scope of only about three hundred configuration items with fifty or so relationships. With a data set this small, we did a physical inventory of each CI every three days of the pilot. With this kind of fanatical attention to data accuracy, we achieved one hundred percent accuracy over a seven-week pilot. While this isn't necessarily the recommended way to keep data accurate, it does show one way to overcome perceptions that the data will always be incorrect.

Finally, during the pilot phase you need to have a strong issue-tracking and resolution process. Keeping track of all issues, regardless of how trivial they might seem, is the best way to increase the satisfaction of your stakeholders. You should announce how issues can be reported, and work with anyone reporting an issue to assign the correct severity to it. Work on the issues of the highest severity first, but be sure to report status on all of the issues. Be attentive to details because, again, the smallest change in the pilot might save you money and time in the longer term.

Some issues might be too big to correct during the original pilot time frame. If the issue is very critical or describes something that simply can't go on in further production, you will have no choice but to extend your pilot or even postpone it until the issue is resolved. If the issue is small enough, however, don't be afraid to let its resolution wait until after the completion of pilot.

Evaluating the Pilot

After the pilot has completed, take stock before rushing on to production. You should evaluate the pilot not just for success or failure, but for lessons that can be learned and improvements that should be made. The evaluation step should help not just to improve your configuration management service, but to help other IT projects in their pilot efforts in the future. Figure 10.4 depicts the components of a complete assessment, which are discussed in the following paragraphs.

The evaluation begins with an analysis of the measurements you decided to track. The measurements should show what is working well and what is not working as well as expected. Use all measurements taken during the entire pilot to compile an overall assessment, including strengths and weaknesses, action plans, and recommendations to proceed or wait. This assessment should be reviewed by the team first, and then provided to your sponsors as a summary of the pilot project.

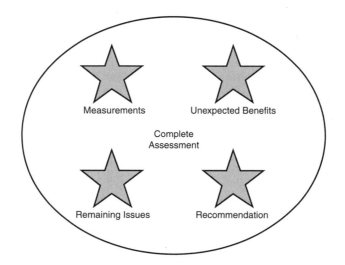

Figure 10.4 There are several key components in a good pilot assessment.

Your assessment should also contain some comments on unexpected benefits from the pilot program. In most projects, you can find benefits that weren't expected, but which are real nonetheless. You might discover during pilot, for example, that you've actually shortened the review time needed for change records. Although you didn't plan to improve the change management process, this can certainly be claimed as a benefit of the configuration management pilot work. Thus, you would expect all other change reviews to be shorter once you've completely rolled out your configuration management service. Spend some time in your evaluation thinking about benefits to the other operational processes that have occurred because of implementing configuration management.

Of course your assessment should also document any issues that remain out of the pilot program. Document the issue clearly, and indicate any steps being taken to resolve the issue. At the end of the pilot program you should close out your issue management by either resolving all remaining issues or documenting in your assessment how they will be handled after the pilot.

In its summary and recommendations, your assessment should provide concrete information about how your project achieved its acceptance criteria. Each criterion you defined before the pilot started should be revisited to assess whether the pilot missed the mark, partially met the goal, or completely satisfied the standard. The recommendation you make should be based on this objective assessment of the acceptance criteria, and if it is, there should be no doubt about whether your recommendation will be accepted.

What Happens When Pilots Fail

Hopefully you will never have to read this section. Maybe your pilot will meet and exceed its goals, and you can sail on smoothly in your implementation. Just in case that doesn't happen, however, this section will describe how to understand and recover from a failed pilot.

The first thing you need to do with a failed pilot is find out what happened. Was this a real failure of the configuration management service, or a case of failing to meet undocumented expectations? In many cases, you'll find that the pilot is declared a failure because you failed to do something you never intended to do in the first place. Someone read your scope document, or perhaps your acceptance criteria, and thought you meant something different than you actually intended. This can be a difficult situation to get out of, because it is difficult to have a retrospective discussion of motives. In many cases, this type of dispute will need to be worked through the issue management process, and if the dispute is significant enough, a new pilot may need to be run with a different scope or acceptance set defined.

If the cause of the pilot failure is not found to be mistaken expectations, you should proceed to do a root cause analysis. Dig beneath the symptoms of failure to find the underlying causes. You might find processes that were inadequately or incorrectly defined, team members who didn't receive adequate training, tools that failed to provide needed functions, or even requirements that were poorly specified. Whatever you find should be documented and worked until you are fairly satisfied that the root cause is well understood.

The integrity of the root cause process can often be enhanced by inviting people outside the project team to participate. If your organization has an independent IT quality group, they would be ideal members of the root cause team. If no such group is available, ask a peer manager or one of your stakeholders from outside the project team to help you really understand the causes of the failure without prejudices associated with having been on the team.

After the root causes have been clearly stated, you can formulate the action plans to address them. Document the actions, including the person taking the action, and definite completion dates. Track this mini-project plan to completion in order to get your configuration management effort back on track. If the actions are going to take a long time to complete, you may need to address some other things before coming back to configuration management. For example, your pilot might have failed because of lack of process discipline among those who resolve incidents.

Some incidents could be resolved with configuration data, but others didn't even have enough basic data to enable the technician to find the right CI.

If you are faced with long-term action items, you need to announce to the organization that although configuration management is a great thing to do, your organization is not yet mature enough to accomplish it. Then go work on the long-term action items and come back to configuration management after those issues are taken care of.

And when your action items are all complete, whether in the short term or after some time, you should run another pilot. It is important to have a successful pilot before moving on to a wider scale roll out of your configuration management service. This is especially true after you've had a failed pilot because the confidence *in* the team and *of* the team will both need to be bolstered. The full recovery cycle is documented in Figure 10.5.

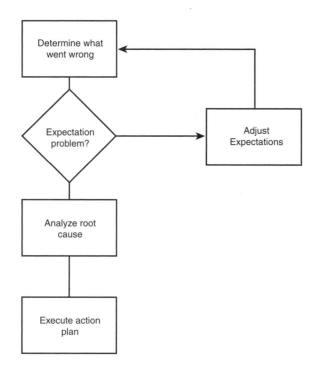

Figure 10.5 Recovery from a failed pilot is possible.

After the successful pilot (even if you've had to try more than once), you'll be armed with real-world experience that will help you tackle a much wider scope. If you're staging in your configuration management effort, your next round might be a lot like the pilot—another small, contained effort. If you are in a fairly small organization, you might be able to move from pilot directly to a complete roll out. Either way, the next chapter will help you move from pilot to production as smoothly as possible by describing ways to extend from a pilot program to your full implementation.

CHAPTER 11

Communication and Enterprise Roll Out

After the pilot has ended and the victory celebration is complete, the long, slow march toward implementation begins in earnest. Although the pilot is a tightly controlled, highly visible environment where everything runs as planned, the production roll out can be just the opposite. Control gets distributed and sometimes slips. Visibility of the effort, even to other parts of the same project team, can sometimes be minimal. Your best-conceived plans are likely to take twists and turns that you would never have dreamed. All of this makes the deployment stage a grand adventure.

The keys to surviving the adventure are planning and execution. Based on the success you've had in the pilot, you can adjust your project plans and really focus on executing them well. In addition, you can build a solid communication plan that can help everyone's expectations stay reasonable. Finally, you can break up the work up into reasonably size pieces to better predict and measure progress throughout a long deployment cycle.

This chapter describes how to move from your simple pilot implementation of configuration management into a full enterprise deployment. If you've been meticulous about everything you've read thus far, the payoff happens now. If you've skipped any steps or thought less deeply about some areas than you should, however, this is the time you'll be caught. At the end of this chapter, we'll consider how strong sponsorship can help to reach into some of the farthest corners of your organization to make sure your implementation is truly complete when you are finished.

Figure 11.1 shows a visual outline of this chapter.

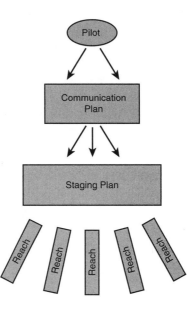

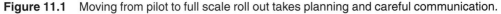

Figure 11.1   Moving from pilot to full scale roll out takes planning and careful communication.

Leveraging the Success of the Pilot

Another reason to always run a pilot is to have a firm foundation to build on. Every effort needs some place to start, and for configuration management that place is the pilot program. Hopefully you followed the advice in Chapter 10, "Choosing and Running a Pilot Program," and kept at the pilot until you reached success. That success is the best possible place to start with your wider scale deployment.

Advertise Your Success

The first step in deployment is to get the word out to a much wider audience. Later in this chapter we talk about an organized communication plan, but for now the first message to get out is that your pilot was a success. This will pave the way for all the other messages, both positive and not, that will come later. Communication has the double benefit of building organizational support and awareness for configuration management and helping the organization understand the benefits of the service.

Start by putting together a slide show, possibly the same one you used in the final stakeholder meeting of the pilot. This presentation should review the key functions that were delivered by the pilot, share some of the lessons that were learned during the pilot, and describe the measurements that declared the pilot a success. The slide show should include some good graphics, and perhaps even introduce marketing elements, such as a logo, that you'll use to represent the entire program during deployment. This kind of branding can help to put your project in people's mind.

When the slides are ready, you should host a kickoff meeting. The kickoff will let everyone know what's coming, and what to expect. Invite the highest level sponsor you can find to open the meeting with a discussion of why the organization feels that configuration management is important. The message is much more powerful when coming from a CIO or even the senior executive from one of your business units. You want to show people that the entire weight of the business is behind the project, so when the project comes back later to disrupt their processes and look for their data, they know you have priority.

You should make sure that representatives from every affected area are part of the kickoff meeting. People won't be excited about what is coming if they don't know about it. Include businesspeople who will be able to benefit from faster incident resolution. If possible, bring together people from different geographies. This can be done physically or using technology to share the same message in different places. If your rollout plan includes different phases to cover different parts of your scope or different spans, by all means invite people from each different phase to the kickoff meeting.

Be sure that the kickoff meeting doesn't end without everyone having the high-level milestones of the rollout in their heads. Present these milestones through the slide show, talk about them both formally and informally, and sometimes it is even effective to hang large charts displaying the milestones on the walls of the meeting room. The whole point is to move people from the success of the pilot to the correct expectations for the deployment; the more they know about the dates and targets for deployment, the more realistic their expectations will be.

As part of the kickoff, you might want to schedule a road show where you or the key members of the deployment team take the message out to the business units. The format of each session will be similar to the kickoff, but the audience will be smaller and the setting more intimate. This is a time for people to ask questions and express their doubts about the project. As deployment team members, keep the message upbeat and positive. You succeeded in the pilot, and now you will succeed in the deployment. Advertising your success is the first of a three-part strategy from moving from pilot to full deployment. All three parts are depicted in Figure 11.2.

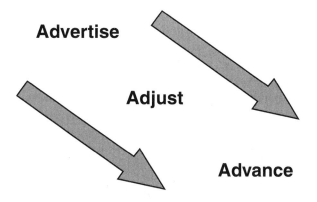

Figure 11.2   Use the success of the pilot as the base for the deployment.

Adjust the Project Plan

The second way in which you can leverage a successful pilot is by adjusting the planning that you did from the first part of this book. While you certainly don't want to throw out all the good work you did, you probably have learned through the pilot which planning steps were less effective than others. As usual, time spent in planning is always better than time spent in rework caused by a bad plan.

When you were defining requirements, you probably made some assumptions that didn't turn out to be true. There may have even been some goals stated that turned out not to be very useful now that you've been through the pilot. Even if nothing has changed, time has passed between the first writing of the requirements and the end of the pilot. Before you rush into the deployment, take time to update your requirements to reflect what you really want to do in deployment.

You should also review and adjust your scope, span, and granularity now that you are more familiar with how configuration management will work in your organization. You might have learned that it will be extraordinarily difficult to track wireless handheld devices, so you will want to take them out of your scope definition. Perhaps you want to change the granularity of servers based on your experiences from the pilot. Document any of those changes that make sense now, and be sure to get your sponsor's approval for the new documentation before going forward.

The process customization efforts have already been reviewed as part of the set of improvements you made while the pilot was going on. We'll consider some changes you might want to make to the data population strategy in the later section, "Growing from Pilot to Deployment."

Of course, each change you make will have implications to your overall project schedule, scope, and cost. Be sure to reflect all changes in the appropriate project documents and reset expectations around project time lines if they are going to be different. It might seem unreasonable to rework all the planning before you get started with the deployment, but experience shows that flexibility in the beginning will lead to greater success in the end.

Advance from the Foundation

The final way you leverage a successful pilot is to build the deployment upon the data foundation already laid during pilot. This might take different forms, depending on how you structured the pilot project. For example, if your pilot project involved capturing server configurations, you might build on this foundation by quickly gathering operating system data and relating all the servers to the correct operating systems.

You gain two strong benefits from building on an existing Configuration Management Database (CMDB) foundation. The first is that you can leverage existing data to infer the need for new data. If you've gathered workstation hardware in the pilot, for example, you can infer that there are local area networks (LAN) at the same locations as the workstations. When you're gathering the LAN data, you know where to start because any place without workstations is either a data center or it doesn't have a LAN. Having a foundation enables you to guess at what other data should be found.

Second, having some data already in your CMDB provides a way to start building out the relationships, which is typically the more difficult part of the population effort. If you defined the business applications in the pilot, you can use those records to start making relationships to the servers as you move into production. Then later in production, you can leverage the server data to make relationships to networks or to middleware. In this way, you can logically build out the chain of related records based on the starting point established in pilot.

This is why it is critical that your pilot be a full, production-ready project and not a simple test project. If you ran pilot in a different environment, or one that wasn't ready to take the full load of production data, you will not be able to gain the benefit of building on the data without some kind of migration effort. Save yourself the bother and enable a seamless transition from pilot to deployment.

If you advertise your success, adjust your project plan, and advance from the solid foundation build in the pilot, you should be able to ease into the full deployment of configuration management. Deployment may still seem like a long, slow journey, but at least you'll have the satisfaction of knowing you've begun by being as well equipped as possible.

Creating a Communication Plan

One of the specific things that should be done early in deployment is to create a communications plan. Communication might have been useful during planning and while running the pilot, but it is crucial during deployment. You could have created a communication plan as part of your overall project planning effort, but only after the pilot will you really know all the messages to be communicated and have an appreciation for the best way to communicate those messages.

A communications plans is basically a matrix. The rows on the matrix are the different messages that need to be communicated. The columns on the matrix are the different audiences that need to know about the configuration management deployment. In each cell where a row and column intersect, you'll either add a specific format that you'll use to deliver the message to that audience, or you'll leave an empty cell to indicate that the message in question doesn't have to be communicated to that audience.

So, what are these messages? They are distinct bits of information you want to send at various times throughout the deployment. If you're doing a physical inventory to gather configuration data, one message will be an announcement to the people who normally work in that area, so they can be aware of what you're doing. There will certainly be a recurring message that contains the status of the deployment project, including any significant issues that the team is facing. Another message might include information about your processes and how they will interface to each business unit. You'll probably want to craft a message about how people can request configuration data and what kind of response they should expect. Anything that the project team will need to communicate to the wider organization should be framed as a message in the communication plan.

Each message should be documented in a format that does not exceed one page. Regardless of the final context used to deliver the message, a single page should be enough to distill the gist of the message so that your team and your sponsors can understand what's going to be communicated. It is important to keep track of these communications to make sure they happen and as a record in case someone comes back to say they weren't informed about the project. The full matrix with messages and audiences is shown in Figure 11.3.

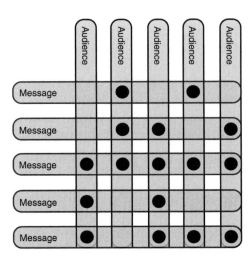

Figure 11.3 A communication plan consists of a set of messages delivered to a set of audiences.

The messages will be communicated to audiences. By audiences, I mean any person or group who can be the target of one or more messages. Some examples might include a specific business unit, your project sponsors, or the information technology (IT) organization as a whole. If you find that the exact same set of messages need to go to two different audiences, it makes sense to combine those into a single audience for the sake of the communication plan.

Defining messages and audiences is an iterative experience. You'll be thinking about a specific message and realize that you need to deliver it to an audience you haven't defined yet. Then you'll be defining an audience and realize you forgot to include an important message. Don't get too granular with messages and audiences, however. The rule of thumb for messages is that they should have enough content to fill a single page, but no more. Try to keep the number of audiences down to 15 to 20 in a very large organization, and 10 to 15 in a medium or small organization. With less than that number, you're probably not communicating widely enough. With more than that, you are spending too much of your project's resources on communicating.

After you determine the correct messages and lay them into a grid with the right audiences, its time to think about how you communicate. Go through each intersection and determine the best way to send the message to the audience. Is there an existing newsletter where you could publish an article? Maybe you can post a news item to a web page where members of your audience are likely to find it. More urgent communications might require that you send an email to every member of the target audience. For complex messages where questions are likely, you might want to schedule a meeting to most effectively transmit the message. For long-lasting information, a document or presentation that you could send might be suitable.

The format information should be documented in each cell of the communication plan matrix. Put in just enough detail so you know how the message will be delivered to that particular audience. A note such as "email" or "meeting" will normally suffice.

After you define which format is appropriate for each combination of message and audience, it will be time for the final piece of the communication plan. This is the element of timing. People tend to hear and comprehend messages best when they need to know the information. Determine when each message should be sent to each audience to maximize their receptivity and understanding. Work out the correct timing for the delivery of each message and use that to interlock your communication plan with your overall project plan. Whether you actually put tasks in the project schedule or just work from the communication plan matrix doesn't matter as long as the communications go out at the right times.

Growing from Pilot to Deployment

The key to successfully deploying configuration management is to break up the work into manageable sized pieces. Because you can't be everywhere and do everything at the same time, you need to define some sort of progression or sequence for completing the work. This section helps you define that progression and understand how to get to the completion of the project.

Choosing the method to move from pilot to deployment should be relatively easy now. Look again at the definitions used for span in Chapter 3, "Determining Scope, Span, and Granularity," Check the advice for choosing a pilot in Chapter 10. You should have enough information to make a good decision about how you want to define the portions of the overall project.

As a review, consider Figure 11.4. You can organize geographically, planning to roll out configuration management location by location. You could also organize by business unit, moving from division to division until everyone is participating fully in configuration management. You could use your scope definition and work on certain classes of configuration items (CIs) at a time, or you might even follow the relationship chain, starting at business applications and then working down to servers and eventually to network equipment.

Hybrid approaches are also quite possible to get to a finer level of detail. If your major approach is technology based, you might want to configure all the workstations in the home office first, then all the ones in a major manufacturing site second, thus combining the technology-driven approach with a geographical approach. Keep driving down the details until you have defined pieces small enough that you are very certain you can accomplish them. After you get to that point, you'll have developed a good approach for production.

So, what do we mean by a "piece" in the preceding context? Think of each piece as a component of your overall deployment project. Each piece will have a scope, although not necessarily one that is formally documented. Each piece will have a set of tasks, and those tasks are likely to be repeated for each piece that is of the same type. For example, each time you gather workstations from a new site, you're likely to repeat tasks for setting up a discovery tool for the site, gathering lists of users at the site, perhaps getting some sort of floor plans to divvy up the discovery work, running the discovery tool, matching the discovered workstations with the users, compiling a site-specific report, and then entering all that data into the CMDB using the data reconciliation techniques from Chapter 9, "Populating the Configuration Management Database."

Each of those tasks will be repeated for each "piece" of work that involves getting workstation data at a site, but the tasks might be slightly different for a different kind of piece.

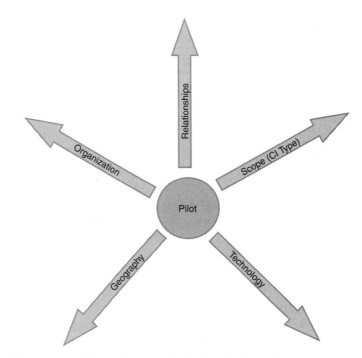

Figure 11.4   There are multiple paths toward a full production roll out.

Rolling out configuration management involves documenting the pieces, delegating them to small work teams for execution, and then managing the communication and the execution through all the different pieces you've defined.

The pilot required a lot of focused attention in order to execute well. Now that you're into deployment, don't let up too much. The first piece of the deployment will require almost as much attention as the pilot. It shouldn't be its own project or necessarily have its own measurements, but you still need to be sure it is executed well.

I wouldn't recommend trying to do the second piece in parallel with the third or any others. It might delay your overall schedule a bit, but the second piece should be executed first before any other pieces are attempted. If the second piece is executed flawlessly, you can then plan to send your work teams out in parallel to speed up the schedule. If there are issues in executing the second piece, then you need to do the third piece individually as well until you feel the deployment is running smoothly.

You should schedule some natural pauses into the overall deployment plan to give yourself time to evaluate and rework the plan as needed. If you have more than two work teams out doing things in parallel, it is especially critical that you schedule one week every several months when your teams plan to not work. That week should be used to gather tips and pointers that the work teams have developed and disseminate that information out to the other teams. Your overall plan will actually be accelerated if you plan these breaks into the schedule and use them to improve the effectiveness of your work teams.

During these pauses in the schedule, you can also evaluate your resource needs against your risk. If you've been going too quickly and your measurements are showing that quality is suffering, you might want to drop one or more work teams to slow down the work and allow the focus to be on quality. This assumes that you've built some degree of flexibility into the overall schedule to allow yourself to slow down. Conversely, you might want to take the break to train some new work teams to help accelerate the pace.

After your deployment activities reach a good pace, it is time to start thinking about being finished. It seems an odd situation, but many times projects don't know when they are finished. This is especially true with configuration management projects in organizations that haven't thought very deeply about this topic before. Perhaps you started with a very simple scope that included just business applications and the servers they run on. Somewhere along the way a sponsor suggested you might also want to collect the operating systems that run on those servers. So, you process a project change request and add that to your scope. But while collecting the operating systems, you find that the line between operating systems and middleware is fairly blurry, so you decide to include middleware as well. Suddenly, what started as a three-month deployment is going on six months, and someone is starting to suggest you get desktop software as well since you already have all the server software.

The overall scope of a configuration management project can creep in many different directions. You should assume it is a compliment when your organization sees the good work that you've done and wants you to continue with a wider scope. The configuration data you're providing is valuable, and when people see the benefits, they assume more data would bring more benefits. But you need to be aware that continuing on the same project forever will eventually wear down your project team and wear out the patience of your sponsors.

The better approach is to start gathering requirements for the next release. When you initially documented requirements, you assumed there would be more than one release. So now is the time to begin pushing new requests into that next release. It is much better practice to have several short duration releases that add function incrementally than to have one very late-running project which adds the functions through change control until your original scope is almost unrecognizable.

Reaching into Corners

Configuration management is difficult for many reasons, not the least of which is that it requires learning things that some people may not want to teach you. To get a complete picture of your IT environment, you need to reach into some corners that are not normally open to IT projects. This section discusses some examples of these corners and how to deal with them.

First, let's consider departmental servers. Every major IT organization issues a policy that all servers are housed in data centers. Then they make a process by which servers are purchased, configured, and deployed. At almost every organization I've worked with, however, at least one business manager decides that following the standard IT process is too expensive or takes too long. Besides, they think, a server is nothing but a beefed-up PC. So, they purchase a workstation with lots of memory and hard disk space and use it to share files, host applications, or take on other server tasks. Thus is born a departmental server.

Because the IT group is not involved in configuring or supporting this beefed-up PC, it doesn't get involved in disciplines like business continuity planning, capacity management, or change management. But when a configuration management project comes along, you want to capture the existence and purpose of this device. You might be able to help the department by implementing the normal operational disciplines, and at the very least you want to capture the business functions that the server supports.

The best way to handle departmental servers is to engage your project sponsor as you enter into a negotiation with the department manager. You can offer the benefits of configuration management as well as the other IT disciplines. They can offer the information about the servers they manage. You either need to make this exchange happen or let your sponsors understand why these servers will remain outside your scope.

Another difficult corner of the configuration management world happens in applications or devices that are no longer supported. Unfortunately, in most large organizations there is at least one application or server that is in a crucial role, but which nobody seems to understand. I've actually had one of our clients tell me about an old IBM Series 1 computer they were still using. Nobody knew how to service it or even how to safely shut it down and restart it. When I asked why they didn't just get rid of it, they told me it was running the application that managed physical security for the data center! Unfortunately, there are many such "turn key" systems that have been installed over the years for specific business purposes. The vendors that installed them no longer support them, or may have even gone out of business, leaving us with the IT relics we can't get rid of.

Dealing with these technology barriers is not easy. The best policy is to move them out of your scope and ignore them like everyone else does. If you aren't allowed to do that, at least insist that a team be assigned to do a thorough analysis of what it would really take to replace the relic with a modern solution. By getting a detailed proposal on the table, you point out to your sponsors the real value of the data they are insisting you gather, and maybe you can even do the whole IT shop a favor and get rid of one of these problems altogether.

Finally, consider the case of items that are just difficult to reach. Perhaps you are in the retail business and have more than eight hundred separate store locations around the world. Can you really afford to send some member of your team to Riyadh to collect configuration information about the one server and six point-of-sale terminals in that store? On the other hand, can you count on the store manager to give you correct information? This is just one example of information that is physically difficult to reach because it is remote. There are many other situations where devices are hard to reach because of geographic barriers.

In most cases, you should get someone who normally works with the devices to give you data. For example, perhaps there is a local Saudi support person who services the POS terminals when they have failures. That person is most likely more reliable than the store manager for finding things such as serial numbers and asset tags. This is an example where you would want to let the data trickle in by integrating your configuration management process with the support process for the equipment. That way, when the support person was again called to the store, he would know about configuration management and how to collect the appropriate data.

These are just a few examples of the various corners that might remain after your main deployment project is ended. In each case, you need to help your sponsors assess the value of the information against the difficulty in obtaining the information. In many cases, you'll find that it is quite acceptable to leave some of these corners for the next release, or perhaps to never include them in any configuration management program.

By the end of deployment, you've done a great thing. Starting from virtually nothing, you will have catalogued all of the IT environment and will now have a team and a process in place for keeping the information up to date and accurate. Now it is definitely time to celebrate!

In the third and final part of this book, we discuss ways to keep the program going and use all the great information you're managing.

PART III

Running an Effective Configuration Management System

CHAPTER 12

Building a Configuration Management Team

Every significant endeavor requires some kind of organization to balance the workload of the team. For configuration management, there is plenty of work to go around, so it is important to clearly define the roles that will help the team operate at maximum efficiency. One set of skills is needed to plan the effort and document what a complete configuration management solution will look like. Additional roles are needed to move the solution from the dream into reality by implementing configuration management for your organization. After implementation, a new set of roles will take over as stewards of the process and tools to actually achieve the business results expected from all the effort. Finally, throughout the lifecycle someone needs to look after the quality of the effort, making sure that the organization's goals don't get lost in the daily grind of getting the job done.

Chapter 8, "Implementing the Process," touched briefly on staffing the configuration management team, but it didn't go deeply into the skills and job descriptions that you want to include. This chapter provides much more complete detail on each role to be played in the overall configuration management effort. Figure 12.1 displays the visual outline of the chapter.

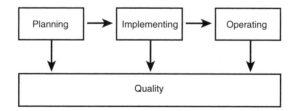

Figure 12.1 Different roles are played at different points in the overall program.

So, what makes an adequate definition of a role? There are three primary aspects to defining any role—a job description, the set of skills needed to succeed in the role, and the responsibilities of the person in the role. The job description should be succinct, descriptive, and helpful in understanding the job described. The set of skills includes not only the technical skills, but also the business skills needed to get the complete job accomplished. The responsibilities should be consistent with the needs of the process work in fulfilling the overall configuration management effort. Many people are familiar with the RASIC model where you define a set of tasks and assign individual roles to be Responsible, to Approve, to Support, to Inform, and to Consult on that task. If your organization is familiar with this model, it can be a helpful tool to organize your team. Each of the following role definitions includes all three of these characteristics.

But creating a configuration management team is much more than assembling a group of individuals. Much has been written about the need for a vision in bringing groups together, and in configuration management this is definitely the case. Every member of the team must understand the big picture of what is being accomplished, must see the business value of accomplishing it, and must be committed to do whatever it takes to achieve that value. Most parts of building the team will fall on the configuration management architect as the technical team leader, so it is extremely important to choose an architect who has the ability to work with people, along with the technical skills to guide and direct the configuration management effort.

Planning Roles

The first set of roles to consider are those needed to plan the configuration management effort. Typically, these are people with higher skills to get your program off to a solid start and to build a foundation for solid progress for years to come. Note that although these roles are designated for planning, they will be important through all the lifecycle phases. The project manager, for example, will be needed during implementation and occasionally during operations as significant enhancements are being made to the configuration management process or tools. These roles are introduced here because they are all necessary in the planning phase of the work.

Configuration Management Architect

The configuration management architect is the technical leader for all configuration management efforts. The key job of the architect is to define the overall configuration management solution, including people, processes, and technology. A secondary job is to lead the technical team that will implement and later operate the solution. The architect should be well respected for both technical depth and leadership skills by both the team and the stakeholders. Clearly, the architect role is a key job for the overall configuration management effort and should be staffed very early in the planning phase. In the IT İnfrastructure Library (ITIL) literature, this role is called the Configuration Manager, but I've chosen to provide the architect title to indicate the level of thinking required to fill this role.

The configuration management architect should be deep in configuration management, but broad in information technology (IT) topics in general. Although it isn't critical to know every nuance of every environment, understanding the key pieces of information in almost every IT domain is certainly helpful. For example, the configuration management architect may not understand the intricacies of every routing protocol, but should understand the importance of a router in the network and what impact a router failure could have in delivering IT service. In addition to this technical breadth, the architect should also have the skill to understand business cases, know the value of configuration information, and participate intelligently in the tradeoff discussions that are an inevitable part of determining scope. Clear written and spoken communications skills, and the ability to relate well to both management and the technical team, are also necessary in the configuration management architect. To have had time to gain all of these skills, the configuration management architect is likely to be a senior technical person with at least ten years of IT experience.

The responsibilities of the architect reflect the broad range of required skills. From the beginning of the project, the configuration management architect participates in the requirements discussions to ensure that all requirements are understood and can be technically achieved. The architect has primary responsibility for the scope and granularity discussions, and documents the results of those discussions, as described in Chapter 3, "Determining Scope, Span, and Granularity." The architect must then work with the process engineer and the requirements analyst to ensure that the configuration management process is defined in a way that meets the requirements. Finally, the selection of a Configuration Management Database (CMDB) tool is the primary responsibility of the architect. In producing the project architecture documents, the configuration management architect considers all these work products: requirements, scope documents, processes, and technology. This overall solution architecture furnishes the guiding principles for the implementation team.

The following table summarizes the configuration management architect role:

CM Architect	Configuration management team leader who is the main technical person and subject matter expert
Skills	*Responsibilities*
Configuration management expert	Define solution
Think architecturally	Lead teams
Read and contribute to business case	Establish scope, span, granularity
Communicate clearly	Select CMDB tool
	Produce architecture documentation

Requirements Analyst

The requirement analyst (RA) role is specific to the planning and implementation phases of the project. As the name implies, the main job of the requirements analyst is to gather and manage the requirements around configuration management. Requirements are critical because they are the best way to understand and document the value of the configuration management effort to the overall business. The requirements engineer is not a configuration management specific role, but someone who might come from a general pool of system engineers. After the requirements have been documented and agreed on by all stakeholders, the role of the requirements analyst is needed only if changes to those requirements are desired. Once implementation is complete, this role is no longer needed.

The key skill for a requirements engineer is the ability to understand the business and imagine the value of configuration management to this business. This involves many people-oriented skills, such as interviewing business managers, communicating with executives around overall business strategy, and facilitating group discussion with those who will use the configuration management data. Standard systems engineering skills such as requirement elicitation, traceability analysis, and requirements management will also be important for this role. A good requirements engineer should have a broad technical background to understand how to take the business-oriented requirements and drive them down to overall system requirements in the areas of performance, reliability, compliance, and manageability. This role should be staffed with a seasoned technical professional with at least five years of experience.

The first responsibility of the requirements analyst is to conduct a workshop in which representatives from all stakeholders come together to define and refine the business requirements for configuration management. This workshop is generally seen as the kickoff for the project and should be sponsored by the senior IT executive, but planned and run by the requirements analyst. The requirements analyst is also responsible for documenting the business requirements that come out of the workshop and working with the technical team to refine those business requirements into system requirements for the overall configuration management solution. After these lower-level requirements have been adequately documented, the requirements analyst leads a series of reviews to make sure that the implementation team understands and agrees with the requirements of the total system. Throughout the lifecycle of the project, the requirements analyst should be available to handle changes to the requirements caused by new understanding of the project or changes in the business climate.

This table summarizes the role played by the requirements analyst.

Requirements Analyst	Systems engineer who can gather and manage requirements for the project
Skills	*Responsibilities*
Understand the business	Gather and document requirements
Interviewing	Plan and lead requirements workshop
Facilitate discussions	Ensure requirements traceability
Manage requirements	Respond to requirement changes
	Control technical baselines

Process Engineer

A process engineer also should be employed during the planning phase of the configuration management project. The key job here is to make sure that the total process—including the part automated by tools and the part done manually—is documented, refined, and implemented. The process engineer works alongside the architect to take a "big picture" view of the effort, but specializes in documenting the key workflows and control points rather than worrying about the infrastructure and tools that are used to accomplish the work. The process engineer role is needed primarily in planning and early implementation.

Business skills are more important than technical skills for a process engineer. The ability to see the business value of configuration management and arrange people and tools to meet those needs most efficiently is the most important task. This requires broad knowledge of the business, an understanding of the culture and roles involved, and the ability to assimilate this knowledge into a cohesive process. Other specific skills required include architectural thinking, process engineering techniques, and the ability to work with a wide variety of people. The process engineer should not be a dedicated configuration management expert, but rather a strong process engineer who has the ability to create processes in a variety of business contexts.

The primary responsibility of the process engineer is to define and document the configuration management process, but the work certainly doesn't stop there. All processes, by definition, are at a high level. The process engineer is also responsible for working with the implementation team to help document lower-level procedures, which will fill in the gaps on how to execute the process. As these procedures are developed, the process engineer is responsible for training one or more trainers and helping to develop a curriculum to teach the entire organization how to do configuration management. The process engineer is also responsible for establishing some objective measures of the effectiveness of the configuration management process. These measures will be used throughout the organization to show the business value being gained by the process and to make incremental improvements as the organization matures.

The process engineer role is summarized in the following table:

Process Engineer	Workflow specialist who helps define the configuration management process
Skills	*Responsibilities*
Understand the organization	Define and document process
Think architecturally	Build lower level work instructions
Document processes and procedures	Train the trainer
Strong interpersonal skills	Define process measurements

Project Manager

The project manager rounds out the configuration management planning team. As would be expected, the project manager coordinates and organizes the actions of the architect, requirements analyst, and process engineer. The project manager role is not specific to configuration management, so no further description is needed here.

Implementation Roles

Implementation is always a transition phase between planning and production. The configuration management project is no different. The following roles reflect this transitory nature, as they are important for a short while during the actual implementation of the process and tools but then become much less important. All operational roles described below will be present during implementation as well, but the following roles are dedicated just to implementing the system.

Logical DBA

The Database Analyst (DBA) role is important throughout the entire configuration management effort, but in transition there is a specific role to be played by the logical database analyst. In the planning phase, the architect created some high-level diagrams to show the scope and granularity of the intended CMDB. The role of the logical DBA is to take these diagrams and turn them into a full database schema that can be implemented by a specific tool. From the high-level diagrams to the actual database description language that will implement the schema, everything related to making the scope and granularity real in software is the domain of the logical DBA.

The most important skill for the DBA is database design. The ability to effectively organize attributes, configuration items (CIs), relationships, and categories into a set of entities and relationships is critical for the overall success of the project. Other skills needed for the complete DBA are a good understanding of the selected CMDB tool, strong communication skills, and the ability to read and understand the system requirements. The logical DBA role should be filled with someone who has at least five to seven years of database design experience.

The responsibilities of the logical DBA are straightforward: Design the perfect structure to hold the critical configuration management data. The DBA begins by attending the scope and requirements reviews in that planning phase to get a good understanding of what the database needs to contain. Then the DBA pulls together a draft design and sends it out for technical review by several other competent database designers. After incorporating changes, a business review is conducted to ensure the high-level business requirements are going to be met by the proposed design. Finally, the DBA commits the design to software and oversees testing and actual implementation of the database schema in the tool.

This table summarizes the DBA role:

Logical DBA	Database engineer who can help design the right layout for the CMDB
Skills	*Responsibilities*
Database design	Design logical database
Tool knowledge	Implement database design
Understand requirements	
Strong interpersonal skills	

Communications Person

It makes sense that you need good communications around your configuration management efforts, but does this really warrant a full person? For a large organization, it might take more than one person. Communications is essential to getting the agreement of all business units to support IT in making the CMDB a success. The communications person is a very visible role that makes sure everyone understands and agrees to the goals and functions of the configuration management system. Without adequate staffing for this role, someone else (most likely the project manager or architect) will try to fill it part time and won't give it the attention it deserves.

Only two skills are needed for a communications person—deep understanding of the business and strong ability to relate technical plans to business leaders. But these skills are not necessarily common. People with a deep understanding of the business—including the current political currents, the unwritten organizational structures, and the personal interplay between business leaders—are not exactly common. It is usually best to choose as communications person someone who is well-thought of in the business community, and this person may not necessarily be the normal IT spokesperson. But be sure the communications person also has the ability to quickly catch the vision of what configuration management is and is not. Unfortunately, many businesspeople have heard the latest hype from the IT department too often and no longer believe in the promises of value throughout the enterprise. The communications person has to understand the IT speak and be able to translate it to the real business value in terms that are believable and compelling.

The responsibilities of the communications person fall into two different categories: defining the message and sharing the message. The communications person begins with getting into the heads of the configuration management architect and the project manager. Getting a deep understanding of the scope and effort and the kinds of business decisions that will be enabled will definitely help in understanding the overall value of configuration management. After the heart of the project is well understood, it is time to look at the schedule and resources in conjunction with the project manager. While the communications person will be telling others about the scope, they also will be answering many questions about the more practical aspects of how and when the project will impact the business units. The third step in preparation is to really understand where to find the most valuable audience and schedule meetings, web page updates, newsletter articles, and any other communication forms that can reach those audiences. Having a detailed plan that targets the entire audience in manageable segments will help ensure complete coverage of the message, and thus, more complete acceptance of the program. Finally, after all the preparation, the communications person should have some fun with sharing the message—be creative, enthusiastic, and even a little silly. Use the best aspects of the corporate culture to get the message out there as best as possible.

Here is a summary table for the communications role:

Communication Coordinator	Public relations person who can effectively organize and deliver the messages about configuration management
Skills	*Responsibilities*
Strong organizational knowledge	Understand project scope and goals
Ability to communicate complex topics	Schedule communications
	Define creative methods
	Communicate proscribed messages

Trainer

Depending on your organization, the communications person may be able to also train all the people who need to use the configuration management system. For larger organizations, the trainer is a separate person. Regardless of who fills this role, the trainer has a great opportunity to influence the acceptance of your configuration management process and tools. Because they get to interact with all of the users, they can be an effective cheerleader for the entire effort, or they can be the corporate equivalent of a wet blanket. Just as with the communications person, the trainer must understand and believe in the vision in order to effectively teach others both the how and the why of the process and tools.

The trainer requires the technical skills to learn the tools, the business skills to learn the process, and the communications skills to effectively teach both of these skills to others. The technical skills become important because even with the best-tested software, it is likely that some student will try something unexpected with the configuration management software. If the trainer gets confused or doesn't know how to recover, everyone gets the message that this new software is difficult to use and confusing. The business skills are equally important because it is critical to not just explain the tools and the process, but to relate them to the actual business areas represented by people in the class. Someone from accounting may not care at all about this IT discipline of configuration management until they realize the value of understanding the "total cost of ownership." The need for communication and teaching skills is obvious to anyone who has endured a very boring corporate training course.

The responsibilities of the trainer are simple: Prepare the training materials, organize the courses, determine the training delivery method, and then deliver the training. The duration of the training role will be determined by the number of people to be trained, the frequency of changes to the process or tool, and the job turnover in your organization. Even in the most static organizations, refreshing the training from time to time will help keep configuration management a vital and maturing process.

The following table describes the trainer role:

Trainer	Educator who can train people on how to effectively execute the configuration management process using the chosen tool set
Skills	*Responsibilities*
Understand the CMDB tool	Prepare training materials
Understand the process	Schedule courses
Communicate creatively	Deliver courses
Teaching	Evaluate effectiveness of education
Organize and schedule training	

Operational Roles

Although all of the previously described roles are important to getting set up, it is the people in operational roles who will determine the long-term success of configuration management for your organization. Unlike the planning and implementation roles, which have a (hopefully brief) time of importance, the operational roles are permanent. One key factor in the success of long-term operations is the understanding of the process and the tools gained by the operational team during the implementation. For this reason, the operational roles should be staffed fairly early in implementation so that they can be a significant part of the deployment effort, and therefore have ownership in the longer term success of the effort.

Configuration Management Integrator

In any IT organization, multiple data sources must be brought together to create a complete CMDB. At the very minimum, you'll have some data about people, perhaps in a corporate directory or a legacy human resources system. But you're also likely to have some asset data in one or more inventory scanning tools, some data about the locations where your company does business, some software license information, and perhaps some information about the IT products that have been purchased—all in separate databases or applications. The job of the configuration management integrator is to oversee the regular transfer of data from all external sources into the CMDB. The integrator, as the title implies, worries about getting all the data, transforming it to a common format, and then populating it in the right place in the configuration management tool. This role is also described in the ITIL literature as a configuration librarian.

The key skill for this role is data integration. This involves a broad knowledge of the various technologies used to get data out of systems and push it into other systems, including XML/XSL, SQL, and the query languages of whatever corporate systems your organization uses. This person must also be detail-oriented and patient to massage large data sets into a format that will be acceptable to the CMDB. There is nothing exciting or glamorous about changing a list of names from "last name, comma, first name" format into "first name, space, last name" format, but without someone to do this work, the data in your configuration database will quickly become a confused jumble that provides no business value.

The responsibilities of the configuration management integrator are many. She must be a detective to find sources of data that others may not have thought of. The configuration management integrator becomes a salesperson to convince the guardians of corporate data to turn it over to this new effort. Then she becomes an accountant, poring over rows and rows of data to look for inconsistencies and discrepancies. Finally, the configuration management integrator becomes a watchdog, guarding the integrity of the data against anyone who wants to transport a mess they've been holding without cleaning it up first. In addition to all of these roles, the configuration management integrator has the day-to-day job of scheduling when the various input feeds will reach the database, checking the logs to ensure they run successfully, and correcting any errors that are found. The configuration management integrator will be a very busy person indeed.

The following table summarizes the role of the configuration management integrator:

Configuration Management Integrator	A data management professional who is responsible for gathering and managing configuration data
Skills	*Responsibilities*
Data integration technologies	Find appropriate data sources
Attention to detail	Negotiate access to data
	Understand inconsistencies in data
	Schedule batch inputs
	Review data transfer logs
	Report on data discrepancies

Configuration Management Tools Support

Because even the simplest of organizations needs an automated tool to support their configuration management efforts, you also need someone to support that tool. The tools support person helps in selecting the tool, is responsible for installing the tool, and then does all the things necessary to maintain the tool. It is unlikely that you will program your own configuration management tool, so you will most likely have a vendor organization to help the tool support person. But there are certain tasks that cannot be done by a vendor, and a whole variety of tasks that the vendor's service organization would charge you too much to perform. Thus, you should maintain at least one person, and perhaps several, who are deep experts in the tools of configuration management.

The skills needed in tools support are among the most technical and specific. This person needs to understand the tool, any middleware required to run the tool (including the database management system), and the operating system on which the tool is going to run. In many cases, you will want to run your configuration management system in a clustered or other highly available environment, so your tools support person should at least be familiar with the specifics of supporting the tool in those kinds of environments. Unless your organization is very large and has dedicated people for support of the server hardware, the configuration management tool support person may have to be knowledgeable of backup and recovery mechanisms and other general hardware operating concepts. The tools support person typically comes from a background of desktop or server support.

The responsibilities of the tools person are simple—keep the configuration management tool available and running at peak performance at all times. This often involves troubleshooting, planning and executing software upgrades and patches, performance tuning, and evaluating new versions from the vendor. Occasionally, the tool support person will also get involved in significant new projects, such as refreshing the hardware under the system or perhaps even moving to a more highly available architecture. In general, the tools support person acts as the guru for anything related to configuration management tools.

This table summarizes the tool support role:

Configuration Management Tools Support	A traditional IT support role with special expertise in the CMDB tool
Skills	*Responsibilities*
CMDB tool expert	Install and set up CMDB tool
Operating systems support	Maintain CMDB tool
Understand clustered environment	Capacity and availability management
	Server administrator

Reporting Specialist

By its nature, configuration management data is complex and difficult to visualize. Although many people will have some knowledge of how to get things out of the CMDB, one person will know the data in great depth and be able to access just the right information very quickly. That person is the reporting specialist. As the name implies, the reporting person will take business queries such as "How many dual-processor servers do we have capable of running the next DB2® version?" and turn them into queries that the database can process. This person is part requirements analyst and part programmer so that they can interpret what business users are asking for and get the system to produce the right data.

The key skills for a reporting specialist are listening and data manipulation. Like the configuration management architect, the reporting specialist must listen to the language of business and translate what he hears into the technical terms needed to get the right data. Like the configuration management integrator, this person must also be able to understand the structure of the data in the CMDB and relate the various pieces of data together to extract meaningful information in the most efficient way possible. Using this combination of listening to the users and navigating the data, the reporting specialist can be a critical and very busy member of the operational team.

The reporting specialist has two broad classes of responsibilities. The first is creating reports that will be executed repeatedly. These standard reports typically have a wide audience and need to be well-defined and easy to read. A large block of standard reports will be created during the implementation of the configuration management process, but additional reports will most likely be needed along the way as the process gets refined and the data becomes more useful. Creating the standard reports and overseeing their execution and distribution are all in the domain of the reporting specialist.

In addition to standard reports, the reporting specialist will most likely need to build ad hoc or one-time reports. Ad hoc reports are useful for many different events in the normal business cycle. Making IT decisions, such as when to refresh servers, requires some configuration information, and thus requires an ad hoc report. Audits often spark queries for specialized data that can be gained from a one-time report. In many cases, these one-time reports need to be created quickly to ensure timely response to a business need. Although the standard reports are more widely read, the ad hoc reports are most likely more urgent and more important. The reporting specialist must have some free time available to handle these requests when they come.

This is a summary of the reporting specialist role:

Reporting Specialist	An expert in retrieving data from the CMDB
Skills	*Responsibilities*
Understand business needs	Define standard reports
Database query languages	Manage production of reports
Understand CMDB tools	Build ad hoc queries
Expert in reporting tools	Help users refine data needs

Impact Manager

Although all the previous roles are fairly common in IT, you need to find a different person to staff the role of impact manager. The impact manager is the person ultimately responsible for making sure the relationships between CIs are accurate and helpful. The impact manager populates data that will help all other IT decision makers to better understand the impacts of a proposed change or a current incident on the overall IT infrastructure. As an example, you will probably learn from an automated inventory discovery tool that a particular server is connected physically to a particular hub, and that the hub in turn connects to a router. The impact manager is responsible for digging deeper to understand that the server hosts your inventory ordering application and the router connects to the primary business location of your purchasing staff. Any proposed change that causes the hub to be out will mean that your company cannot order replacement inventory. The role of the impact manager is to bring the business sense to the mass of information in the CMDB, and to code that business knowledge into the relationships stored in the CMDB.

The impact manager should be skilled in understanding all primary functions of the business. They need to be able to communicate freely with each set of IT consumers to really understand the value of IT to the overall business. Skills such as systems analysis, business analysis, process evaluation, and financial management are the key ingredients to a good impact manager. The technical skill of capturing the discovered relationships into the CMDB can be learned, but the business skills should be hired.

The responsibilities of the impact manager are likely to evolve as your configuration management capability matures. Initially, the impact manager will mostly find facts and capture data. As the database gets more accurate and thus more useful, the impact manager will be called on to help evaluate any significant change or ongoing problem. Later on, the impact manager will fade to the background as more of the relationships are documented in the CMDB and users gain confidence in using this data directly without an interpreter. The impact manager never fully goes away, however, because each new project will add another web of complexity that needs to be assessed and documented.

The impact manager role is summarized in the following table:

Impact Manager	**Data analyst who can express the business side of configuration management**
Skills	*Responsibilities*
Deep business understanding	Analyze configuration data
Systems analysis	Assist in impact analysis
Enterprise architecture	Ongoing assessment of new projects
Financial management	Define new relationship types
Process design	

Quality Role

Over the life span of your configuration management effort, the quality of the process and the data determine the value of the work. The quality role is described last, but it is one of the most important roles. The quality person uses all the tricks available—audits, inspections, reviews, and more—to make sure that the overall configuration management process has integrity. Acting as a guiding conscience, the quality manager validates that the plans developed early will lead to a quality system, then checks that the implementation is done according to the plan, and finally monitors the process and the data in an ongoing basis to make sure that everyone can be extremely confident in the value of the information that is your CMDB.

The quality manager needs skills very much like those of other quality assurance or quality control professionals. The most important are a driving passion to make the project a success, the independence to speak up when things are going wrong, and an eye for details that others might overlook. Quality can sometimes become a very lonely role, so it is critical that the person chosen for this role have strong support from management and a good ability to handle confrontation constructively.

The responsibility of the quality manager is simple. She simply has to make sure that everything about the configuration management process, tools, people, and data is top notch. This involves watching how people work, looking at the outcome as represented in the data, analyzing the process to see inefficiencies, and auditing everything to make sure there are no organizational failures. The role will mature over time and eventually can be included in a shared IT quality department. But to begin, the quality manager should be a specifically named individual who everyone on the configuration management planning and implementation teams should recognize.

The following table summarizes the quality manager role:

Quality Manager	An independent party who oversees the quality of the configuration management service
Skills	*Responsibilities*
Quality assurance process	Define requirements for measurements
Auditing	Assess quality of planning stages
Data analysis	Assess quality of implementation
Using measurement data	Oversee quality controls for data
Conflict resolution	Assess skills of the organization

Some Notes on the Roles

To close this chapter, let's observe a few things about these roles. First, we've represented a fairly large and complex team. Depending on the size of your enterprise or the complexity of your scope, you might not need a dedicated person for each role. In fact, some roles can be combined in a single person as long as that one person has all the skills needed. It wouldn't be unusual, for example, for a single person to be both the reporting specialist and the impact manager because those are related roles.

For very large organizations with a high degree of complexity, additional roles might be needed, or different aspects of a single role might be split among multiple people. You might have one project manager to focus on getting the tools and processes ready, for example, and a second project manager focus on data integration and population.

To move from these role definitions to a specific staffing plan, you need to use the process work you've done to create more specific responsibility lists. Then estimate the number of hours per week needed for each responsibility, and you will begin to see how many hours of work might be required. Don't forget to account for vacations and other work absences that are normal in your organization. Divide the number of hours needed by the number of hours a typical IT person works for your organization, and you'll get a good picture of how many people should be on your team.

When you actually start to put people into the team, some flexibility will be required to account for different skill mixes. You might have defined a specific job position that puts the trainer and the communications person roles together, but if you cannot find a single person with both sets of skills, you might have to rearrange your staffing plan. Figure 12.2 shows graphically how you build a staffing plan.

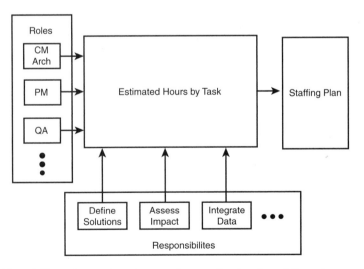

Figure 12.2   The staffing plan springs from a clear understanding of the roles and responsibilities.

Also note that the roles described in this chapter are limited to IT people or people working directly with the core configuration management team. There are many roles outside the team that will be impacted by configuration management. Change coordinators and change approval board members need to understand how to use configuration data to assess the impact of the changes they are proposing and reviewing. Incident managers and people who resolve incidents will likewise learn to use configuration data in assessing the severity or impact of IT incidents. Department leaders will get new understanding of which IT components are servicing their business functions, and this new knowledge will enable their decision making.

Although all these people, and many more, could be said to have roles in configuration management, they are extant roles that are simply augmented by the existence of configuration data. The people in these roles are important for the communications and training plans, but not the staffing plan.

Finally, you should think a bit about how the configuration management team will be organized. During planning and implementation, they will most likely be organized as a project team, with a project manager and architect taking the lead. Governance of the team will be accomplished through your normal project governing practices.

When you move into production operations, however, there are some decisions to be made. Do you create a department for configuration management, complete with a department manager? Or do you put the configuration management people into an existing operations department, such as the server administrators or the service desk? To some extent, these decisions are dictated by your corporate culture, but in general the configuration management team should be as closely related to the incident and change management teams as possible to allow the synergies inherent in ITIL.

Obviously, no book can tell you how to build out a staff. Hopefully this chapter has at least given you a basic outline of the skills and roles you should be thinking about as you build a configuration management organization.

CHAPTER 13

The Many Uses for Configuration Information

The most significant reason for instituting a configuration management service within your organization is to be able to use the data produced by the service. If you didn't need to use the data in any way, you wouldn't need to do configuration management at all. But as indicated in the opening words of this book, the key reason for configuration management is to enable better information technology (IT) decisions, and using the data gathered in the Configuration Management Database (CMDB) is how those decisions get better.

Of course, the primary way that data is used is by producing reports. This chapter explores the various kinds of reports that you might want to produce from your configuration management data. We'll examine standard reports that get produced on a regular basis, and then we'll explore four of the different ways that ad hoc reporting might be useful. Of course, we could have explored dozens of different uses for ad hoc data, but the ones chosen here are most representative of the ways most organizations use their newly created configuration data.

The intent of this chapter is not to be an exhaustive catalog of all the ways you can produce reports or use configuration management data. Instead, the chapter will spur your thinking as you consider the best possible approaches for your own implementation and use of configuration management.

As usual, the first figure (Figure 13.1) provides the visual outline for the rest of this chapter.

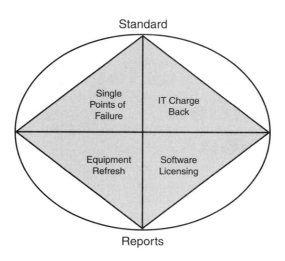

Figure 13.1   There are many different uses for configuration management data.

Standard Reports

Reporting begins with creating a set of standard reports. By standard, I mean that these reports run on a periodic basis with minimal changes. The reports may be posted on a web page or distributed via a standard email distribution list.

There are two types of standard reports for configuration management, as shown in Figure 13.2. The first type deals with configuration items (CIs) and the relationships between them. These reports generally reflect the configuration of some piece of the environment at a point in time. The other type of report provides measurement data about the configuration management service and process. These are most likely reports about events and processes that change or use the configuration data in some way. Both types of reports are considered in this section.

Reports about Configurations

The first reports most people think of producing are what I'll call allocation reports. Any reports that break down CIs to parts of the business fall into this category. On the technical side, this probably includes a report of all CIs by responsible party, to indicate who supports each individual piece of your configuration. If you capture the appropriate data, you can also produce a report of CIs by user community, which can be extremely useful when determining the impact of a particular incident.

For the business side, the most common standard report is a listing of CIs by financial responsibility. We'll talk more about this report later, but the general idea is that each department or business owner can get a listing of the items they are paying for within the IT world. Clearly this report can then be rolled up to higher levels to produce line-of-business or division-level reports. Given the right data, you might also want to produce business benefit reports to show which business units are served by each IT component regardless of who is paying for that component.

Even the most simple allocation report will lead you to understand the amount of data that your CMDB contains. Seeing the huge mountain of data should lead you to start thinking about the next category of reports, which I'll call exception reports. These reports provide data about the completeness of your database.

The first exceptions to consider are the very technical ones. For example, if you are tracking servers and also tracking operating systems as two separate types of CI, you can produce an exception report showing all servers that do *not* have a relationship to at least one operating system. A server without an operating system clearly would be an error. Depending on how you provision servers, a server with multiple relationships to operating systems (indicating more than one operating system (OS) per server) might be an error as well.

With a bit of brainstorming, you should be able to produce a wide variety of exception reports specific to the scope, granularity, and span of your database. Some reports will be very technical, such as a router without attached LAN segments. Others will be oriented toward the business to find things like desktop PCs without a departmental owner. Each exception report will help you improve the accuracy of your CMDB and also give the organization confidence that configuration management is truly under control.

The third class of reports could be called environment reports. These are specific reports that describe a complete IT environment from top to bottom. Normally, they start with a business application, or perhaps even a business process which is related to multiple business applications. The report then proceeds to walk through the relationships for that application to specify the complete environment. Depending on what structure you've chosen for the CMDB, this might include components of an application, the servers that each component runs on, the databases used, the middleware components used, and down through the logical and physical network that supports the environment.

Seeing a complete environment report for the first time can be an eye-opening experience for business application owners. Perhaps they have a vague idea that the application is complex, but a report can highlight that complexity in a whole new way. In many cases, a single environment report can help to define which changes will and will not be approved for a given environment. It can also be a lifesaver when debugging a particularly thorny incident in a complex environment.

Some of the more advanced configuration management tools today are beginning to offer graphical views of an environment report. It shouldn't be far in the future when you can point to a specific CI and get a single page drawing of the environment in which that CI operates. This is the ultimate goal of the environment report.

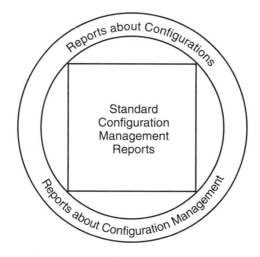

Figure 13.2   Standard reports fall into two categories.

Reports about Configuration Management

We've seen that there are many examples of reports which contain either CIs or relationships—the core of the CMDB. But there is another entire class of reports that doesn't contain data about configurations, but instead report on the health of the configuration management process.

By now you should understand that the configuration management process is best viewed in relation to other IT Infrastructure Library (ITIL) process areas. So, it should be no surprise that the best way to understand the health of configuration management is to understand its impact in other areas. This section provides examples of standard reports that can be created to assess the effectiveness of configuration management.

In your planning, you defined a relationship between configuration management and change management. For most organizations, the goal of that relationship is to reduce the number of changes that fail. Logic dictates that the more you know about an environment before starting the change, the less likely the change will fail due to unexpected discoveries. Given this goal, it is fairly simple to imagine a report showing the number of failed changes as a percentage of total changes attempted. You might even go so far as to create a new code in your change management tool to allow people to give a reason for failed changes, and then you could report on changes that failed due to poor configuration data. That would allow you another objective measure of the maturity of the configuration management service.

One way to assess the completeness of your CMDB would be to create a report of changes that don't refer to at least one CI. In most circumstances, a change that doesn't affect any CIs would be considered a mistake, so such a report would show one of two things. Either the correct CI wasn't in the CMDB to be referenced, or the person recording the request for change didn't know how to find the appropriate CI. Both say something about the effectiveness of your configuration management service.

Of course, change management isn't the only process related to configuration management. You can also look at incident management to help assess the effectiveness of configuration management. Incidents without associated CIs can provide as good a measurement as changes without CIs do. If an incident occurs and nowhere can someone indicate which CI is broken, people clearly don't understand the appropriate use of the CMDB as an incident resolution tool.

In incident management, the time taken to resolve the incident is the ultimate measurement, so it would make perfect sense to track whether the configuration management service is improving resolution times for your incidents. One way to get this kind of report would be to track incident resolution times before configuration management, and then after it is implemented. This measurement could either be done as a combined average or broken out into by teams to better understand which teams are benefiting the most.

You could also create reports in other ITIL process areas that might help you better understand configuration management. A useful report might show the CIs that are not part of a business continuity plan. Another report could be produced to show excess capacity by CI type, allowing capacity planners to know when they have underutilized resources. There are many examples of reports that can help highlight the effectiveness of configuration management by tracking the impact of configuration data on other ITIL processes.

But you don't need to stop your reporting efforts at ITIL processes. Most organizations will need compliance reports from the CMDB. For example, you might have an IT standard that says you use only certain versions of an operating system. A standard report might be one that shows all installed operating systems that don't meet that standard. Similarly, you can produce reports of hardware older than its specified refresh cycle, PCs that have a restricted encryption program, or even business applications that must meet Sarbannes-Oxley standards. Many internal standards, industry regulations, or legislative mandates can be considered using standard reports from the configuration management database.

Analyzing Single Points of Failure

Standard reports can be used for a wide variety of things, but they represent only half the power of configuration management data. Rather than waiting for monthly reports to be produced, many people are going to have more specific queries they will want to run on demand. The ad hoc queries can be used for a variety of purposes, and the rest of this chapter explores some of those purposes.

One very common use for ad hoc queries against the CMDB is to analyze environments for single points of failure. Essentially, this is an attempt to proactively identify the risk of failure in a given environment so those risks can be avoided.

A single point of failure analysis begins with an environment report, as described earlier. This report can be very broad, focusing on a very large part of the IT environment, or very narrow, focusing on just a few CIs. The scope of the analysis will dictate the breadth of the report needed.

After the needed configuration information is available, the analysis can begin. Basically, you look at every CI on the report and consider the possible failures that could affect that component. Start by simply brainstorming what could possibly go wrong. What happens if the power goes out? What would happen if a virus were introduced? How about a denial-of-service attack against the network? What if a wide area network circuit suddenly met a backhoe? The more IT experience your team has, the more failures you're likely to have experienced, and thus the better your analysis can be.

For each failure that has a nontrivial chance of happening, prepare a risk statement. The risk statement should include your estimate of the likelihood of this particular failure, and some statement of what the impact of the failure would be. You may have a very detailed risk management process that calculates the likelihood and impact based on many factors. On the other hand, you may want to simply indicate high, medium, or low for each risk and leave the risk statement there. Your organization's policy will dictate how you go about actually assessing the risk.

After all risk statements have been created and reviewed, you can formulate an action plan. The action items should address those risks that are most likely or will have the most impact. In some cases, a single action might address multiple risks, whereas other risks might each need their own action to be addressed. Each action should include an estimate of the cost of implementing that action in terms of both money and time. The analysis concludes by making recommendations to indicate which risks are worth avoiding, which should simply be known, and which can be ignored. Combine information on the current environment, the potential failures, the risk statements, potential action items, and recommended action items into a single package. That package becomes your single point of failure analysis.

In order to make this analysis more real, let's take a real-life example from one of the customers I've worked with. Imagine an architectural and engineering firm whose primary output is drawings. Of course, they have a fairly sophisticated CAD environment, including a storage area network for holding the files, redundant application servers, a web server for quickly displaying the files for customers, various middleware products, engineering workstations, and the CAD program itself. The environment report as it might appear graphically can be found in Figure 13.3.

Even in this simple environment, we can imagine a whole series of things that might go wrong. Any individual piece of hardware might break down, including the storage device, a workstation, a server, or even the network hub. In addition to a complete failure, any one of these devices might run short on capacity—perhaps with too many users trying to view the web server at the same time, or a single drawing being too big for the memory on one of the workstations. Any of the various pieces of software might contain a bug that will stop it from being used. Depending on the granularity of analysis desired, we might separately consider the failure of smaller components, such has hard disk drives, network interface cards, or system memory. The list of potential failures in this very small environment could easily grow to more than a hundred possibilities.

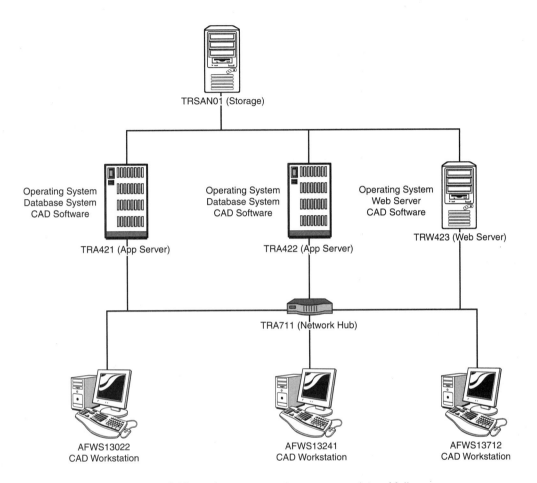

TRSAN01 (Storage)

Operating System
Database System
CAD Software

TRA421 (App Server)

Operating System
Database System
CAD Software

TRA422 (App Server)

Operating System
Web Server
CAD Software

TRW423 (Web Server)

TRA711 (Network Hub)

AFWS13022
CAD Workstation

AFWS13241
CAD Workstation

AFWS13712
CAD Workstation

Figure 13.3   Even a simple CAD environment can have many points of failure.

The next step is to prepare a risk statement for each identified failure. For example, we might assess the risk of the storage device losing a hard drive as high, but the impact of such a failure as low because it is running as a redundant array of inexpensive disks (RAID). We might assess the likelihood of a network hub failure as relatively low, but realize that such a failure would have the highest possible risk on our users' ability to make and view drawings.

We can dig deeper into the configuration management data for some risk assessments. For example, the likelihood of an operating system having a bug will be higher if the OS is relatively new to the marketplace or if maintenance hasn't been applied as regularly as it should. The risk of software problems with the CAD application might be assessed by looking at the vendor's web site to find errors other installations have reported. Ultimately, we can develop a good set of risks around the total environment.

After the risks have been assessed, we can formulate actions that will correct each of them. One such action might be to build out a second RAID array to eliminate the possibility of a single storage failure making all drawings disappear. Another action might be to implement a second network hub along with a second network interface to all servers to protect against a simple network failure. Assessing each of these actions would show that the additional storage is a very expensive option which protects a risk that has a very low likelihood of occurring. Implementing the redundant network, however, is relatively inexpensive and protects against multiple failures that each have a moderate chance of happening.

Hopefully this simple example has given you a better appreciation for the power of having configuration information available. Although you could certainly have started your single point of failure analysis by doing a physical inventory of the environment, it is much simpler if you can simply query the CMDB when you need information about the configuration of devices and their relationship to one another. This makes it much more likely that you will actually do such analyses and significantly less expensive to do them.

Enabling IT Chargeback

Analyzing an environment for single points of failure is an inherently technical task, and you would probably imagine configuration management data would be well suited to technical tasks. In this section, we consider a more business-oriented task—charging within the organization for IT services.

Although financial functions generally are the responsibility of the asset management service, configuration management can play a significant role, as we'll see. This section is written from the perspective of an organization that either doesn't have asset management data or doesn't trust it enough to base their chargeback system on it. We'll see how configuration management data can be stretched to serve a financial purpose.

The first piece of enabling chargeback is to establish an IT service catalog. Creating and using a service catalog is a very broad topic which is described in Chapter 14, "Measuring and Improving CMDB Accuracy." For this section, what I mean by a service catalog is simply a list of the things that you will charge for, and the rate charged for each of them.

For example, you might want to charge for access to network printers. In order to set up the service in the services catalog, you need to answer a number of fundamental questions. First, you must define exactly what is being charged for. Will you charge simply for access to a printer, or attempt to have a charge for actual printing? Will you charge per page, or per megabyte sent to the printer? If a user has access to both a color printer and a network printer, is that two different access charges? The answers to all these simple questions need to be provided in order to establish the printer service in the service catalog.

After you establish the unit for charging, you need to be sure that unit can be linked to configuration data or some event that can actually be measured. Let's say you want to have a specific charge for each page printed regardless of how many network printers are available. To do so, you need to know how to track each printed page back to a user or a specific workstation. If you want to charge an access charge for each accessed printer, different data needs to be acquired. The charge itself dictates the data you need to acquire in order to allocate the charges.

Notice that much of the data you need can be tracked through a combination of configuration management and the other service support processes. Incident data, change data, problem data, capacity data, and release management data can all be great sources of information to help you measure the utilization of the services and thus allocate charges for them.

Going back to our printer example, if you're already doing capacity management of the network printers, you probably already know how many pages are being printed. Now you just need to combine that information with the network name of the device sending the print to get the full picture. Fortunately, that network name is most likely already contained in your CMDB if you're tracking workstations. Using the two together enables you to allocate specific numbers of pages to specific workstations, and thus to users.

When the end of the billing cycle comes around, all you need to do is use the organizational information associated with your CMDB to allocate charges back to the correct organizations. So now that you know which workstations sent how many pages to each printer, you can find the relationships of those workstations to departments to prepare the monthly billing report of printer usage by department. Look into the services catalog to get the cost for printing a page, and you have a complete charge ready to be sent out to the department or to your internal financial organization.

The best practice for IT chargeback is to start small. Rather than defining hundreds of individual services, start with a few simple ones such as an office telephone, a workstation, file storage on the local area network, and printing service. After those services are clearly understood and the basic mechanism for chargeback is in place, you can begin getting more elaborate and offering sets of differentiated services, such as international telephone service or color printing. It isn't that you withhold services; it's just that you don't charge for every service at the beginning so you don't end up with mountains of data and no comfort that the charges are equitable.

The general flow of IT chargeback and its relationship to the CMDB is depicted in Figure 13.4.

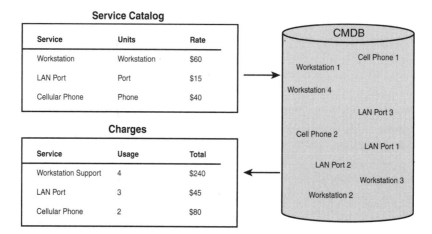

Figure 13.4   Charging for IT costs consists of the interplay between a service catalog and the CMDB.

Planning Equipment Refresh

Another use for configuration management data is planning for the refresh of your IT equipment. Everyone understands the pace of technology—there is always a better widget available for sale. The decision of when to move to that better widget can be made more intelligently if you have solid configuration management data. This section describes different approaches you can use to decide when to retire your old equipment and replace it with new technology.

Fixed Refresh Cycles

The simplest way to establish dates for refreshing equipment is to create a fixed cycle. This is by far the most common method, especially for people who don't trust their configuration information. The fixed cycle simply says that you'll replace equipment based on its age.

One approach to a fixed cycle is to simply choose a period for all equipment refreshes across your company. You could establish a policy, for example, that says all equipment is refreshed every three years. The CMDB can help you here because it can record the date any piece of equipment went into service, and it will be easy to produce a simple report of all equipment that went into service more than three years ago.

The downside of this simple approach is that it doesn't recognize that different kinds of technology advance at different speeds. A three-year-old disk storage unit might barely be broken in, but a three-year-old cell phone is practically a relic.

Many organizations choose a different fixed cycle for each category of equipment. This is where the CMDB starts to be genuinely helpful because you've already categorized your equipment when you defined the scope of the CMDB. Leveraging those categories should allow you to create a standard report to show when equipment in each category is due for replacement.

Variable Refresh Cycles

But age is not the only criteria that can be used to determine when to refresh equipment. Some machines get used harder than other machines, and just like with any other purchase, it is always possible to get a "lemon" that never seems to be working correctly.

Basing the refresh decision on factors other than age is possible only when you begin to combine configuration management data with data from other operational processes. You can achieve a variable cycle, meaning that equipment is refreshed based on factors that will change from machine to machine. Here we'll consider just two of the ways you can create a variable equipment refresh cycle.

One obvious approach is to look at the number of incidents that occur for any given piece of equipment and establish a threshold value to indicate refresh is necessary. For instance, you could create a policy which dictates that any server with more than 100 incidents should be replaced. The threshold can be different for different types of equipment; using the data from the incident management process, you could distinguish between the primary or only CI involved in an incident and secondary CIs.

You can extend this kind of refresh logic by including information from the change management process. Factoring in the number of times a piece of equipment has been changed will help eliminate incidents caused by human error and focus on just those that actually indicate hardware failures. You can also analyze the length of changes and the success rate of changes to get a good estimate of how expensive a piece of equipment is to maintain. Putting together incident data with change management data will give you a very clear picture of which pieces of hardware should be refreshed, and will even help you decide when your refresh program should include switching to a different manufacturer to get more reliable equipment. This is a very powerful use of configuration management data to make important IT decisions.

Although incident and change data help you assess the historic reliability of equipment, you can do even better by using configuration data to predict the future. Combining capacity monitoring data with configuration data enables you to understand how much each machine actually is used. Viewing this utilization information with statistics on the mean time to failure (MTTF) rating of the equipment will help you predict when your IT components are likely to fail.

For example, you might find from doing root cause analyses across a group of problems that disk drives from a particular manufacturer are failing at an unacceptable rate. Spotting a trend like this is part of the problem management discipline; but after the trend is spotted, your configuration management data will be invaluable in quickly determining which other equipment have these disks, and what the cost would be to proactively replace all of them.

Being able to predict failure will give you the option of replacing equipment before failures happen, making your refresh program a contributor to the quality of your IT environment instead of just an expense that must be incurred. This is one of the examples of how the configuration management data can be used to improve the business value of IT.

Leverage capacity monitoring data to determine how much equipment is used, and that can help assign a criticality. This technique can be used in combination with single point of failure analyses. A summary of different ways to approach equipment refresh is shown in Figure 13.5.

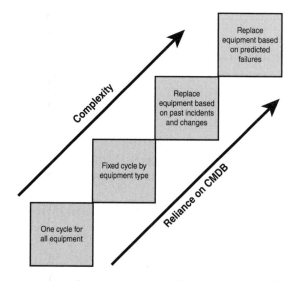

Figure 13.5   Equipment can be refreshed based on either fixed or variable cycles.

Understanding Software License Compliance

As we learned in Chapter 5, "Planning for Data Population," software license management may or may not be done using configuration management data. As you'll recall, to fully understand whether you are in compliance with software licenses requires three different pieces of data, which often come from three different sources. You need to know which licenses and which type of licenses were purchased, and this information is best gained from you asset management database. If at least some of your licenses are concurrent or usage based, as often happens with server-based software, you need to know what software is actually executing on which processors at any given point in time. This information is usually obtained from a dedicated software metering solution. Finally, for almost any other kind of license (the norm for desktop software) you need to know which computers have which software installed. That is the domain of configuration management, and specifically the relationships between software packages and processors. This section describes how configuration management can be used along with other types of data to determine whether you are in compliance with software licensing policies.

As stated above, the CMDB is useful only for managing those kinds of licenses that are based on installation of the software. If your license agreement is not concerned with where the software is installed, but only with how many times it executes, you will be better off using a software metering tool that includes an agent running on each system to tell you when each software product is actually executing on that machine. The rest of this section assumes that you want to manage installation-based licenses.

We'll also assume that you chose a complex model for holding software data in the CMDB. Under this model, you will have a CI for each installed software package and a CI for each license you've purchased. A simple relationship will be used to indicate when a license is in use by an installation. A license CI without any relationships is available, whereas a license with multiple relationships might indicate a license violation.

Using this kind of scheme allows a very simple lifecycle to be tracked for each software license. When you make a purchase, new CIs are created to reflect the licenses you have acquired. These new CIs have a creation date, and can have other attributes to track the information you want to know about your software licenses. When licenses expire or are abandoned, you can mark the status of these CIs to indicate that the licenses are no longer active.

When software is installed on a PC, the installer can look in the CMDB for available licenses, and make the association between the newly installed package and the license it will consume. This kind of discipline among all of your software installers will ensure that you never use more licenses than you've purchased. You can also run reports to show numbers of unused licenses by product to know when it is time to purchase additional licenses.

When a machine is retired or a software package is no longer needed, the relationship with the license is removed, thus making that license available for another machine to use. This complete lifecycle is enabled by using the CMDB cleverly to track software packages and the licenses that enable you to install those packages.

As we've seen in this chapter, there are many different ways to leverage configuration management data to improve your overall IT services. As your CMDB gets more mature and your organization grows to rely on configuration information more, you will find entirely new ways to use the data. The value of the CMDB grows with age as long as the data stays current and accurate.

CHAPTER 14

Measuring and Improving CMDB Accuracy

We've touched on the issue of data accuracy many times already. More than anything else, the accuracy of your data will determine the amount of trust your organization places in the Configuration Management Database (CMDB). A trusted CMDB opens the door to a world of benefits, whereas a mistrusted CMDB will simply become another expensive information technology (IT) effort without significant payback.

But exactly how to do you make sure that the data in the CMDB is accurate? Clearly we begin by defining what we mean by accuracy. It may seem strange, but data accuracy is often misunderstood. Once we've established a working definition, we need to measure accuracy in a way that doesn't negatively impact the overall configuration management service. After baselines have been established through a solid measurement system, we can track the sources of errors, and eventually reduce the number of errors to improve the overall accuracy.

These four steps—define, measure, track, and improve—are described in this chapter, and depicted in the visual outline shown in Figure 14.1.

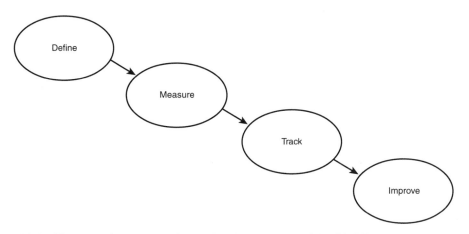

Figure 14.1   There are four steps to improving the accuracy of the CMDB.

Defining Accurate Configuration Data

The definition you choose to use for the accuracy of your CMDB is quite important. If the definition is too stringent, you will spend significant resources trying to achieve accuracy in unimportant details. If the definition you choose is too lax, you will be declaring your database very accurate when people depending on your data know it isn't. This section helps you strike a balance that will work for your organization by balancing validity, correctness, and timeliness.

Accuracy of Attributes

The immediate thought when people think of CMDB accuracy is that the attributes of each configuration item (CI) are correct. This is a good start, but we'll see that it is not nearly complete enough. Suppose that for every server, you are tracking the server name, number of CPUs, physical memory installed, and the status of the server. You find that one of the machines has the wrong number of CPUs, so there is an error in one of the specific attributes of that server.

You may find out, however, that a change was executed on the server just yesterday, so what looks like an error may actually be an issue of timing. The normal cycle for updating the CMDB in your process might be several days, and during those days there will be a discrepancy between what is recorded and reality. These timing errors are different from errors where data is inaccurate, and your policy on measuring accuracy must account for them. In most cases, you'll want to exclude timing errors from any measures of CMDB accuracy.

Your accuracy policy will also need to further distinguish between errors and invalid entries. Using the previous example, the status of the server is probably one of a specific set of values. The tools and database constraints will ensure that one of those values is always assigned, so in some sense you could say that the value in the status attribute will always be valid. However, if the status is "production" but the server is really disconnected from the network and in a storage location, the status is not correct even though it is valid. So, you need to make a distinction between attributes that are invalid and those that are inaccurate.

You should also think about your position on empty attribute values. In some cases, an attribute is clearly in error if it is empty, such as in number of CPUs. In other cases, such as the date of the most recent audit, an empty attribute might be a perfectly valid value. There should be a difference between saying that no value is possible or available and saying that you simply forgot to put a value into an attribute. Perhaps you want to define "n/a" as a valid value in some places, and ensure that your procedures help everyone understand exactly when to use it. Whether or not an attribute can be empty is most likely defined in your database, but you should also think about it in terms of errors in the database. Empty values may or may not be errors, depending on your definitions.

Accuracy of Configuration Items

As stated in the preceding section, simply knowing whether attributes are accurate is not nearly enough to define the accuracy of your CMDB. It is also quite possible that a CI itself can be inaccurate.

One obvious error in CIs is incorrect classification. Although it would be relatively rare for someone to mistake a router for a server, classification errors will spring up with less tangible kinds of CIs, such as business processes, documents, or even compliance audits. Each CI can have only one classification, but it's sometimes difficult to determine which classification applies. Your definition of database accuracy should define what is meant by an error in classification.

CLASSIFICATION ERRORS

One client I worked with wanted to define network file shares as CIs. Unfortunately, they also wanted to define *permissions* to network file shares as a separate configuration item. Although I told them this much detail might be expensive to maintain, they persisted and we went into production with this schema.

We soon learned that it was extremely difficult for even the IT people to tell the difference between a file share and the permission to use a file share. We were constantly getting errors in classifying the CIs, and people were confused by any search or report that showed both groups.

If you put too many categories, or categories that are too closely related, into your scope definition, you're just inviting classification errors in the future.

Another common problem with CIs is that they aren't in the CMDB at all. This is the most difficult of all errors to find because you never know what might be missing. Anyone who has spent any time in the IT field knows that as hard as you try, equipment will often get moved around without any record. We've all heard the stories of opening the door to a closet to find a whole room full of equipment that we never knew about.

The positive side of discovering new CIs is that at the very moment you make the discovery, you can collect data, and thus the error is corrected. Part of your policy around defining database accuracy should define how this is handled. At the very minimum, you should keep a count of the number of newly discovered CIs so that you can discover trends and form an educated opinion about how many more CIs you may be missing.

Accuracy of Relationships

The third part of the CMDB that must be considered for accuracy is the relationships between CIs. Just like attributes and CIs, there are several ways that relationships can be inaccurate.

By far the most common inaccuracy in relationships is that they grow stale. By stale, we mean that the relationship was broken in the real world, but the CMDB was not updated to reflect that fact. This happens because many organizations believe that "simple" changes do not need to be controlled as tightly as more complex changes, and this policy allows for many kinds of modifications to the environment that are not tracked.

As one example, consider a desktop PC with four software packages installed on it. A workstation discovery tool will find this PC, and faithfully record the PC with relationships to each software package. In most organizations, however, users will be allowed to remove any of these software packages whenever they like. When a user removes a package, the relationships recorded in the CMDB will still exist and be stale until the discovery tool is executed again and finds that the software is no longer installed on the workstation and removes those old relationships.

So, it is quite possible that relationships will be stale as a matter of timing, but it is also possible that someone will simply forget to update the CMDB. Timing issues probably will not be classified as an error, but forgotten updates are obviously errors. This is a distinction that should be made in your accuracy policy for the CMDB.

The opposite of stale relationships can happen as well—that is, it is possible that you will connect two things in the real world but not indicate the newly created relationship in the CMDB. This also can be a timing issue because a user has downloaded and installed a new software product on a desktop, but the discovery tool hasn't run yet to update the CMDB. Undocumented relationships can also happen simply because the organization is not accustomed to thinking through all the implications of the changes being made.

Consider a more complex situation where a new database server is being installed to support databases for several different applications. The server CI is captured, and a separate CI is captured for each database. It is quite easy to forget to define the relationships between the server and the databases, or perhaps between the databases and the business applications that use those databases. IT professionals need to learn to think in configuration terms to remember to record all the different relationships being formed. While this learning is taking place, you will need significant help from the configuration manager to examine each of the changes being made and ensure that configuration information is being updated appropriately.

Finally, relationships can be in error because they are recorded as the wrong type. Just as CIs have a category, so do relationships. If you are implementing a SAN device and want to indicate the physical connection between a server and the SAN, it would be inaccurate to use a relationship type of "logical connection" rather than "physical connection." Just as with CIs, the way to avoid this mistake is to have a smaller number of relationship categories, and clearly differentiate those categories so everyone understands when to use each one.

Figure 14.2 displays the different areas where errors can occur in the CMDB.

Ultimately, you need to create a policy that defines what is meant by accuracy of the CMDB. This policy is the foundation for being able to measure and report on accuracy, as described in the next section.

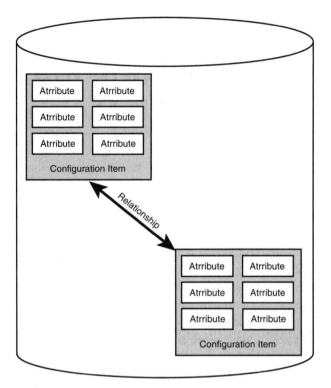

Figure 14.2   Errors can occur in attributes, configuration items, or relationships.

Ways of Measuring Accuracy

Now that you're armed with a well-considered way to define accuracy, you can move on to measuring the accuracy of the CMDB.

Defining accuracy was about policy and documentation, whereas measurement is about practical action. This section describes in detail how to go about measuring accuracy in your environment.

Counting Numbers of Errors

The first part of measuring the accuracy of your CMDB is to count the number of errors.

You know what an error is, but how do you find errors? The most reliable way is by comparing the data in the CMDB with other data to see whether there are differences. You can think of these as data audits or spot checks.

The sample size you use to conduct these spot checks will shrink as you find higher levels of accuracy and grow if you start to see less accuracy. A good rule of thumb is to spot-check 5 percent of your database. If you are finding very few errors with this sample, you should assume your overall CMDB accuracy is good and reduce the sample size to 2 percent or so. On the other hand, if your original sample of 5 percent shows numerous errors, grow the sample size to 10 percent for the next spot check and continue to grow until you've identified the major sources of errors.

There are several good sources to use for comparison. If you originally got the data from a discovery tool, you can compare the data in the CMDB to the same data in the discovery tool. If you are reconciling discovery data with your production CMDB daily, you should find very few errors.

Another possible source is to do a physical comparison back to the actual item being compared. For software, this could be as easy as selecting "Help" and "About" to determine the version of the software and comparing that to the version listed in the CMDB. For hardware, this might mean going to where the hardware is located and finding characteristics such as the serial number and model number printed on the case.

When doing this kind of comparison, it is clearly impossible to verify every single CI and relationship monthly. You will need to select a representative sample and extrapolate to determine the number of errors in the whole database. You'll want to choose a large enough sample so that a single error doesn't skew your results too far. If you compare only ten items and find that one is incorrect, you have a 10 percent error rate. Adding another 90 items to the comparison without finding another error brings your error rate down to only 1 percent. The larger the sample size, the longer it will take to do the comparison and investigate the differences. A larger sample will get you closer to the true accuracy of your database, however. Finding the proper balance of sample size and effort is a matter of maturity and may take some time.

In addition to finding errors by actively looking for them, you will be able to discover some errors by using the configuration data in your operational processes. Each time someone raises a request for a change, they should be looking at configuration data to assess the impact of the proposed change. Many times this person raising the request for change (RFC) will be very knowledgeable about the environment and will be able to spot some errors just by looking at the data. You need to train your staff to avoid the tendency to simply get frustrated in silence at this phenomenon. Instead, people finding errors while looking at the data should be rewarded and encouraged to report the error. It wouldn't be out of the question to even put a "bounty" of some kind on each error, rewarding people for paying attention to details and improving the accuracy of the data.

The incident management process often results in someone digging deeply into a particular part of the environment. These people should be encouraged to take a few extra seconds to compare what they find with the CMDB. If they will do this comparison before resetting a router or rebooting a server, you will get many of the benefits of a physical inventory without having to incur the cost. By helping improve the accuracy of the CMDB in this way, you also improve the IT staff's confidence IT in the data. The more people who feel responsible for accuracy, the higher your accuracy is likely to be. Figure 14.3 summarizes these three ways to detect CMDB errors.

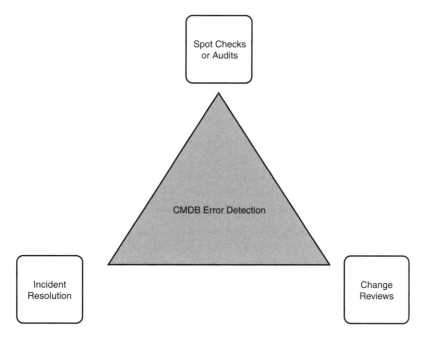

Figure 14.3   There are three ways to actively find errors in the CMDB.

Your operational processes are also the most likely place to find undiscovered CIs and stale relationship kinds of errors. As people become more experienced in using configuration data, they will begin to sense when pieces of the environment are not described completely. You'll start to hear people say things like "I know there should be a router here, but it's not described in the CMDB." At this point, you know that the organization has really embraced configuration management and is maturing in their understanding of the interrelationships of all the processes.

Spot checks and operational processes should work together to give you the best possible coverage of your entire database. You should specifically select your physical audit data to include things that haven't been involved recently in one of the operational processes. Likewise, if you have selected something to participate in a spot check and realize that a technician had just checked that CI recently, you can remove it from the list. Seeing both sides as part of the same effort helps to reduce your costs and increase coverage.

The important part of finding errors is having a good means of logging them. Some organizations like to create a special type of incident to track errors they find with configuration data. This allows you to use the incident tracking system you probably already have, but it requires that you work out reports and dashboards to not include these tickets that really don't represent degradation of service to any of your IT consumers.

Another possibility, if your tool is flexible enough, is to create a table in the CMDB to track the errors. This has the benefit of easily relating the errors to the CI or relationship involved, but requires that you create input screens to enter the data. Of course, if neither the incident system nor the CMDB is a suitable place for you to store error information, you can always use a spreadsheet to do your tracking. The tool you choose is not nearly as important as the information you track.

For every error, you should capture the person who found it, the way it was found, the CI or relationship identifier where the error is found, and the date and time the error was uncovered. This information will help you determine the source of the error and find ways to prevent it from happening in the future.

Investigate and Sort Errors

After you have found and logged all errors, the next step is to investigate them to determine whether they truly are errors. This is where you take into consideration the timing situations described earlier. Each of your various operational processes is likely to have a different cycle, so you can't simply check whether the error occurred some number of days after the last incident or change. Instead you need to consider each discovered error, understand when the data should have been changed by your standard processes, and then eliminate each one that has a valid explanation for the data inconsistency.

Investigating errors is a time-consuming process. You should actively look for opportunities to automate it as much as possible. For example, if you can create a clever query that cross-checks data between the CMDB, the incident ticketing system, and the change management tool, you could produce a report that shows the most recent change and incident for each CI that has an error. Such a report can help to eliminate many timing errors very quickly. As you consider the policy for defining accuracy, you're likely to see other opportunities to build reports or queries that can sort the false errors from the real ones more quickly. It will probably not be possible to completely automate the error investigation, but you should get as close as you can.

When you have investigated all errors, you should indicate in your tracking system which ones remain as errors and which ones can be explained. Usually this can be accomplished with a simple status field for each error.

Reporting Overall CMDB Accuracy

Most senior IT managers want to think of CMDB accuracy in terms of a single percentage. In my experience, people want to talk about the CMDB as being somewhere between 90 and 100 percent accurate. That's a great measurement, but getting there from a simple list of discovered errors is not straightforward.

The formula for percentage accuracy is going to be the number of errors discovered divided by the number of opportunities for error. It's that second number that takes some consideration. Let's think about how to define the denominator of the formula shown in Figure 14.4.

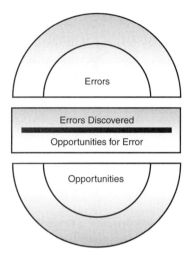

Figure 14.4   There is a simple formula describing the accuracy of the CMDB.

Most organizations start out with the idea that they will simply divide the number of errors by the number of CIs in the database. This is simple to understand, but leads directly to a quandary. If a CI has12 attributes associated with it and two of them are incorrect, is that 2 errors or 1? If you are simply dividing by number of CIs but counting each attribute or relationship as a possibility of an error, you can actually have more errors than CIs.

You could simplify your definition of accuracy to say that if any attribute or relationship of a CI is incorrect, that whole CI is wrong and counts as a single error. That is a case of making the measurement easier at the expense of losing the ability to really understand what is going wrong. If you don't track the individual errors, you can't be sure to fix them all.

So, the next possibility is that each attribute and each relationship is an opportunity for error. Even in a very small database, the denominator will quickly grow quite large, which will result in a much higher percentage of accuracy than just counting the CIs.

Note, however, that even adding all the existing relationships and attributes does not represent all the opportunities for errors. You could still have errors that are introduced as new CIs are discovered and missing relationships are added. When these are discovered, you will add to the numerator (number of errors) and the denominator (opportunities for error) at the same time, making these the most significant kinds of errors.

Like so many other things in IT operations, you should decide how to measure CMDB accuracy based on practicality. Initially, it might make sense to track each error individually, but calculate accuracy as the number of CIs with any error divided by the number of total CIs. As you grow in maturity, you can move on to dividing total errors on any aspect by the total number of attributes and relationships. When your configuration management service has been operating for a while, you can even use historical trends to predict how many errors will be found as new CIs or relationships are discovered, and create a formula to factor those into the overall error calculation.

The important thing is that you create a measurement that your stakeholders will understand and appreciate. Don't simply publish the number, but be sure to explain exactly how you calculate the number. Unfortunately, the industry hasn't yet selected a single method to calculate accuracy, so you will need to make people aware that a comparison with other organizations may not be as simple as comparing their percentage to yours.

Improving Accuracy

So now that you know how accurate your CMDB is, you can calculate the accuracy to several decimal places. Whatever your number turns out to be, you will immediately be challenged by someone to make it better. After all, operations people are never satisfied with less than perfection!

The next step is to understand how the errors came to be in your database. This involves a bit of detective work and a lot of understanding of your processes. With some experience, you'll realize that the type of the error often determines what caused the error. In this section, we look at the various causes and work backward to what types of errors are likely to be seen with these causes. The results are summarized in Figure 14.5.

Error Class	Discovered By	Removed By
Clerical	Spot Checks	Training
Process	Reports or Spot Checks	Control Points
Programming	Reports	Testing

Figure 14.5   Different classes of error require different handling.

Clerical Errors

Clerical errors are the most obvious. It is very easy to see most typographical or transposition errors. Clerical errors can also occur whenever a person uses a direct interface to create or update configuration data. This can involve choosing the wrong value from a drop-down list, selecting the wrong radio button, or any other such mistake made on an entry screen.

Errors can be introduced any time manual entry is needed, but the error may not actually be introduced in data entry. Many times we ask technicians to gather configuration information when they are in a data center server room or at a user desktop. Because most technicians don't carry a laptop or other entry device with them, they pull out a pencil and write down the needed information; or worse yet, try to remember it until they get back to their desk. When they try to re-create the information, they have either lost the paper, can't read their own handwriting, or have simply forgotten what they tried to remember.

Clerical errors are the most difficult kind of errors to detect, but perversely they are the simplest to correct. These errors are usually subtle, like the transposing of two digits in the serial number of a piece of equipment, or having the wrong location specified. These errors normally cannot be identified through clever queries or searches in the CMDB, but only through careful comparison or spot checks.

The best way to prevent clerical errors is to automate more of the process. This can take many different creative forms. You can implement a scanning tool on each piece of equipment so technicians do not have to write down information. You can even issue hand-held devices so that technicians can electronically scan external characteristics like asset bar codes and device serial numbers. You can implement electronic links from procurement or software licensing systems to create new CIs without having to manually enter them. Any way that you can avoid a person writing down or typing in configuration data will be one less way that clerical errors can be introduced into the database.

It is probably not possible to eliminate all manual activities from the configuration management process. You can also eliminate some clerical errors by increasing the training of your key people who will manually be handling or entering data. Teach people not to try to remember information, give them at least a clipboard and a paper form to capture data accurately, and train them to double-check data as they enter it. It is surprising how even these low-tech safeguards can improve the accuracy of the CMDB.

Process Errors

A second class of errors to be aware of are process errors. These occur typically when some process has failed or hasn't been followed well. For example, there are organizations that fail to properly link the change management process with the incident management process. The service desk gets a call that a desktop PC won't power on. An incident is opened and sent to the desk side support queue. A technician goes to the desk and finds that the system board on the computer is bad, so a replace computer is needed.

The correct step would be to branch to the change management (or Install/Move/Add/Change) process at this point and follow that until the appropriate configuration update is made before coming back to incident management to indicate resolution. In organizations that don't have well-integrated processes, the new PC may be acquired from a storage or redeployment locker without consideration of the configuration database update. The result is an incorrect state for both the broken machine and the machine that has been newly called into service—errors introduced because of a failed process.

The most common process errors are introduced because of unauthorized changes. People who decide that the "needs of the business" supersede the need for a change record will rarely update the CMDB to reflect the environment after they've gone ahead with their change. When these changes are made, errors are introduced to the CMDB, and the rest of the IT organization suffers with inaccurate data. There are also cases where people are honestly trying to follow the operational processes, but overlook steps that provide correct configuration data. All these are cases of process errors.

Some process errors can be found through standard operational reporting or special queries designed to look for certain types of errors. Other process errors, such as unauthorized changes, are found through scanning technology or spot audits. The difference is that processes should yield predictable results—you can often use this fact to find errors by finding where the results are not predictable. Several times already we've considered a report that shows recently completed changes and whether the CMDB has been updated after the change. This same report can often be used to find process errors.

The primary way to avoid process errors is to create more control points in the processes and to train all of your people to follow the processes. Each control point is another opportunity to have a report that might find whether process errors have been made. Of course, more control points and measurements will also cause more process overhead, driving up the cost and slowing down the process. Use these control points judiciously to minimize your errors, but then relax them as your people are more accustomed to the discipline of configuration management.

Programming Errors

The final kind of error we'll consider is the programming error. Hopefully these will be the rarest form of error in your CMDB, and the easiest to spot. Programming errors potentially could be introduced by your CMDB tool itself or by the underlying database management middleware, but those would be very rare situations. In most cases, programming errors are the result of some integration software that is trying to pull data from other sources into the CMDB or federate data and reflect that data into the CMDB. These integration programs can be written in a variety of ways, and often aren't built with the full rigor your business applications use.

Programming errors can be spotted with reporting. Normally they show up as impossible inconsistencies in the data. For example, you might see all workstations added on a single day as having two gigabytes of memory, when you know your environment is more heterogeneous than that. Keeping an adequate report of what CIs are added or changed by each execution of your integration tools is extremely important to protect against the possibility of programming errors.

Programming errors are eliminated through stronger testing of your integration work. If the programs are tested adequately, preferably in a development or testing environment first, there should be very few cases where programming causes errors in the CMDB.

Finding errors that exist, and preventing errors from creeping into the CMDB in the first place, should be a significant investment area for you for the first several years of your configuration management effort. Only after your accuracy is consistently better than 97 percent should you start directing your investments toward higher business value. After all, the value of all other processes and projects depending on configuration data will be diluted if your accuracy is not high enough.

CHAPTER 15

Improving the Business Value of Configuration Management

By now you have all the information you need to implement and run a successful configuration management service. You've done the planning, lived through the implementation, and started to mature your operational service. Maybe you even did all that before you picked up this book. This chapter gives you some suggestions for what might be the next step.

We will consider three different projects that are possible only when your Configuration Management Database (CMDB) is fully populated and trusted. These are all projects that can add significant value to your information technology (IT) operations by moving IT closer to the business you support. The projects aren't presented in any particular order—they are equally important and equally difficult to implement. Each should be considered in light of the business case for your organization. Some organizations will do all three of these projects and get huge benefits from them. Other organizations will only do one or maybe even none of them. Let the value obtained be your guide for how many are right for you. Figure 15.1 depicts these projects which can supplement the CMDB to bring significant extra value to your organization.

Some of the benefits you can expect from implementing these or other projects based on solid configuration data include:

- Clarified expectations leading to higher user satisfaction with the IT service
- Lower cost of providing services because of reduced support costs
- Improved compliance with business mandates, including government regulations
- Stronger linkage between the services provided by IT and the needs of the business units

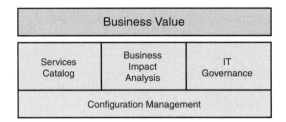

Figure 15.1   The business value of configuration management depends on how you use the data.

An IT Services Catalog

The IT industry in general, and IT functions within large corporations in particular, are continually being pressed to reduce cost and justify the expenses they incur. One common trend in the responses of most IT organizations is that they are choosing to define their services more clearly. Organizations find it much easier to understand the value of IT when they can see all the available services and can make sure they are not paying for more than they need.

The technique of defining and organizing IT services is rapidly gaining popularity, and is called the IT services catalog. Defining and building a complete catalog are beyond the scope of this book, but it is important to understand how the services catalog leverages the information in your CMDB. This section describes how the IT services catalog improves the business value of your configuration management service.

Defining IT Services

Let's consider what is meant by IT services. The simplest example is a service desk that takes a call and resets a user's password. This is a very foundational service for most organizations, but it actually captures all the elements we need to define an IT service. There is a service name, which is "password reset" or "UNIX password reset." There are entitlements, or rules about who can request the service and who cannot. In the password-reset example, only people who have a user ID can request the password-reset service. The service has defined inputs that must be received in order to satisfy the service, such as a user ID in this case. The service has a defined workflow, which in this case consists of just the two steps of receive the request and fulfill the request.

It may also be important to your organization to understand the cost structure of a service. If you think about it long, you'll realize that a password reset actually has at least two costs. The first cost is what the service requester should expect to pay. In most organizations, this is zero for a password reset. The service also has a cost to fulfill, which may be very small, but is not zero because the password reset requires that the phone system be in operation, that a service desk agent be present, and several other components. If the service desk has been outsourced, there may also be a cost from the service provider back to the organization. The key element is that each service can have one or more costs that are defined as part of the catalog. Cost structure is shown in Figure 15.2 as one of five elements of the complete definition of an IT service.

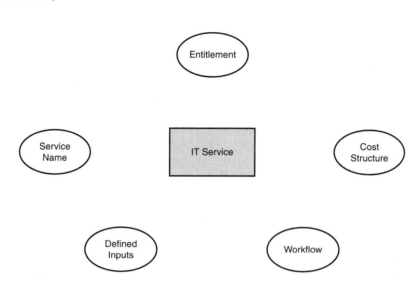

Figure 15.2 There are five key components to an IT service definition.

While password reset is the simplest example of an IT service, there is almost no upper limit to what an IT service might consist of. Any situation where we can define a service name, entitlements, defined inputs, defined workflow, and a cost structure can be defined as an IT service. We could, for example, define a complex service that involves everything IT needs to do to respond to a new employee joining the organization—acquiring and installing a PC, setting up email, defining user IDs, and whatever else needs to be accomplished.

One of the interesting things about IT services is that they can build on one another. After you've defined installation of a UNIX server, a database management system, and a storage device, you can more quickly build a service for deploying a user database out of these components. Actually, one of the more challenging parts of building an entire service catalog comes from separating these "component" services from the "combination" services.

The Place of Configuration Items in Service Definitions

So, what does all of this have to do with the CMDB? Where appropriate, the services should tie to the configuration items (CIs) that are critical to providing the service. In this way, you can always be aware of the importance of the CIs based on what services they provide to your organization. Let's explore how to make that linkage appropriately.

In the simple example of a password-reset service, there are several candidates that might be CIs. The phone system, or more specifically the automated call director and the voice routing unit, are likely to be CIs, possibly along with the wide area network circuits that route voice traffic from your users to the service desk. You might have an administrative tool used by the agents to reset passwords, and that tool would be in your CMDB. Interestingly enough, the actual user IDs and passwords are probably too detailed to be part of the CMDB, so those would not be able to be linked to the service.

In a more complex service, the linkages become even more important. If the service involves recovering from a natural disaster, for instance, it will be critical to point to the exact CIs you will bring into play to help the recovery effort, and to indicate which CIs need to be recovered. These definitions help everyone providing the service to quickly understand exactly what needs to be done.

Many IT services add new CIs or relationships to an environment. A service to bring a new employee on board might add a computer, a telephone, and a PDA, for example. So in addition to depending on some CIs to be able to perform the service, this definition also provides new CIs to the overall IT environment.

The reason you want to make these connections between IT services and CIs is twofold. First, these connections will help you assess the impact of either a planned change or an unplanned outage. If you know which CIs are involved in providing a service, you will be able to quickly determine which services are interrupted by an outage. This can be valuable information when deciding the severity of the incident or the risk of a change.

The second reason for linking services with CIs is to make sure that the CMDB gets updated appropriately as services are provided. When a service creates or modifies a CI or a relationship, you can create a report that shows the number of times the service is used against the number of updates or creates in the CMDB. You'll have change records for those updates as well, but this ability to check service requests against changes and updates gives you a very strong control point to keep the CMDB accurate.

You can build a services catalog even if you don't have a CMDB, but you will lose the benefits of the association of services with CIs. The catalog and the CMDB work much better together.

Benefits of a Services Catalog

There are many benefits to having a services catalog, not the least of which is that it imposes order on top of the many activities of the IT function. Once the organization begins thinking in terms of IT services, you'll find that the criteria for what projects to pursue become simpler. If a project provides a service your IT consumers need at a cost they are willing to pay, then it becomes a good project. This attitude aligns your IT function more closely to the business and helps you to put the business side of IT on a much more solid footing.

Another key benefit of a services catalog is that it brings order to the many tasks the IT organization must perform. Technicians often get the impression that they do the same task day by day with little forward progress. Defining these tasks as part of bigger service will bring some sense of accomplishment and order. But even more importantly, defining these sets of services helps you implement measurements based on service and gives the technicians a reason why they have to achieve their tasks on time—the overall service has a service level that must be achieved.

Another benefit of services is that users can approach IT more clearly because they know exactly what to expect. After you have defined a services catalog, you can offer the users "catalog shopping" through a single web portal. Users can choose from the catalog those services they are entitled to have, and because you have clearly defined workflows, much of the fulfillment of those services can be automated. Even for services that cannot be completely automated, expectations and costs can be made clear on the web portal.

If you want to charge business units for IT services rendered, the catalog becomes indispensable. The ability to classify the services and understand the cost structures is fundamental to sorting out the various charges that will be allocated. When a business user requests a service, they can clearly understand the impact to their budget and know what they will be charged.

Ultimately, the value of an IT services catalog is that it brings order and precision to the business of IT, helping your entire organization understand what value IT brings at what cost.

Business Impact Analysis

Another exciting area you will be able to explore with solid configuration data is business impact analysis. You've heard a lot about impact analysis throughout this book, but in this section we'll concentrate on understanding the impact of an incident or potential change to the business of your organization, not just to other IT components.

Higher Order Relationships

The foundation for achieving this kind of analysis lies in extending the basic CMDB to include business objects in addition to IT objects, and then creating the relationships between the business and IT. I refer to this as creating "higher order" relationships.

Most organizations have a set of custom business applications at the top level of the technology stack, with servers and network components at the lower layers. To go above the technology stack and into the business, you need to think about what the interface is between those custom applications and the functions of your wider organization outside of IT.

In most cases, you'll find that business applications have been built to automate business processes. Depending on what your organization does and how you've chosen to organize, you may have several very broad business processes, or you may have many very specific processes. If you have very broad business processes, you want to group applications together into subprocesses that can be combined to make up the complete processes.

Above the process level are the products and services your organization produces. These should not be confused with IT services, as described in the previous section. These products and services are the output of your organization and the reason you are in business. The products and services might be strictly external things like refined petroleum or canned foods, or you may choose to represent internal products and services, such as financial statements and marketing materials. What is important is that you define these as real products that are important to your enterprise and not as simple abstractions for the sake of the tools.

The complete hierarchy from the network through the business products is shown in Figure 15.3.

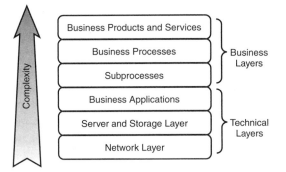

Figure 15.3 Adding business layers helps to track what's really important in your CMDB.

Connecting Business and IT

Building the appropriate CIs to populate the business layers is difficult enough, but the task of building the relationships between the CIs in these layers is even more challenging. The secret is to go slow and steady, and add more complexity only as the business value warrants it. As always, business value should be measurable in costs saved or additional revenue generated. Making connections from the IT components to your business functions should allow you to measure the real costs of downtime or the real revenue value of new IT services.

If you already have a clearly defined set of products and services for your business, you should prioritize these and work on the most important products or services first. Say that your organization is an electricity generator. Your important product would be electricity, but your services might include electrical distribution, billing, meter reading, and advertising. You prioritize the product and services and determine that your key priority is to understand the impacts on billing for any IT service disruption. By improving billing, you reason, you can directly increase the speed at which you collect revenue for the business.

In looking at the billing function, you determine that it is made of one process for tracking consumer electricity usage, another process for tracking commercial usage, and a third process for applying the rates to produce the invoices that go out to your customers. When these processes are built out as CIs, you create relationships between them and the billing service. These relationships allow for a clear understanding of exactly which IT components drive commercial billing and which components drive consumer billing, allowing you to optimize one over the other if desired.

Next, you analyze each of these processes and realize 12 different subprocesses are involved. Some of these may have relationships to one another because they call and depend on one another to make up the complete process. In addition, you create the subprocess CIs and relationships of the subprocesses to the processes. Getting to this level of granularity helps you optimize in ways that would not be possible if you hadn't done the decomposition and understood exactly how IT was supporting the overall billing process.

Finally, you must determine exactly which business applications link in to which of these subprocesses. A good rule of thumb is that if a single application facilitates more than one of the items you've defined as a subprocess, you probably have too granularity in your definition. On the other hand, if you have large, monolithic applications, you may find that the same application links to multiple business processes. Whichever case you find yourself in, it is important that you create the appropriate relationships between business applications and either processes or sub-processes to complete the linkage from the IT layers to the business layers. Now that the billing business function is completely understood, you may learn that adding extra capacity to a specific server will allow you to offer commercial customers different rates for prime-time kilowatt hours and nighttime kilowatt hours, leading directly to improved revenue and customer satisfaction. That is just one example of the significant business value that can be driven by combining business analysis with configuration data. Figure 15.4 shows an example of decomposing a single business service into its IT components down to the network layer.

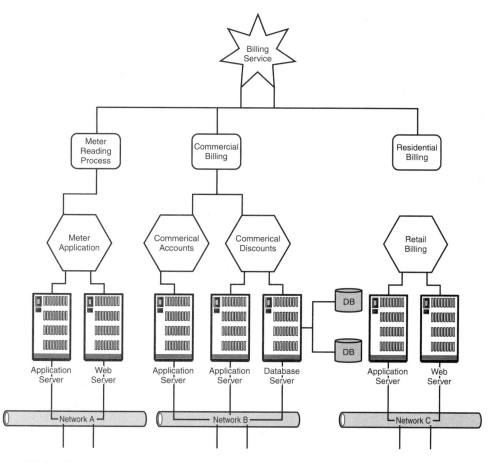

Figure 15.4 It is possible to decompose each business product or service into its contributing IT components.

It is important to remember that the value gained from business impact analysis is incremental. That is, you can get some value even if you completely analyze only one product or service, and you will eventually run into a situation where further analysis and breakdown of your business does not provided significant extra value. Just as in so many other areas of IT, don't pedantically strive for full coverage, but instead plan to achieve the degree of coverage that balances the cost of implementation with the value you will get.

The Benefits of Business Impact Analysis

Setting up the relationships between IT components and business components takes some effort, and maintaining them adds to the effort. Just like relationships between other components, you need to define processes that keep the business relationships updated as changes occur. This involves building a bridge between the IT change management discipline and the business change management discipline, thus aligning IT closer to the rest of the organization.

This alignment between IT and the core functions of your enterprise is a key benefit of business impact analysis. Instead of talking about a change only in terms of minutes of server downtime, you can talk about the number of lost engineering hours or the number of widgets that won't get produced. The ability to follow the chain from any piece of the IT infrastructure to the corresponding product of service allows these impacts to be clearly understood.

Understanding the relationships also allows more clear definition of the severity of incidents. Studying the CIs and relationships in the CMDB will allow you to know precisely what part of the business cannot function when any IT component is out of service. These impacts can be coded in advance of a failure as part of the CI record for each CI, and thus when an incident does occur, you'll know the business impact as soon as you isolate the failing CI.

Most organizations find that the ability to perform business impact analysis changes the way IT decisions are made. You'll no longer be limited to cost or IT risk as the key influencing factors. With alignment of IT to the rest of the organization, you can begin assessing wider business factors, such as productivity improvements, additional product opportunities, and risk to the business. Looking at decisions in this new light will help put IT decisions in a broader context and help you see the long-range consequences of decisions. This ability to make better decisions is exactly where this book started and is the key business value that can be added with solid configuration management data.

IT Governance

Another aspect of making solid decisions can be found in the IT governance space. This is yet another area that is sparking much interest now that configuration management programs are gaining a foothold in many organizations. By IT governance, we mean the establishment and management of standards to help in creating a consistent and logical environment. Good configuration information will help to both establish and maintain your IT standards.

Establishing IT Standards

Standards promote consistency and leverage economies of scale. We all know from experience that it is easier to drive any car because the automotive industry has established standards for where the steering wheel and brake pedal are located. Similarly for IT standards, it is easier to manage a set of servers when they all run the same operating system and easier to configure routers when they all come from the same manufacturer.

In many organizations, however, the IT environment is built piecemeal from a series of disconnected projects instead of holistically from a set of carefully considered standards. This leads to a problem when gathering configuration information, but after you've done the hard work of sorting out all the complexity, you can then use that configuration information to establish new standards.

You can, of course, simply say that whatever item in each category you already have the most of is the standard for that category. Or you can leverage your configuration information a bit more to calculate the reliability of different manufacturers or the cost of operation of different types of equipment. Using this information, you can make intelligent decisions about which particular type should be a standard for your environment.

Setting IT standards allows you to make some decisions much easier. Instead of having to perform a trade study each time you acquire a component, you can simply choose the standard component with full confidence that it will meet your needs.

Automating Audits

After you have defined the standards in each critical IT space, you can begin to compare future project architectures against those standards. This can be done in an architectural review, but it is much easier with a CMDB to automate the audit process.

You start by marking certain CIs as IT standards. By indicating that these are standards, you allow everyone to observe with a simple check of the CMDB whether something is standard or not. You also pave the way for automated audits of IT standards.

When a project is proposing new IT components that will become CIs, you simply request that they provide a "bill of materials." This listing of proposed new components can be compared quickly against the CMDB to determine which items are standards and which are not. For those items proposed by the project that aren't standard, you can do extra review or can ask the project team to prepare extra documentation indicating why the deviation is needed.

These automated audits allow for the architecture review board to focus on the bigger picture rather than on the details of whether the project is adhering to the standards.

Benefits of IT Governance

Just as IT services catalogs and business impact analysis, the benefit of IT governance is better decision making. If you understand what an ideal, standard environment would look like, you can make decisions about each project or proposed addition to the environment. You can decide whether the addition will fit into the standard or violate it. You can determine whether exceptions should be made, or new standards proposed. Ultimately, you can decide whether the project should go forward or change its direction.

Governing IT decision making will help build a discipline into your entire organization that is both healthy and educational. People will learn to use the standard building blocks, and this will enable them to focus on the novel aspects of any new solution and spend less time worrying about the standard aspects. This should lead to higher quality architectures, resulting in more robust infrastructure.

There are probably other high-value activities that can be initiated after you are comfortable that you have solid configuration management data. This chapter has chosen several activities and demonstrated the value they can bring to your entire organization. After you've built a solid foundation of configuration management, you'll probably be able to think of dozens more projects and initiatives that can more closely align your IT function with the rest of your business—and that will ultimately lead to better business decisions.

Index

A

accuracy of data, 193
  defining, 194-197
    attribute accuracy, 194
    configuration item
      accuracy, 194-195
    relationship accuracy,
      195-197
  during pilot programs, 144
  improving, 202-205
  measuring, 197-202
    counting errors,
      197-200
    investigating
      errors, 200
    reporting measure-
      ments, 200-202
advertising success of pilot
  programs, 150-151
allocation reports, 180-181

ambiguity of requirements, 22
analyzing requirements,
  31-36
  derived requirements,
    33-34
  prioritization of
    requirements, 31-32
  scope of project, determin-
    ing, 34-36
  sizing requirements, 32-33
application management,
  relationship with configuration management, 6
architecture documents in
  project plans, 95
asset databases, populating
  CMDB from, 71-73
asset management, configuration management versus, 71
associations. *See*
  relationships

attributes, accuracy of, 194.
  See also granularity
audiences, in communication
  plans, 154
auditing
  automating audits, 215
  CMDB in standard ITIL
    framework, 59
  procedures for, 62-63
automating audits, 215
availability management, 4

B

baselining project plans, 96
batch loaders, 82
bottom up schedules,
  building, 94
boundaries. *See* span
budgets, development of, 94

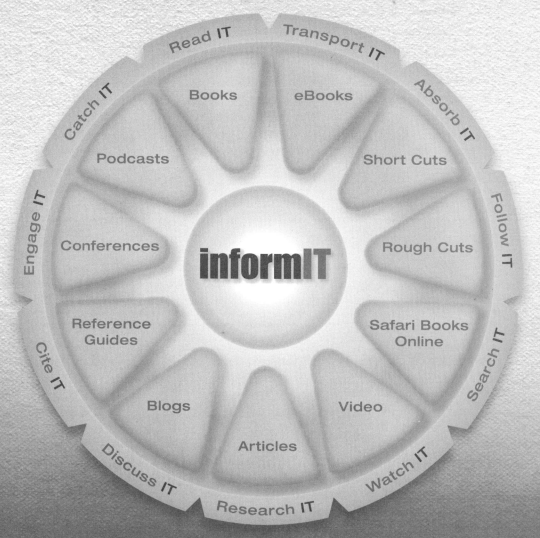

THIS BOOK IS SAFARI ENABLED

INCLUDES FREE 45-DAY ACCESS TO THE ONLINE EDITION

The Safari® Enabled icon on the cover of your favorite technology book means the book is available through Safari Bookshelf. When you buy this book, you get free access to the online edition for 45 days.

Safari Bookshelf is an electronic reference library that lets you easily search thousands of technical books, find code samples, download chapters, and access technical information whenever and wherever you need it.

TO GAIN 45-DAY SAFARI ENABLED ACCESS TO THIS BOOK:

- Go to **http://www.prenhallprofessional.com/safarienabled**
- Complete the brief registration form
- Enter the coupon code found in the front of this book on the "Copyright" page

If you have difficulty registering on Safari Bookshelf or accessing the online edition, please e-mail customer-service@safaribooksonline.com.

PRENTICE
HALL